THE AGE STRUCTURE OF
THE CORPORATE SYSTEM

Publications of the
Bureau of Business and Economic Research
University of California

THE AGE STRUCTURE
OF THE
CORPORATE SYSTEM

BY

WILLIAM LEONARD CRUM

UNIVERSITY OF CALIFORNIA PRESS
BERKELEY AND LOS ANGELES
1953

UNIVERSITY OF CALIFORNIA PRESS

BERKELEY AND LOS ANGELES

CALIFORNIA

❖

CAMBRIDGE UNIVERSITY PRESS

LONDON, ENGLAND ◆

To

Dr. Thomas C. Atkeson of the Bureau of
Internal Revenue, United States Treasury, who has, during many years, contrib-
uted greatly to enlarging the scope and
refining the quality of *Statistics of Income,*
this book is respectfully dedicated.

Preface

TWO MAIN PURPOSES *are intended to be served by publication of this book, which reports my first analysis of an entirely new body of facts concerning the age of corporations and certain characteristics related to age. One purpose is to present various findings which seem to be fairly dependable and to have large importance for an understanding of the corporate section of the private enterprise system and for the consideration of certain policies, not only private policies of corporations but also public policies toward corporations. I am aware that some of these findings may be debatable, and that other and more competent investigators may reach conclusions somewhat different from those reported here. One of my reasons for showing the details of the analytical steps more fully than one might expect in an ordinary research report is that the later work of other investigators may thereby be facilitated.*

A second purpose is to awaken an interest in the vital statistics of corporations by showing how various significant inferences can be drawn from one limited body of such statistics. I hope that this book will lead to a more extensive compilation of corporate vital statistics, so that numerous important obstacles to analysis encountered in preparing the book will, in the course of time, be largely removed through the coming to hand of statistics more extensive in scope and more elaborate in detail. I hope also that methods of analysis described here will offer a stimulus to other investigators, so that later studies can derive from a growing body of factual information more significant inferences than I report in the following pages, and can also have the benefit of important improvements upon these methods. I do not regard this book as definitive, but rather as a pioneer work; and, with the accumulation of new and better data and with the more effective interpretation of those data through the efforts of scholars who find in these pages a challenge, the book may be expected soon to become obsolete. This result will convince me that the second purpose has been fully realized.

Preparation of the book has been forwarded by much able assistance made available to me. Mrs. Harriet Ross, of Wollaston, Massachusetts, handled much of the arithmetical work on the 1946 tabulations. The Bureau of Business and Economic Research of the University of California at Berkeley assisted similarly with work on the 1945 tabulations and also aided me in preparing the text, tables, and charts for publication. I am grateful for this help, which has enabled me to share the heavy burdens of so large a task; but the responsibility for any errors that may damage the published results and for any misapprehensions in the interpretation of results can not be shared, and rests upon me alone.

W. L. CRUM

Berkeley
June 23, 1952

Contents

[xi]

CHAPTER I

The Problem and the Relevant Data

THE CORPORATE SYSTEM at any particular time is a population, each member of which has a life span that began at some date in the past with birth—incorporation—and may end at some date in the future with death—dissolution. The life span may be marked at various stages by morbidity of various sorts and in varying degrees. The membership of the corporate population, and of each of its parts, changes from time to time because of the entrance of new corporations through births and the exit of other corporations through deaths; and these changes, as well as the march of time, effect changes in the age structure of the system. A comprehensive and continuous system of vital statistics of corporations would supply information on births and deaths, length and perhaps expectation of life, age structure at any particular time, and morbidity and mortality from various causes for the entire corporate population and various important sections thereof. Such vital statistics would be immensely helpful guides in attempts to understand the functioning of a major, and in some respects dominant, section of the private enterprise system. Such statistics would also assist in formulating policies, public and private, designed to improve that functioning. Unfortunately, despite the elaborate recording which is an essential incident of corporate activity, no such systematic body of corporate vital statistics yet exists.[1]

---

[1] We may well bear in mind that the present system of vital statistics pertaining to the human population is the outcome of a long period of growth and development, during which investigators, while striving to make the utmost valid use of existing fragments of information, engaged in a continuing effort to secure more comprehensive and detailed and more nearly accurate data and to insure that the various types of data would be sufficiently comparable to permit study of important interrelations. One of the incidental purposes of the present investigation is to suggest, in the course of examining one large section of corporate vital statistics, how still more useful inferences could be drawn from a well-rounded body of such statistics.

[1]

1. *An important recent addition to corporate vital statistics.*—
A long step forward has, however, recently been taken in the publication by the United States Treasury of statistics on dates of
incorporation as reported on corporate income-tax returns. These
statistics enable us to describe and examine the age distribution of
the corporate population and certain relationships between age
distribution and other characteristics of the population. The new
tables appeared in *Statistics of Income for 1945*, Part 2, and similar
tables appeared in *Statistics of Income for 1946*, Part 2 (these docu-
ments are hereafter designated as *1945 S. of I.* and *1946 S. of I.*).[2]
Reported herein is an analysis of these statistics with attention particularly to: the age distribution of the entire corporate population
in terms of number and total assets, variations in age by size of corporation, variations in age by line of industry, relation of size to
profitability in 1945 and 1946, extent to which incorporation reflects change in legal form of previously existing enterprises, and
some narrowly limited implications as to corporate births and
deaths and related matters.[3]

The age distribution of 477,949 corporations active in 1946 is
shown in figure 1. The time periods on the horizontal axis indicate
the intervals—annual since 1939, and longer intervals before
1940—in which the various corporations were chartered. The light
line in the figure classifies the *number* of corporations by periods of
incorporation; the heavy line classifies the *total assets* held in 1946
by periods of incorporation.[4] The figure readily indicates that a
remarkably large fraction of the total number of corporations is
made up of very young corporations, whereas the maximum concentration of assets owned (in 1946) is among corporations chartered in 1925–1929. Further comment on the implications of these
results appears in chapter ii.

[2] *Statistics of Income for 1945*, Part 2, Washington, U. S. Treasury Dept., 1950, pp.
18–35; *Statistics of Income for 1946*, Part 2, Washington, U. S. Treasury Dept., 1951,
pp. 17–33. On p. 18 of *1945 S. of I.*, appears the statement (italics mine): "The corporation income tax return provides for reporting the date of incorporation and in this
report there is published *for the first time* a classification of the returns by year of
incorporation. The year of incorporation furnishes an indication of the length of
time that *the corporation* has been in business but *does not measure*, in every instance,
the entire business period since many incorporations merely represent a change in
form of a previously existing business." No such tables appear in *Statistics of Income
for 1947*, Part 2.
[3] These six parts of the analysis are reported in chaps. ii to vii, respectively.
[4] The heavy line refers only to 432,657 corporations which filed balance sheets with
their tax returns. A full explanation of the derivation of the materials on which the
figure is based appears in chap. ii.

The date-of-incorporation tables in *1945 S. of I.* and *1946 S. of I.* are almost identical in form.[5] The descriptions of the tables, comments on the nature and limitations of the data, and explanation of the computations, as presented at various points in this report, relate specifically to 1946; but they are also applicable, by obvious

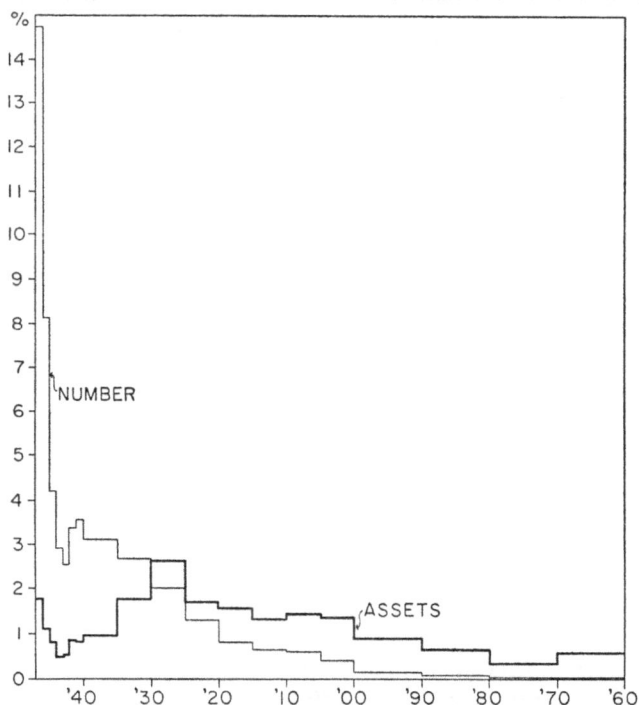

Fig. 1. Percentage distribution among periods of incorporation, of dated corporations active in 1946, in terms of number of such corporations and of the estimated total assets held in 1946.

SOURCE: Data from line *f* of tables 4 and 8. Percentages for Before-1860 not shown.

adaptations, to 1945 except as indicated by notes herein to the contrary. The *results* of most parts of the analysis, however, are presented for each of the two years; and the commentary on the results relates generally to both years or to each separately and ordinarily

[5] One significant difference is that the 1946 tables include a size classification of the material on previously existing form of business, whereas the 1945 tables do not (see chap. vi). An obvious difference in form between the two sets of tables arises because the 1946 tables relate to corporations "active" in 1946 and therefore include figures on incorporations in 1946.

includes notes comparing the two years. But important parts of the commentary give greater emphasis to the 1946 results because, as is explained in chapter v, 1946 is in some respects a less abnormal year than 1945.

2. *Limitations in coverage.*—Although the coverage of the corporate system by these date-of-incorporation statistics is so nearly complete that we may regard the findings below as approximately valid for the whole system, some restrictions in coverage should be noticed. These statistics, like most statistics appearing in annual issues of *Statistics of Income*, Part 2, are compiled from corporate

TABLE 1

Number of Returns on Forms 1120, 1120L, and 1120M, for 1945 and 1946*

		1945	1946
a	Returns with net income..........................	303,019	359,310
b	Returns with no net income......................	118,106	131,842
c	All active returns (a+b).........................	421,125	491,152
d	Inactive returns.................................	33,335	35,211
e	All returns (c+d)...............................	454,460	526,363
f	Per cent inactive (d/e)..........................	7.34	6.69

* Source: *1945 S. of I.*, pp. 2 and 6; *1946 S. of I.*, pp. 2, 5, and 6.

income-tax returns; and their coverage therefore cannot reach beyond corporations required by law to file such returns.[6] The coverage reaches in effect over approximately the entire system of American *business* corporations.

The returns include those of active corporations, which show income data, and those of inactive corporations, which show no data.[7] Returns of inactive corporations constitute a substantial frac-

---

[6] "Every domestic and every resident foreign corporation not specifically exempted by Section 101, whether or not having any net income, must file a return. The term 'corporation' is defined by the Code to include associations, joint-stock companies, and insurance companies. Receivers, trustees in dissolution, trustees in bankruptcy, and assignees, operating the property or business of corporations, must make returns of income for such corporations." From *fac simile* of Form 1120, *1946 S. of I.*, p. 461. Certain life insurance companies file on Form 1120L, and certain mutual insurance companies file on Form 1120M. Returns on these forms, as well as those on Form 1120 (which are the great bulk of the corporate returns), are included in the tables here studied. The exemptions in Section 101 of the Code cover a range of organizations having a form legally defined as corporate, but distinguished from ordinary business corporations by the fact that they are not designed to yield profit for the benefit of shareholders or other individuals.

[7] "The returns for inactive corporations are filed in accordance with the regulation that a corporation having an existence during any portion of a taxable year is required

tion of total corporate returns, as indicated by table 1; and the fraction varies markedly according to line of industry.[8]

The date-of-incorporation statistics tabulated in *1945 S. of I.* and *1946 S. of I.* relate only to active corporations. If similar statistics were available for inactive corporations, certain unanswered questions in the present analysis (see especially chaps. vi and vii), particularly questions involving comparisons with statistics of incorporations published in non-Treasury sources, might be subject to examination.[9] As indicated by table 1, the active returns are separated into two broad categories, those showing net income and those showing no net income (hereafter designated as net and nonet corporations or returns); and these categories are shown separately for each of the classes—according to line of industry or to size or to type of predecessor organization—shown in the tables here under study.

Apart from the fact that these tables cover only active returns, we must note another deficiency in coverage, arising from failure of certain returns of active corporations to include answers to the questions on the tax form about date of incorporation and related matters. These cases of failure to report are covered in a column headed "Not stated" in the *S. of I.* tables, and the percentages in table 2 indicate the extent of the deficiency in reporting. The percentages in sections A and C of the table vary greatly according to line of industry, and those in section B and the footnote to section C vary according to size of corporation (these variations are reported in chaps. iv and iii); and the table indicates marked variations be-

---

to make a return." From *1946 S. of I.*, p. 4. The two main categories of inactive corporations are previously active corporations which are in process of liquidation or dissolution and have ceased income-producing activities, and recently incorporated companies which have not yet commenced such activities. Some doubt may exist as to whether the requirement of filing returns is effectively enforced for inactive corporations, and particularly for the second category (see chap. vii).

[8] In view of the fact that line of business is determined, for corporations engaged in more than one line, by the amount of total receipts (chap. iv), and in view of the fact that inactive returns show no accounting data, some question may exist as to the precision of the industrial classification of inactive returns. In fact, slightly more than ⅓ of the inactive returns for 1945, and slightly less than ⅓ of those for 1946, were classified as "Nature of business not allocable." (*1945 S. of I.*, p. 6; *1946 S. of I.*, p. 6). This means that the industrial classification is much more nearly precise for active returns than for all returns.

[9] This deficiency may perhaps not be susceptible of removal by a mere tabulation of date-of-incorporation data from the inactive returns, since such returns may to an exceptional degree fail to state the date. Danger always exists that a return, which in any case involves no tax liability, will omit reporting facts which would ordinarily be supplied on a return likely to be scrutinized in the Treasury's testing of tax liability.

TABLE 2

	1945	1946
A. All active returns		
Net	303,019	359,310
No-net	118,106	131,842
Total	421,125	491,152
Date of incorporation not stated		
Net	9,253	7,486
No-net	6,653	5,717
Total	15,906	13,203
Per cent not stated		
Net	3.06	2.08
No-net	5.63	4.33
Total	3.78	2.69
B. All balance-sheet returns		
Net	281,244	334,042
No-net	93,706	106,708
Total	374,950	440,750
Date of incorporation not stated		
Net	6,683	5,572
No-net	2,980	2,523
Total	9,663	8,095
Per cent not stated		
Net	2.37	1.67
No-net	3.19	2.36
Total	2.58	1.84
C. All incorporated in current year†		
Net	11,485	42,666
No-net	11,058	27,781
Total	22,543	70,447
Whether successor not stated		
Net	2,758	4,499
No-net	2,482	3,984
Total	5,240	8,483
Per cent not stated		
Net	24.0	10.5
No-net	22.4	14.3
Total	23.2	12.0
All stated to be successors		
Net	2,459	20,654
No-net	1,665	6,485
Total	4,124	27,139

TABLE 2—*Continued*

	1945	1946
Type of predecessor not stated		
Net	46	1,442
No-net	24	600
Total	70	2,042
Per cent not stated		
Net	1.87	6.98
No-net	1.44	9.25
Total	1.70	7.53

* Source: *1945 S. of I.*, pp. 19–34; *1946 S. of I.*, pp. 18–30.
† *1946 S. of I.* gives also (pp. 32–33) balance-sheet returns for corporations incorporated in 1946 as follows:

	Incorporated in 1946	Whether successor not stated	Per cent not stated
Net	40,263	4,154	10.3
No-net	24,415	3,373	13.8
Total	64,678	7,527	11.6

	Stated to be successors	Type of predecessor not stated	Per cent not stated
Net	19,790	1,368	6.91
No-net	5,744	522	9.09
Total	25,534	1,890	7.40

tween 1945 and 1946 and between the net and no-net categories. These variations suggest that the returns for which the facts are stated may not be entirely satisfactory samples of all corporations, even though such returns include high percentages of all corporations (of the various sorts listed in the table). The percentages not stated are fairly low (the percentages stated are fairly high) in all cases shown in the table except those relating to whether the corporation is a successor for 1945 (22.4 to 24 per cent) and for 1946 (10.5 to 14.3 and 10.3 to 13.8 per cent), and those relating to type of predecessor for 1946 (6.98 to 9.29 and 6.91 to 9.09 per cent). The analyses which follow will assume that the samples, for which the information was reported and tabulated, are adequate for the date-of-incorporation data, and acceptable with reservations (see chap. vi) for the data distinguishing between new and successor enterprises and among various types of predecessors.

Another deficiency in coverage appears in those parts of the tables classifying corporations by size. This classification is available only for returns which include balance sheets, and not all active corporations supply this accounting statement on their returns. For 1945, 46,175 among the 421,125 active returns showed no balance sheets;

and for 1946, 50,402 among 491,152 (table 2). The indicated deficiencies in coverage are: for 1945, 11, and for 1946, 10.3 per cent. Although the *number* of balance-sheet returns is from 10 to 11 per cent smaller than the number of active corporations, the deficiency in coverage in terms of such a measure of importance as total compiled receipts is much smaller—about 1.1 per cent for 1945, and 1.7 for 1496.[10] Percentages, showing deficiency in balance-sheet coverage, vary as between the net and no-net categories, and among lines of industry; and we may suspect that they also vary, although we have no direct evidence on this point, among corporations of different sizes.[11]

Nevertheless, the deficiencies in balance-sheet coverage are so small that we shall regard the date-of-incorporation statistics for the size classes of corporations as thoroughly valid samples.

---

[10] These are derived from *1945 S. of I.*, p. 9, and *1946 S. of I.*, p. 8:

Total Compiled Receipts (in millions of dollars)	*1945*	*1946*
All active returns	255,448	288,954
Returns without balance sheets	2,811	5,037
Per cent deficiency	1.10	1.74

In terms of compiled net profit (a less suitable measure of importance), the deficiency is still smaller:

Compiled Net Profit (in millions of dollars)	*1945*	*1946*
All active returns	21,345	25,399
Returns without balance sheets	126	374
Per cent deficiency	0.59	1.47

Roughly comparable percentages, indicating the deficiency in balance-sheet coverage, have prevailed for many years.

[11] Indirect evidence—indirect because amount of net income or deficit is only partly trustworthy as an indicator of corporate size—is found in data (*1945 S. of I.*, p. 10; *1946 S. of I.*, p. 9) classified by amount of net income or deficit.

Per cent of active returns showing balance sheets	*1945*	*1946*
Net income:		
Less than $1,000	83.11	83.27
More than $10,000,000	100.00	98.92
Deficit:		
Less than $1,000	74.48	75.40
More than $10,000,000	100.00	100.00

And the percentage rises almost steadily as amount of net income, or of deficit, increases.

Other indirect evidence, much less convincing, appears from variations in the deficiency of balance-sheet coverage among lines of industry: corporations in certain lines of industry are generally smaller than those in others, and higher deficiency percentages tend to appear in certain lines where corporations are typically small.

3. *Fiscal-year and part-year returns.*—The tables in *1945 S. of I.* do not apply strictly to corporations active during the entire calendar year 1945, and a similar remark applies to the 1946 tables. The bulk of the returns do in fact apply to the calendar year, but the inclusion also of fiscal-year and part-year returns blurs slightly the timing of the accounting summations tabulated in *Statistics of Income.* Strictly, the tabulations pertain to the specified taxable year (1945 or 1946, as the case may be) or part thereof, the accounting period to which the corporate return applies. The accounting period for a fiscal-year return is a year ending on the final day of some month, other than December, ranging from July of the calendar year bearing the same numeral as the taxable year to June of the following year. The fiscal-year returns are of large significance in terms of number, and of roughly equal significance in terms of such a measure (imperfect though it be) of importance as amount of net income or deficit, as appears from table 3. Although fiscal-year returns constitute about one quarter of all active returns, the *average* taxable year to which all active returns apply is very close to the calendar year. This is because the fiscal-year returns for 1945 (or 1946) are distributed fairly evenly over the annual accounting periods ending from July, 1945 (or 1946) to June, 1946 (or 1947).[12]

The inclusion of part-year returns in the tabulations also blurs, but in still less significant degree, the timing of the accounting data tabulated.[13] The number of part-year returns is a moderate fraction of all active returns: 22,175 out of 421,125 in 1945; 46,727 out of 491,152 in 1946.[14] Although we have no specific data as to how the

---

[12] Actually, the concentration of fiscal years ending after December is somewhat heavier than those ending before December. Hence, the average taxable year for all active returns does not center at July 1 of the calendar year, but about $\frac{1}{6}$ of a month later. The importance of fiscal-year returns (among all active returns) varies greatly for different lines of industry, and the balance of concentration before and after December also varies among lines of industry. Hence, the average taxable year for certain lines of industry differs by more than $\frac{1}{6}$ month from the calendar year. See *1946 S. of I.*, pp. 38–53.

[13] The chief ways in which a part-year return can arise are through: new incorporations (the company involved is "active" during only a part of the first taxable year in which it becomes active); liquidations (the company on the road to dissolution is active during only a part of the last taxable year in which it is active); reorganizations (both the old company and the new company may be active during only a part of their respective taxable years); changes from calendar-year to fiscal-year basis of accounting (or vice versa) or from one fiscal year to another; certain admissions to, or withdrawals from, affiliated groups of corporations which file consolidated returns. (See *1946 S. of I.*, p. 54.)

[14] Figures are for active returns only. See *1945 S. of I.*, p. 54. A part-year return is tabulated for the year in which the greater part of the accounting period falls.

TABLE 3

COMPARATIVE IMPORTANCE OF CALENDAR-YEAR AND FISCAL-YEAR RETURNS,
FOR 1945 AND 1946*

	Number of returns		Net income or deficit	
	Number	Per cent	Amount (in millions of dollars)	Per cent
1945				
All active returns				
Net....................	303,019	....	22,165	....
No-net.................	118,106	....	1,026	....
Total.................	421,125	....	21,139	....
Fiscal-year returns				
Net....................	79,873	26.3	5,353	24.2
No-net.................	24,499	20.7	251	24.4
Total.................	104,372	24.8	5,102	24.2
Calendar-year returns				
Net....................	223,146	73.7	16,812	75.8
No-net.................	93,607	79.3	776	75.6
Total.................	316,753	75.2	16,037	75.8
1946				
All active returns				
Net....................	359,310	....	27,185	....
No-net.................	131,842	....	1,992	....
Total.................	491,152	....	25,193	....
Fiscal-year returns				
Net....................	98,824	27.5	7,159	26.4
No-net.................	33,537	25.4	488	24.5
Total.................	132,361	27.0	6,671	26.5
Calendar-year returns				
Net....................	260,486	72.5	20,025	73.6
No-net.................	98,305	74.6	1,504	75.5
Total.................	358,791	73.0	18,522	73.5

* SOURCE: *1945 S. of I.*, pp. 2 and 39; *1946 S. of I.*, pp. 2 and 37. Inactive returns are excluded; part-year returns, included.

accounting periods for these numerous part-year returns of 1945 and 1946 are distributed with reference to the pertinent calendar year, we may perhaps assume that their effect on the centering of the average taxable period for all active corporations is small.[15]

4. *Preliminary description of the source tables.*—The foregoing comments concerning limitations in coverage and imperfections in timing of the data here under study should be borne in mind in examining the ensuing analysis and its results. The analysis nevertheless proceeds on the assumption that these limitations and imperfections are negligible, except as specifically noted at pertinent points below.

The factual data used are provided by tabulations from active returns of the answers to two questions appearing on the income-tax form. Question 1 calls for the date of incorporation, and Question 3 reads:

If incorporated in 1946, indicate whether (a) completely new business (- -), or (b) successor to previously existing business, which was organized as (1) corporation (- -), (2) partnership (- -), or (3) sole proprietorship (- -), or (4) other (indicate) .... If successor to previously existing business, give name and address of previous business organization ....[16]

Tabulations from Question 1 are the basis of the analysis in chapters ii, iii, iv, v, and most of vii, and tabulations from Question 3 are the basis for chapter vi and part of vii.[17] The tabulations from

---

[15] With respect to certain other averages which one might be tempted to compute, however, the inclusion of the part-year returns in the tabulations may be a significant bar to precision. Thus, for 1946, the 491,152 active returns showed aggregate net income of 25,193 million dollars; and this implies an approximate average per return of $51,300. Entirely apart from other serious objections to this average, which need not be outlined here, this figure cannot be taken as the average net income for an *annual* period, because its size depends significantly on the inclusion of 46,727 returns for periods *less* than a year in length.

[16] Question 1 appears on Forms 1120, 1120L, and 1120M for both years. Question 3 appears only on Form 1120, and tabulations from Question 3 do not therefore cover those life insurance companies or mutual insurance companies filing Form 1120L or 1120M. On the 1945 Form 1120, of course, 1946 is replaced by 1945 in Question 3. We may note that the form in which the first part of Question 3 appears would lead one to expect that, if a return indicates that it is a successor, the type of the predecessor organization would be automatically indicated—the Not-stated category, as to type of predecessor, would be nonexistent. The second part of the question, however, makes it possible for the Not-stated category to arise; if this part of the question is answered without answering the first part in various cases, the type of predecessor would not be clearly indicated.

[17] The first set of tabulations appears in *1945 S. of I.*, pp. 19–29, and *1946 S. of I.*, pp. 18–27. The second set appears in *1945 S. of I.*, pp. 31–35, and *1946 S. of I.*, pp. 28–33; and for 1946 this set includes a size classification not included for 1945.

Question 1 classify the active corporations according to date of incorporation into 20 periods (19 for 1945): annual periods back to 1940, five-year periods 1935–1939 to 1900–1904, ten-year periods, 1890–1899 to 1860–1869, and an indefinitely long period before 1860. Returns on which the date was not reported are classified as Not stated. Returns for which the date of incorporation was stated and tabulated are hereafter designated dated corporations (or returns). The tabulations from Question 3 classify active corporations which were incorporated in 1946 (or 1945) between those which were new enterprises and those which were successors to previously existing enterprises; and the latter category is further classified according as the predecessor was a corporation, partnership, sole proprietorship, or other form of business organization. Returns on which the relevant information was not reported are covered in Not-stated columns of the tables.

All the tables show separate data for the net and no-net categories; and, for each of these two categories, all active returns are separately classified by 85 lines of industry (of which 74 are mutually exclusive—see also chap. iv), and the balance-sheet returns are separately classified by 10 size classes.[18] All the tabulations are in terms solely of the *number* of corporations (returns) in each class or group: they do not distribute any of the accounting items appearing on the return among the classes and groups. Our analysis, therefore, runs mainly in terms of number of corporations. We are able, however, by using certain data appearing in other tables of *Statistics of Income,* to work out the approximate age distribution of corporations in terms of such a measure of importance as total assets, and such estimates appear below in chapter ii.[19]

[18] The size-class tabulation from Question 3 appears only for 1946.

[19] One might suggest that the date-of-incorporation statistics of *S. of I.* would be more informing if not only the number of returns but also certain important accounting items were tabulated. As the inclusion of such information, however, would greatly increase the job of tabulation and might not have much value for purposes of tax administration or the planning of tax policy, one may pause before recommending this elaboration of the date-of-incorporation tables.

CHAPTER II

Shape of the Age Distribution

THE AGE DISTRIBUTION of corporations can helpfully be examined first with reference to the entire corporate system. Fortunately, we are able to present this over-all age distribution in terms not only of the number of corporations, but also of the aggregate amount of assets held, in each age group. The basic method of analysis developed below for describing the age distribution of the entire corporate system is used in subsequent chapters for analyzing various classes within the system, classes in terms of size and of type of business.

5. *Basic method of analysis.*—Table 4 illustrates the procedure followed in the basic analysis of corporate age. The figures of this table pertain to the entire system of active corporations in 1946, without regard to industrial or size classification. A similar analysis was carried out separately for 1945 and 1946, for each of 10 size classes and each of 85 industrial classes; and the results are reported in chapters iii and iv. Table 4, except for the two summary blocks in the lower right corner, includes 23 blocks of seven rows each. The *a* line of each block is an abbreviated descriptive designation of that block. The three upper blocks in the left column include: all active corporations regardless of what the date of incorporation was, or whether it was stated on the return; those for which the date was not stated; and all for which the date was stated (herein called the dated corporations) regardless of the date. Items *b*, *c*, and *d* of the third block are obtained by subtracting corresponding items of the second block from those of the first. The next 20 blocks—hereafter designated period blocks—pertain to the specific years, or other periods, in which the stated dates of incorporation fall. The sum of items *b* in these 20 blocks is item *b* of the third block, and similarly for items *c* and *d*.

In each block, lines *b* and *c* are, respectively, the numbers of net and no-net corporations in the class indicated by line *a;* and these

TABLE 4

ANALYSIS OF DATE-OF-INCORPORATION STATISTICS OF ALL ACTIVE
CORPORATIONS FOR 1946*

a	All returns	1944	1935–1939	1910–1914	1870–1879
b	359,310	14,197	56,031	12,695	668
c	131,842	5,797	18,638	2,802	110
d	491,152	19,994	74,669	15,497	778
e	26.8	29.0	25.0	18.1	14.1
f	....	4.2	15.6	3.2	0.2
g	....	27.0	55.0	92.4	99.7

a	Date not stated	1943	1930–1934	1905–1909	1860–1869
b	7,486	9,885	49,589	12,026	711
c	5,717	3,986	14,336	2,581	92
d	13,203	13,871	63,925	14,607	803
e	43.3	28.7	22.4	17.7	11.5
f	....	2.9	13.4	3.1	0.2
g	....	29.9	68.4	95.4	99.9

a	All stated	1942	1925–1929	1900–1904	Before 1860
b	351,824	8,385	37,423	8,304	456
c	126,125	3,778	10,600	1,589	115
d	477,949	12,163	48,023	9,893	571
e	26.4	31.1	22.1	16.1	20.1
f	....	2.5	10.0	2.1	0.1
g	....	32.5	78.5	97.5	100.0

a	1946	1941	1920–1924	1890–1899	Quartiles
b	42,666	11,617	25,343	5,719	1944
c	27,781	4,550	6,181	1,108	1936
d	70,447	16,167	31,524	6,827	1926
e	39.4	28.1	19.6	16.2	3
f	14.7	3.4	6.6	1.4	11
g	14.7	35.9	85.1	98.9	21

a	1945	1940	1915–1919	1880–1889	Loss points
b	25,372	12,259	15,982	2,496	1.495
c	13,437	4,760	3,469	415	0.685
d	38,809	17,019	19,451	2,911	1860–1869
e	34.6	28.0	17.8	14.3	1940
f	8.1	3.6	4.1	0.6	1935
g	22.9	39.4	89.1	99.5	1940

* See accompanying text for description of items.

Except for the Quartiles block, which is described in section 7 and the Loss-points block, which is described in section 19, the meanings of the items in each block may be summarized as follows:

a. A description of the groups of 1946-active corporations, or of the period of incorporation, covered by the block.

b. The number of net-income corporations in the group designated by line *a.*

c. The number of deficit corporations in the group.

d. The sum of lines *b* and *c.*

e. The percentage ratio of line *c* to line *d.*

f. The percentage ratio of line *d* of the particular block to line *d* of "All stated."

g. The cumulation of line *f*, from 1946 backward over the whole range of time.

figures, for all blocks except the third (for which they are computed by subtraction, as indicated above), are transcribed directly from the table published in *1946 S. of I.* (pp. 18–25). Line *d* is the sum of lines *b* and *c*, and gives the number of corporations in the block without regard to the distinction between net and no-net. Line *e* is the percentage ratio of line *c* to *d* and is the primary basis of the study (see chap. v, below) of the relation between age and profitability. For the 20 period blocks, two other lines appear. Line *f* is the percentage ratio of line *d* of the particular period block to line *d* of the third block; it is the fraction, of all dated corporations active in 1946, incorporated in the particular period. Line *g* is the cumulative total of line *f* figures, the cumulation running from 1946 backward over time (the line *g* figures in this, and other 1946 tables may not check in the final digit as cumulatives of line *f*, since the actual cumulations were carried to hundredths of per cent before rounding). The summary figures of the two lower blocks of the fifth column are described below, section 7 and section 19, in connection with discussion of the results of the analysis.

The corresponding table for all active corporations in 1945, table 5, is exactly similar in form to table 4, except that the 1946 block is missing. The age-distribution results for both 1945 and 1946 are reported in this chapter, but certain important inferences which can be drawn by comparing the 1945 and 1946 distributions are reserved for examination in chapter vii.

6. *Numerical importance of very young corporations.*—Line *f* of table 4 shows the percentage, for each period (year, or other), of all active dated corporations, incorporated in such period.[20] The incorporations in 1946 may have occurred at various times during that

[20] If we may assume—and this is debatable—that the "date not stated" corporations had the same age distribution, we may say that line *f* shows the age distribution for *all* active corporations in 1946. See chap. vii.

TABLE 5

ANALYSIS OF DATE-OF-INCORPORATION STATISTICS OF ALL ACTIVE
CORPORATIONS FOR 1945*

a	All returns	1944	1935–1939	1910–1914	1870–1879
b	303,019	13,917	55,884	12,476	648
c	118,106	7,518	22,071	3,314	142
d	421,125	21,435	77,955	15,790	790
e	28.0	35.1	28.3	21.0	18.0
f	....	5.3	19.2	3.9	0.2
g	....	10.9	45.7	90.9	99.7

a	Date not stated	1943	1930–1934	1905–1909	1860–1869
b	9,253	10,490	48,886	11,870	695
c	6,653	4,472	16,905	2,965	105
d	15,906	14,962	65,791	14,835	800
e	41.8	29.9	25.7	20.0	13.1
f	....	3.7	16.2	3.7	0.2
g	....	14.6	61.9	94.6	99.9

a	All stated	1942	1925–1929	1900–1904	Before 1860
b	293,766	8,994	36,713	8,137	519
c	111,453	4,191	12,764	1,869	91
d	405,219	13,185	49,477	10,006	610
e	27.5	31.8	25.8	18.7	14.9
f	....	3.3	12.2	2.5	0.2
g	....	17.9	74.1	97.1	100.1

a	....	1941	1920–1924	1890–1899	Quartiles
b	....	11,771	24,899	5,646	1940
c	....	5,291	7,411	1,242	1933
d	....	17,062	32,310	6,888	1924
e	....	31.0	22.9	18.0	6
f	....	4.2	8.0	1.7	13
g	....	22.1	82.1	98.8	22

a	1945	1940	1915–1919	1880–1889	Loss points
b	11,485	12,422	15,836	2,478	1.785
c	11,058	5,432	4,123	489	0.764
d	22,543	17,854	19,959	2,967	1860–1869
e	49.1	30.4	20.7	16.5	1935–1939
f	5.6	4.4	4.9	0.7	1932
g	5.6	26.5	87.0	99.5	1935

* See table 4 and accompanying text for description of items.

year, but we may assume that on the average the 70,447 corporations classified as incorporated in 1946 were about one-half year old at the end of their 1946 taxable year.[21] Similarly, the 74,669 corporations in the 1935–1939 class were on the average about nine and one-half years old at the end of their 1946 taxable year; and a corresponding rough conversion from date-of-incorporation to age basis can be made for the other periods.[22]

As periods of incorporation before 1946 are identically defined in terms of calendar years for the 1946-active corporations (table 4) and the 1945-active corporations (table 5), the conversion of a particular period to the age basis differs by one year depending on whether we are using the 1946 or the 1945 table. Thus for the 1946 data, corporations incorporated during the 1935–1939 period are on the average about nine and one-half years old at the end of the 1946 taxable year; for the 1945 data, about eight and one-half years old at the end of the 1945 taxable year.

Among all dated corporations active in 1945, many were very young: 5.6 per cent were chartered in 1945 and 26.5 per cent were chartered during the years 1940–1945 (line g of table 5). Still more surprising is the corresponding situation for dated corporations active in 1946: 14.7 per cent were chartered in 1946, and 27.0 per cent in the years 1944–1946. For 1945, more than 5 per cent were not more than a year old, and more than 25 per cent were not more than six years old; for 1946, more than 14 per cent were not more than a year old, and more than 25 per cent were not more than three years old. These facts are emphatic indication of the comparative youth of a substantial fraction of the entire corporate system and of the fluidity with which the corporate system adapts itself—in a legal milieu marked by nearly complete freedom of in-

---

[21] Such an average is only approximate. The number of incorporations may vary greatly from month to month during a year (see chap. vii). And the fact that not all taxable years are calendar years introduces another variable into the average.

[22] The figures in lines *b, c,* and *d* of the 20 period blocks of table 4 should *not* be read as the *total* numbers of incorporations in the stated periods. The figures of table 4 represent *only* the incorporations in the various periods of those corporations which not only survived in or into 1946 but also filed an active return for that year (and stated their dates of incorporation). Many companies chartered in some early period, such as 1935–1939, had disappeared through dissolution by 1946 or were in process of liquidation and filed no active return for 1946. Many corporations chartered in 1946, and perhaps in certain other very recent years, were not yet active in 1946 and, since they filed no active returns for that year, were not tabulated. (See *1946 S. of I.,* p. 60, n. 45.) In connection with this last point we may observe that at least 16,266 (38,809−22,543: line *d* of the 1945 blocks of tables 4 and 5) corporations chartered in 1945 which were not active in 1945 were active in 1946. Actually the figure is higher than 16,266, because some corporations chartered and active in 1945 undoubtedly became inactive in 1946. See chap. vii for more detailed comment on this point.

corporation—to the developing needs and opportunities of free enterprise. That evidence of youthfulness is much more striking in the 1946 than in the 1945 data can be explained by the enormous wave of incorporations which began after the close of the war in 1945 and was more fully developed in 1946. This huge increase, probably unprecedented, in the number of new incorporations reduced the average age of the system between 1945 and 1946.

We note, nevertheless, that 24.9 per cent of the 1945-active dated corporations were chartered before 1925 (were more than twenty-one years old), and that 21.5 per cent of the 1946-active dated corporations were chartered before 1925 (were more than twenty-two years old). Also, for the 1945 data 1.2, and for the 1946 data 1.1, per cent were chartered before 1890—were more than fifty years old. Thus, more than 20 per cent of the dated corporations active in 1945 or 1946 had survived more than twenty years, and one per cent had survived more than fifty years, presumably under their present charters.[23] Although the corporate system, as stated above, comprises a large number of very young members, it also includes a very substantial number of companies which have existed for many years. As will be brought out below (chap. iii), these older corporations are on the average larger, and many of them much larger, than the very young corporations. The "small company" problem, which has received much attention in recent public discussions, is predominately a young company problem; and policies, public and private, effectively designed to aid new and young corporations will in the main benefit small corporations.

7. *Quartile ages.*—The foregoing citation of isolated figures summarizes in some respects the age distribution. A more systematic summarization can be expressed in terms of the quartile dates and the quartile ages. I define the quartile dates and quartile ages, with reference to the 1946 data (similar definitions, with obvious adaptations, apply to the 1945 data), as follows. The first quartile date

---

[23] We are obliged to say "presumably." Question 1 on Form 1120 seems to imply that a corporation return should report the date when *that* corporation was chartered, and Question 3 seems to make this implication unmistakable. But the returns of certain corporations which were successors to previously existing corporations may have given the date when the business was *first* incorporated. This possibility may be important because of the understandable tendency of officials to take pride in the age of the enterprises for which they are responsible, and because one could not readily see how accuracy in the answer to Question 1 would have any bearing on the corporation's tax liability. Such cases of faulty reporting, which are probably not numerous, would contribute to a slight overstatement in the average age of the corporate system or parts thereof. Age here refers, of course, to currently active *corporations* and not necessarily to the enterprises owned or operated by such corporations.

is a date such that 25 per cent of the 1946-active dated corporations were incorporated after that date, the second quartile (median) date is such that 50 per cent were incorporated after that date, the third quartile date is such that 75 per cent were incorporated after that date. For practical purposes we cannot specify the quartile date more precisely than to the nearest year; and the quartile years, as specified and discussed hereafter, are the calendar years within which the quartile dates as defined above fall. The quartile age is the number of years from the beginning of the quartile year to the end of the particular year (1946 or 1945, as the case may be) to which the tabulated statistics apply. For example, from line *g* of table 4, 27.0 per cent of the 1946-active dated corporations were incorporated after the beginning, and 22.9 per cent were incorporated after the end, of 1944. This means that the first quartile date falls sometime within 1944, and the quartile year is 1944. The first quartile age is accordingly three years, the time elapsed from the beginning of 1944 to the end of 1946. This means that 25 per cent of the 1946-active dated corporations were not more than three years old, and corresponding interpretation can be applied to the various other quartile ages.

When a quartile date, such as the first quartile for 1946 data, falls within a calendar year, the quartile year can at once be identified from line *g* of table 4. When, however, the quartile date falls within a longer period, the quartile year must be estimated. Such estimate is based on the assumption that the relevant incorporations within the longer period are spread uniformly among the years of that period.[24]

Thus, line *g* of table 4 shows the second quartile (median) date for 1946 data within the five-year period 1935–1939: 55.0 per cent

[24] The "relevant" incorporations are those of dated corporations active in 1946. The assumption made is *not* equivalent to assuming that *all* incorporations in the period are spread uniformly among the years of the period. If this were true, the assumption made above would almost certainly not be valid, because companies actually incorporated in the early years of the period would be more likely to become inactive by 1946 than those incorporated in the later years of the period. Actually, total incorporations within any five-year or ten-year period probably vary markedly from year to year, because of cyclical or other influences bearing upon the launching of new companies. (See chap. vii, for further details on this last point.) These year-to-year variations in the annual number of actual incorporations result in corresponding, though not necessarily similar, variations in the relevant incorporations (those of corporations active in 1946). Accordingly, the assumption made above is not entirely valid; and the resulting location of the quartile year may be in error, though the consequent error in the quartile age is unlikely to exceed one year if the period is only five years long (and very few quartile dates encountered in chaps. iii and iv fall in ten-year periods).

were incorporated after the beginning of that period, and 39.4 per cent after the end. The 15.6 per cent incorporated within the period 1935–1939 are assumed to be spread uniformly over the five years: approximately 3.1 per cent in each year. On this assumption, 51.9 per cent were incorporated after the beginning, and 48.8 per cent after the end of 1936; and 1936 is therefore the quartile year. A similar procedure has been followed in all cases, in this chapter and in chapters iii and iv, where the quartile date falls in a period longer than one year.

The quartile years and corresponding quartile ages are brought together in the Quartiles block of table 4. The first, second, and third quartile years for 1946-active dated corporations are respectively 1944, 1936, and 1926; and the corresponding years for the 1945 data (table 5) are 1940, 1933, and 1924. The quartile ages for 1946 (3, 11, and 21) are lower than the quartile ages for 1945 (6, 13, and 22). This is another indication that the population of active dated corporations in 1946 was younger than that in 1945 (see section 12 and n. 43). One further summary figure, having some significance in the study of certain classes of corporations in chapter iv, can be drawn from the quartile years. The "middle-aged" corporations (among the active dated corporations in 1946, or those in 1945) are those incorporated between the first and third quartile dates. As 25 per cent were incorporated after the first quartile date, and 25 per cent before the third quartile date, 50 per cent were incorporated between those two dates. As we do not state those dates except to the nearest year, we may say that the 50 per cent of all 1946-active dated corporations which constitute the middle-aged group were incorporated between the beginning of 1926 and the end of 1944, a span of nineteen years. The age of these middle-aged corporations ranged from somewhat more than two (one year less than the first quartile age) to somewhat less than twenty-one years (the third quartile age). Half the 1946-active dated corporations were between two and twenty-one years of age. Similarly, half the 1945-active dated corporations were between five and twenty-two years of age.

Summaries of the sort shown in the Quartiles block of table 4 afford the main basis of the commentary on differences in age distribution among the various lines of industry, in chapter iv; because space does not permit the inclusion of a very large number—the line-of-industry classes are more than 80 in number—of exhibits such as table 4 and figure 2. Although the complete list of percentages, given in line *f* of the 20 period blocks of table 4, more adequately describes the age distribution, the summary in terms of quartile ages is sufficient for most comparisons among age distributions of the various classes.

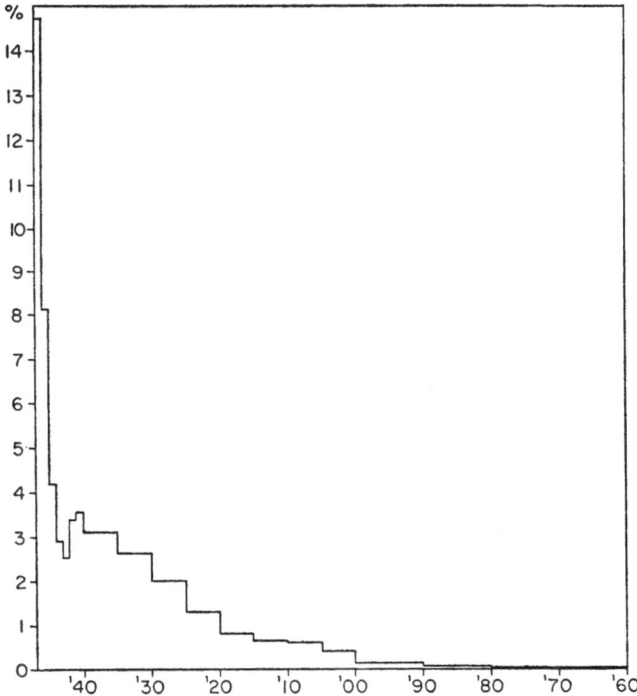

Fig. 2. Percentage distribution among periods of incorporation, of dated corporations active in 1946, in terms of number of such corporations.

SOURCE: Data from line *f* of table 4. Percentage for Before-1860 not shown.

8. *Shape of the age distribution, in terms of numbers.*—Figure 2 shows the percentages of line *f* of table 4 in graphic form, except for the period of indefinite length before 1860.[25] The curve of this figure is identical with the light-line curve of figure 1. The figure facili-

---

[25] For those periods longer than one year, the percentages of line *f* of table 4 have been adjusted to an annual average basis for each such period, before plotting. Hence the *areas* of the various rectangles standing upon the various period segments of the horizontal axis are proportional to the numbers of 1946-active dated corporations in those periods. Because of the indeterminate length of that period, no rectangle appears in the figure for the period before 1860, which included 571 incorporations, or somewhat more than 0.1 per cent of the total of 1946-active dated corporations.

tates an over-all examination of the 1946 age distribution, such as can be made with somewhat greater difficulty directly from line *f* of table 4. From the level of nearly 15 per cent for incorporations in 1946, the curve drops sharply and steadily to 1942. Then, after somewhat higher figures for 1941 and 1940, the curve declines more gradually and without any interruption until 1870.[26] The fact that percentages for 1941, 1942, and 1943 are less than, and that of 1944 only moderately more than, that of 1940 can be accounted for mainly by wartime obstacles to the launching of new companies: difficulties in securing funds, materials, and manpower undoubtedly prevented the chartering of many companies which might otherwise have been created in those years. If we were considering 1940–1944 as a single five-year period, the percentage for that period (corresponding to line *f* of table 4) would be 16.6, which is more than the 1935–1939 figure of 15.6; and the course of the curve plotted on this basis would be steadily downward toward the right, without revealing the dip to 1942 shown by the annual figures.

If the various periods, longer than one year, before 1940, had been broken into annual periods in the *S. of I.* tabulations, and the resulting annual percentages corresponding to line *f* of table 4 had been plotted on figure 2, the curve might have shown various minor fluctuations besides that of 1941–1943. Such fluctuations before 1940, except for those in the 1915–1919 period, would be caused not by wartime obstacles to creation of corporations but by cyclical and other peacetime factors influencing financial and economic conditions and prospects. In spite of such fluctuations, however, the general course of the whole curve would be downward to the right, with the decline generally more sharp in the left than in the right part of the curve.

This sweep of the curve, downward to the right, indicates emphatically the conclusion drawn above from an examination of specific figures: a very large fraction of the corporate system is characterized by youth. The great bulk of the area under the curve lies near the left boundary, in the rectangles pertaining to the few most recent years; and this area represents corporations which were, at the date when the 1946 tax returns were filed, very young. Although the lower levels of the long stretch of curve reaching to the right reflects the presence of moderate numbers of corporations

---

[26] The curve shows 1860–1869 at the same level as 1870–1879. Actually, as shown by line *d* of table 4, 1860–1869 was very slightly higher than 1870–1879, and this constitutes a very slight interruption in the otherwise steadily downward course for periods before 1940.

of considerable age, the most striking inference from the figure is that the system as a whole is dominated—in terms of number of corporations—by the young members. That the corporate business of the nation is, however, not dominated by these youthful members is brought out in section 10 below.

I emphasize again that all these statistics on age, derived from the *S. of I.* data on dates of incorporation, reflect the age of existing *corporations,* and not necessarily the age of the enterprises owned or operated by such corporations (see, however, n. 23). In many cases of incorporation, the new corporate entity merely takes over an existing business (see chap. vi for limited evidence on this point); and in such cases the age of the corporation, if strictly reported, understates the age of the business enterprise. The provisions of the Internal Revenue Code relating to consolidated returns may have a particular bearing—though not of large moment for the system as a whole—upon the relation between the reported date of incorporation (presumably of the "parent" which files the consolidated return) and the ages of some or all of the subsidiaries as well as the possibly longer ages of the economic enterprises which they operate. The parent may be a fairly old corporation and still have some very young subsidiaries. Or, the parent may be a fairly young corporation, possibly organized at the time when consolidation was effected; whereas one or more of the subsidiaries may be much older, whether in the corporate form or in some other and earlier form of organization. (See chap. vii for further details on consolidated returns.) We cannot stress too much the point that these date-of-incorporation statistics furnish no dependably precise guide to inferences concerning the age of the economic enterprises represented.

9. *Allocation of total assets by periods.*—Thus far we have been discussing the age distribution in terms of the *number* of corporations which were incorporated in each period. A large part of the present investigation of corporate age and related matters must be confined to an analysis in terms of number, since the *S. of I.* tables on date of incorporation do not allocate any of the accounting items (but allocate merely the number of corporations) among the various age periods or other groups. Fortunately, however, we can, by combining certain evidence in these tables and evidence published in other *Statistics of Income* tables, develop a highly important *estimate* of the allocation of one accounting item—total assets—among the age periods. Such an allocation provides an informing picture

of the corporate age distribution in terms of importance, rather than of mere number, of corporations of each age. This estimated allocation is the subject of the present section.

Table 6A shows the method of estimate, for the most recent date-of-incorporation period (1946) for the 1946-active net corporations (table 6B shows the corresponding estimate for no-net corporations).

TABLE 6A

Estimated Total Assets, at End of Taxable Year 1946, for Net Corporations Active in 1946 Which Were Incorporated in 1946*

(a) Lower limit of size class (in thousands of dollars)	(b) Number of returns	(c) Aggregate total assets (in thousands of dollars)	(d) Average total assets (c/b) (in dollars)	(e) Number incorporated in 1946	(f) Estimated total assets (d×e) (in thousands of dollars)
0.	127,609	3,019,887	23,665	18,870	446,559
50.	62,601	4,489,292	71,713	8,664	621,321
100.	65,285	10,340,778	158,390	8,002	1,267,437
250.	29,861	10,462,740	350,380	2,909	1,019,255
500.	18,375	12,894,875	701,760	1,203	844,217
1,000.	22,392	48,810,390	2,179,800	560	1,220,688
5,000.	3,944	27,531,276	6,980,500	40	279,220
10,000.	3,066	62,338,534	20,332,000	13	264,316
50,000.	422	29,660,167	70,285,000	2	140,570
100,000.	487	207,296,199	425,659,000	. . . . . .	. . . .
All classes combined. . .	334,042	416,844,058	. . . .	40,263	6,103,583

* Source: Columns *b* and *c*, *1946 S. of I.*, p. 216; column *e*, *1946 S. of I.*, p. 26.

The 1946-active corporations covered include only those for which the tax returns showed balance sheets, but the balance-sheet returns cover so nearly the entire list of active corporations (see sec. 2, above) that we shall regard the findings as valid for the entire system. One of the *1946 S. of I.* tables (pp. 26–27) gives the date-of-incorporation breakdown of the total number of balance-sheet returns separately for each size class of corporations. The size classes are determined by the amount of total assets shown on the balance sheet (pertinent to the end of the taxable year 1946), which is included in the tax return; and column *a* of table 6A indicates the lower boundaries, in amount of total assets, of the ten size classes. Thus, each corporation in the smallest-size class had total assets between zero and $50,000, and each in the largest-size class had total assets of more than $100,000,000. Column *b* of the table gives the total number of 1946-active net balance-sheet corporations—regardless of what the date of incorporation was or whether it was stated—in each size class; and column *c* gives the aggregate total assets of these corporations. These two columns of table 6A do not come from the date-of-incorporation tables of *1946 S. of I.*, on which this investigation is mainly based, but from one of the standard

TABLE 6B

ESTIMATED TOTAL ASSETS, AT END OF TAXABLE YEAR 1946, FOR NO-NET COR-
PORATIONS ACTIVE IN 1946 WHICH WERE INCORPORATED IN 1946*

(a) Lower limit of size class (in thousands of dollars)	(b) Number of returns	(c) Aggregate total assets (in thousands of dollars)	(d) Average total assets (c/b) (in dollars)	(e) Number incorporated in 1946	(f) Estimated total assets (d×e) (in thousands of dollars)
0......	71,467	1,176,053	16,456	17,864	293,970
50......	14,220	1,001,580	70,435	3,271	230,393
100......	11,307	1,752,773	155,020	2,179	337,789
250......	4,403	1,534,678	348,550	608	211,918
500......	2,428	1,689,778	695,950	285	198,345
1,000......	2,226	4,564,263	2,050,400	192	393,677
5,000......	297	2,095,972	7,057,100	8	56,457
10,000......	275	5,557,075	20,208,000	7	141,456
50,000......	41	2,796,836	68,216,000	1	68,216
100,000......	44	15,692,107	356,639,000	......	....
All classes combined...	106,708	37,861,115	....	24,415	1,932,221

* SOURCE: Columns *b* and *c*, *1946 S. of I.*, p. 218; column *e*, *1946 S. of I.*, p. 27.

tables, showing accounting items classified by size of corporation, which have appeared for many years in *Statistics of Income*. Column *d* is computed from columns *b* and *c* and gives the average total assets per return (for net corporations) in each size class.[27]

The fundamental assumption on which the estimates rest is that the average total assets (column *d*), as computed from data (in columns *b* and *c*) for all active balance-sheet corporations (separately for net and no-net categories) in the size class, is valid for those corporations which were incorporated in the stated period (the most recent period, 1946, in the estimate illustrated in table 6A). Thus, for the smallest-size class, the average total assets of $23,665 is assumed to be valid for those, among the whole list of 127,609 net

---

[27] In computing these averages, the divisions were carried to five significant digits except where one or more further digits were needed to express the result to the nearest $1,000.

corporations in that size class, which were incorporated in 1946. Those incorporated in 1946 are shown in column *e* as 18,870 in number. Column *e* for each size class is taken from that part (*1946 S. of I.*, pp. 26–27) of the date-of-incorporation tables which classifies by age the number of balance-sheet corporations in each size class. The validity of the assumption depends partly upon the width of

TABLE 7A

ESTIMATED TOTAL ASSETS, AT END OF TAXABLE YEAR 1945, FOR NET CORPORATIONS
ACTIVE IN 1945 WHICH WERE INCORPORATED IN 1945*

(a) Lower limit of size class (in thousands of dollars)	(b) Number of returns	(c) Aggregate total assets (in thousands of dollars)	(d) Average total assets (c/b) (in dollars)	(e) Number incorporated in 1945	(f) Estimated total assets (d×e) (in thousands of dollars)
0......	114,813	2,629,990	22,907	6,738	154,347
50......	49,254	3,520,096	71,468	1,974	141,078
100......	50,370	7,980,522	158,440	1,339	212,151
250......	23,608	8,279,878	350,720	424	148,705
500......	15,490	10,917,242	704,790	187	131,796
1,000......	20,108	43,928,294	2,184,600	118	257,783
5,000......	3,684	25,749,568	6,989,600	6	41,938
10,000......	3,002	61,373,517	20,444,000	6	122,664
50,000......	403	28,181,256	69,929,000	1	69,929
100,000......	512	223,300,079	436,133,000	......	....
All classes combined...	281,244	415,860,443	....	10,793	1,280,391

* SOURCE: Columns *b* and *c*, *1945 S. of I.*, p. 220; column *e*, *1945 S. of I.*, p. 28.

the size class: validity is higher for the small-size classes than for the large-size classes, for the smallest-size class which is $50,000 wide than for the next-to-largest-size class which is $50,000,000 wide. (The largest-size class is of indefinite width, and validity of the assumption there may be lower than in any of the other classes.) The validity depends also upon the number of incorporations in the size class (column *e*): it is higher where the number is large, as in the small-size classes, than where it is small, as in the large-size classes. For example, the chance that the average total assets of the two corporations of the $50,000,000 class which were incorporated in 1946 is identical with, or even close to, $70,285,000 is much lower than the chance that the average total assets of the 18,870 corporations of the smallest-size class incorporated in 1946 is identical with, or close to, $23,665. On both counts, validity of the assumption is less likely to be high for large-size than for small-size classes.[28] This finding means that the specific class estimates in column *f*—which is the product of column *d* by column *e* for each size class—are less dependable for larger-size than for smaller size classes. As, however, the aggregate of column *f* for all classes, shown in column *f* under all classes combined, which is the objective of the estimating process,

TABLE 7B

ESTIMATED TOTAL ASSETS, AT END OF TAXABLE YEAR 1945, FOR NO-NET CORPORA-
TIONS ACTIVE IN 1945 WHICH WERE INCORPORATED IN 1945*

(a) Lower limit of size class (in thousands of dollars)	(b) Number of returns	(c) Aggregate total assets (in thousands of dollars)	(d) Average total assets (c/b) (in dollars)	(e) Number incorporated in 1945	(f) Estimated total assets (d×e) (in thousands of dollars)
0......	62,975	1,017,670	16,160	7,272	117,516
50......	12,177	858,750	70,522	1,195	84,274
100......	9,938	1,545,819	155,550	731	113,707
250......	3,975	1,386,628	348,840	286	99,768
500......	2,179	1,519,614	697,390	119	82,989
1,000......	1,949	3,979,107	2,041,600	77	157,203
5,000......	264	1,841,811	6,976,600	4	27,906
10,000......	195	3,961,333	20,315,000	1	20,315
50,000......	24	1,653,026	68,876,000	......	....
100,000......	30	7,837,065	261,236,000	......	....
All classes combined...	93,706	25,600,826	....	9,685	703,678

* SOURCE: Columns *b* and *c*, *1945 S. of I.*, p. 222; column *e*, *1945 S. of I.*, p. 29.

is a sum in which positive errors (due to the faulty assumption) for some size classes may tend to offset negative errors for others, this combined estimate may not be seriously damaged by imperfections in the fundamental assumption.

An analysis similar to those of tables 6A and 6B was carried out for each of the 20 periods, from that for 1946 (shown in the tables)

[28] We may observe that the average total assets in any class (column *d*) is invariably below the middle point of the class: for example, $23,665 is below $25,000. This reflects the shape of the distribution according to size (a shape somewhat similar to that of figure 2, though the horizontal variable there is age instead of size). For such a shape, which the statistician calls J-shape, the class average is typically smaller (larger, if the high end of the curve is at the right) than the mid-point of the class. We may observe also that, except for the $5,000,000 class, the averages for the no-net corporations (table 6B) run below those for the net corporations (table 6A). This reflects the fact that the size distribution of the no-net corporations is more sharply J-shaped than that of the net: a greater concentration of small corporations exists in the no-net than in the net category.

TABLE 8

AGE DISTRIBUTION, IN TERMS OF ESTIMATED TOTAL ASSETS HELD AT END OF TAXABLE
YEAR 1946, OF ALL 1946-ACTIVE BALANCE-SHEET CORPORATIONS*
(Lines *b, c, d,* in millions of dollars, *e, f,* and *g* in percentages)

a	All Returns	1944	1935–1939	1910–1914	1870–1879
b	416,844	2,141	18,445	28,158	14,784
c	37,861	1,559	2,945	2,036	724
d	454,705	3,700	21,390	30,194	15,508
e	8.3	42.1	13.8	6.7	4.7
f	....	0.8	4.7	6.7	3.4
g	....	3.7	11.1	56.3	89.4

a	Date not stated	1943	1930–1934	1905–1909	1860–1869
b	3,541	1,748	36,201	30,487	25,537
c	169	370	3,472	2,212	405
d	3,710	2,118	39,673	32,699	25,942
e	4.6	17.5	8.8	6.8	1.6
f	....	0.5	8.8	7.2	5.8
g	....	4.2	19.9	63.5	95.2

a	All stated	1942	1925–1929	1900–1904	Before 1860
b	413,302	1,932	55,021	29,111	18,083
c	37,692	402	4,580	1,929	3,441
d	450,994	2,334	59,601	31,040	21,524
e	8.4	17.2	7.7	6.2	16.0
f	....	0.5	13.2	6.9	4.8
g	....	4.7	33.2	70.4	100.0

a	1946	1941	1920–1924	1890–1899	Quartiles
b	6,104	3,462	36,609	38,229	1928
c	1,932	370	2,023	2,779	1914
d	8,036	3,832	38,632	41,008	1894
e	24.0	9.7	5.2	6.8	19
f	1.8	0.8	8.6	9.1	33
g	1.8	5.6	41.7	79.5	53

a	1945	1940	1915–1919	1880–1889	Loss points
b	3,933	3,170	31,764	28,384	2.876
c	1,060	606	3,702	1,143	0.806
d	4,993	3,776	35,466	29,527	1930–1934
e	21.2	16.0	10.4	3.9	Before 1860
f	1.1	0.8	7.9	6.6	1913
g	2.9	6.4	49.6	86.0	1921

* See accompanying text for description of items.

back to that before 1860, and also for the group of corporations for which date of incorporation was not stated. For each of the 20 periods, and for the Not-stated group, a pair of columns appears corresponding to columns *e* and *f* of table 6A; but the one set of figures in columns *b* to *d* is applicable without change to all 21 cases for the net corporations (and correspondingly the one set in table 6B is applicable to all 21 cases for no-net corporations). Corresponding analyses were also carried out for the balance-sheet corporations active in 1945, covering each of 19 periods and also the Not-stated group. Tables 7A and 7B show, for net and no-net balance-sheet returns filed for 1945, analyses of this sort for the most recent date-of-incorporation period (1945). These tables are of the same form as tables 6A and 6B; and are shown primarily in order to include in this record the average total assets (column *d*) by size classes for active returns in 1945 and the figures from which such averages are derived.

As already indicated, the objective of each of the analyses illustrated and listed above is the column *f* figure under all classes combined—the aggregate of the separately estimated total assets in the various size classes. These figures (rounded to the nearest million dollars), for the 20 periods and the "Not stated" group, are brought together for the 1946-active balance-sheet corporations, in lines *b* and *c* of the various blocks of table 8. The blocks of that table are arranged similarly to those of table 4; but, whereas lines *b, c,* and *d* of table 4 show *numbers* of corporations, lines *b, c,* and *d* of table 8 show estimated *total assets* of corporations (for net, no-net, and both combined, respectively) in the various groups specified by the block titles (line *a*). One other significant difference between table 4 and table 8 should be noted: in table 4, lines *b* and *c* of the third block (All stated) are obtained by subtraction of corresponding lines of the second block from those of the first block; in table 8, lines *b* and *c* of the third block are obtained by adding corresponding lines of the 20 period blocks.[20] Lines *d* to *g* of table 8 are derived from

---

[20] Any discrepancy, between the figures shown in the third block of table 8 and those figures as they would stand if obtained through subtraction of the second block from the first, reflects the magnitude of the aggregate of estimating errors in the various periods (and in the Not-stated group); and such discrepancy is very small. The figures actually shown in the third block may not check in the final digit with the sums from the 20 period blocks, since the figures shown were rounded from sums of the period-block figures stated in $1,000 units. I may remark that the third block figures of table 4 could be obtained either by subtraction of the second from the first block, or by adding the 20 period blocks; and the two results would be identical because no estimating is involved in the data of table 4.

TABLE 9

AGE DISTRIBUTION, IN TERMS OF ESTIMATED TOTAL ASSETS HELD AT END OF TAXABLE
YEAR 1945, OF ALL 1945-ACTIVE BALANCE-SHEET CORPORATIONS*

(Lines *b*, *c*, *d* in millions of dollars; *e*, *f*, and *g* in percentages)

a	All returns	1944	1935–1939	1910–1914	1870–1879
b	415,860	2,292	18,529	29,062	14,102
c	25,601	721	2,289	1,189	1,034
d	441,461	3,013	20,818	30,251	15,136
e	5.8	23.9	11.0	3.9	6.8
f	....	0.7	4.8	6.9	3.5
g	....	1.1	8.5	54.3	88.6
a	Date not stated	1943	1930–1934	1905–1909	1860–1869
b	4,932	1,541	35,869	30,811	25,911
c	204	400	2,373	1,354	565
d	5,136	1,941	38,242	32,165	26,476
e	4.0	20.6	6.2	4.2	2.1
f	....	0.4	8.8	7.4	6.1
g	....	1.6	17.3	61.6	94.7
a	All stated	1942	1925–1929	1900–1904	Before 1860
b	410,929	1,861	56,092	29,709	21,446
c	25,397	418	2,778	1,369	1,603
d	436,326	2,279	58,870	31,078	23,049
e	5.8	18.3	4.7	4.4	7.0
f	....	0.5	13.5	7.1	5.3
g	....	2.1	30.8	68.8	100.0
a	....	1941	1920–1924	1890–1899	Quartiles
b	....	3,326	35,507	38,618	1927
c	....	345	2,660	2,473	1913
d	....	3,671	38,167	41,091	1893
e	....	9.4	7.0	6.0	19
f	....	0.8	8.8	9.4	33
g	....	2.9	39.5	78.2	53
a	1945	1940	1915–1919	1880–1889	Loss points
b	1,280	3,086	32,315	29,571	6.096
c	704	394	1,829	900	0.675
d	1,984	3,480	34,144	30,471	1930–1934
e	35.5	11.3	5.4	3.0	Before 1860
f	0.4	0.8	7.8	7.0	1912
g	0.4	3.7	47.3	85.2	1920

* See accompanying text for description of items.

lines *b* and *c*, in successive steps by exactly the same procedure used in table 4. Table 9 shows, for the 1945-active balance-sheet corporations, a compilation corresponding to table 8, just as table 5 is the 1945 exhibit corresponding to table 4.

10. *Shape of the age distribution, in terms of importance.*—The estimated allocation of total assets by periods, as presented and analyzed in table 8 (or table 9), indicates the age distribution of the corporate system in terms of aggregate importance. Aggregate importance is here measured by total assets held at the end of taxable year 1946 (or 1945) of the corporations chartered in the various periods.[30] The results in line *f* of table 8 and table 9 are compared with those of table 4 and table 5 in table 10. Even a brief glance at table 10 brings out the striking contrast between the age distribution in terms of total assets and that in terms of mere number of corporations. The 1946-active corporations chartered in 1946 represented, by number, 14.7 per cent of the total; they represented, by total assets, only 1.8 per cent. Those chartered before 1860 represented, by number, 0.1 per cent of the total, and by total assets, 4.8 per cent. For 1946, the quartile ages in terms of number are 3, 11, and 21, whereas in terms of total assets they are 19, 33, and 53. Similar contrasts appear for the 1945-active corporations. All these comparisons support emphatically a major conclusion: the age of the corporate system is much greater in terms of total assets held than in terms of numbers of corporations of different ages.

The fundamental reason for this sharp contrast between the age distribution in terms of total assets and that in terms of number is that large corporations tend on the average to be older than small corporations, and very large corporations very much older than very small corporations. Detailed evidence on this point, and some discussion of its implications, appears below in chapter iii. Another way of describing the same fundamental cause is: the size distribution (size being measured in terms of total assets) of young corporations tends to show a greater concentration in the small-size

---

[30] That the total assets here represented pertain to the end of the taxable year (1946 or 1945, as the case may be) for which the date-of-incorporation data are tabulated, must be emphasized. These figures do not purport to estimate, for each period, total assets *at time of incorporation* of corporations incorporated in such period. The initial assets are likely to be lower than the assets held in 1946 (or 1945) for all except the very youngest corporations (and many of these may not be exceptions), and to be very much lower than the assets held in 1946 (or 1945) for all or nearly all moderately and very old corporations. Accordingly, when we speak here of an age distribution in terms of importance, we are reckoning importance for all corporations regardless of age, at a single date—the end of 1946 (or of 1945).

classes than does that of old corporations. Thus, table 6A shows that, among 40,263 net corporations chartered in the 1946 period, 18,870 (nearly 47 per cent) were in the smallest-size class and only 2 (less than 0.01 per cent) were in the next-to-largest-size class. Cor-

TABLE 10

PERCENTAGE AGE DISTRIBUTIONS AND QUARTILE AGES, IN TERMS OF NUMBER OF COR-
PORATIONS AND OF TOTAL ASSETS HELD AT END OF FINAL PERIOD, FOR 1946-ACTIVE
AND 1945-ACTIVE DATED CORPORATIONS*

Period of incorporation	1946-active corporations		1945-active corporations	
	Number	Total assets	Number	Total assets
1946....................	14.7	1.8	...	...
1945....................	8.1	1.1	5.6	0.4
1944....................	4.2	0.8	5.3	0.7
1943....................	2.9	0.5	3.7	0.4
1942....................	2.5	0.5	3.3	0.5
1941....................	3.4	0.8	4.2	0.8
1940....................	3.6	0.8	4.4	0.8
1935–1939..............	15.6	4.7	19.2	4.8
1930–1934..............	13.4	8.8	16.2	8.8
1925–1929..............	10.0	13.2	12.2	13.5
1920–1924..............	6.6	8.6	8.0	8.8
1915–1919..............	4.1	7.9	4.9	7.8
1910–1914..............	3.2	6.7	3.9	6.9
1905–1909..............	3.1	7.2	3.7	7.4
1900–1904..............	2.1	6.9	2.5	7.1
1890–1899..............	1.4	9.1	1.7	9.4
1880–1889..............	0.6	6.6	0.7	7.0
1870–1879..............	0.2	3.4	0.2	3.5
1860–1869..............	0.2	5.8	0.2	6.1
Before 1860.............	0.1	4.8	0.2	5.3
First quartile age........	3	19	6	19
Second quartile age......	11	33	13	33
Third quartile age.......	21	53	22	53

* Summarized from line *f* of the period blocks, and from the Quartiles block, of tables 4, 5, 8, and 9.

responding figures (*1946 S. of I.*, p. 26) for the period 1925–1929 show: among 34,932 net corporations, 10,627 (more than 30 per cent) were in the smallest-size class, and 63 (nearly 0.2 per cent) were in the next-to-largest-size class. For the period before 1860, among 428 net corporations, 18 (4.2 per cent) were in the smallest-size class and 17 (4 per cent) in the next-to-largest-size class. The complete record of differences in size distribution among the various periods is presented and discussed in chapter iii.

Another, and somewhat indirect, indication of the concentration in the small-size classes, for younger corporations compared with

TABLE 11

Period of incorporation	1946-active returns			1945-active returns		
	Number	Total assets		Number	Total assets	
		Aggregate (in millions of dollars)	Average (in thousands of dollars)		Aggregate (in millions of dollars)	Average (in thousands of dollars)
1946..........	64,678	8,036	124	......	......	......
1945..........	35,033	4,993	143	20,478	1,984	97
1944..........	18,189	3,700	203	19,307	3,013	156
1943..........	12,541	2,118	169	13,580	1,941	143
1942..........	10,849	2,334	215	11,683	2,279	195
1941..........	14,496	3,832	264	15,216	3,671	241
1940..........	15,249	3,776	248	15,910	3,480	219
1935–1939......	66,934	21,390	320	69,720	20,818	299
1930–1934......	57,193	39,673	694	58,624	38,242	652
1925–1929......	43,301	59,601	1,376	44,594	58,870	1,320
1920–1924......	28,929	38,632	1,335	29,663	38,167	1,287
1915–1919......	17,785	35,466	1,994	18,303	34,144	1,865
1910–1914......	14,054	30,194	2,148	14,295	30,251	2,116
1905–1909......	13,278	32,699	2,463	13,488	32,165	2,385
1900–1904......	9,103	31,040	3,510	9,217	31,078	3,372
1890–1899......	6,302	41,008	6,507	6,379	41,091	6,442
1880–1889......	2,740	29,527	10,776	2,782	30,471	10,953
1870–1879......	722	15,508	21,479	738	15,136	20,509
1860–1869......	749	25,942	34,636	747	26,476	35,443
Before 1860.....	530	21,524	40,611	563	23,049	40,940

* Number of returns from line *d* of tables 12 and 13 (in chap. iii), aggregate total assets from line *d* of tables 8 and 9.

older, is afforded by the estimated average total assets per corporation for the various periods. Thus, line *d* of the 1946 block of table 8 shows estimated total assets for this youngest group of corporations as $8,036,000,000. The number of balance-sheet corporations incorporated in 1946 is 64,678.[31] Hence, the average total assets per

[31] See chap. iii, where the age distribution of all 1946-active dated balance-sheet corporations, considered as a single group, is presented in greater detail than in table 11, together with corresponding data for 1945.

corporation, for corporations chartered in 1946, was $124,000. Similarly derived averages, for all age periods, for 1946-active and 1945-active balance-sheet corporations, appear in table 11. With very slight exceptions, average total assets increases steadily with increasing age, ranging from about $100,000 for the youngest corporations to more than $40,000,000 for the oldest. We may in fact say that the estimated total assets for each of the various periods, as obtained by the process illustrated in tables 6A and 6B and shown in line *d* of table 8, is the joint result of the number of 1946-active balance-sheet corporations chartered in such a period and of the average total assets held (at the end of the taxable year 1946) by such corporations. The differences in age structure according to size of corporation—or in size structure according to age of corporation—completely account for the difference between the age structure of all corporations regardless of size in terms of total assets (table 8) and that in terms of number (table 4).[32]

Certain matters of detail in the results in table 11 are worthy of notice. For both the 1946-active and the 1945-active corporations, interruptions to the steady increase of average total assets with increasing age appear for periods 1943, 1940, and 1920–1924. The peculiarity for 1943 may reflect extraordinary wartime conditions which had a greater impact on companies chartered in 1943 than on those chartered in the other war years, but the peculiarity for 1940 cannot be readily explained. The peculiarity for 1920–1924 may, in truth, reflect merely a peculiarity for 1925–1929: the average total assets for the latter period may be abnormally high because the then current speculative boom encouraged the launching of an unusual number of fairly large corporations. A second noteworthy point is that, for any particular period with few exceptions, the average total assets is higher for 1946-active than for 1945-active corporations. This probably reflects mainly the accumulation of additional assets by the average corporation with a one-year advance in age during a period of high prosperity, but it may reflect, in part, the probable fact that corporations which disappeared from the active list between 1945 and 1946 were in general small.[33] Evi-

[32] Strictly, a slight additional source of difference may exist: table 4 relates to *all* active corporations, and table 8 only to balance-sheet corporations. The difference in age structure, in terms of *number* of corporations, between all balance-sheet corporations and the somewhat more inclusive list of all corporations (comprising those which did and those which did not file balance sheets) is slight, as shown in chap. iii.

[33] In making comparisons among the figures for average total assets shown in table 11, small differences should not receive much attention. The reason is that the average

dence on this second explanation is not entirely conclusive, but some evidence is discussed in chapter vii. A third sort of comparison, not involving the figures for average total assets, may be suggested by table 11: comparisons, for the various periods, between the number (or the estimated aggregate total assets) of the 1946-active corporations and that of the 1945-active corporations. These matters receive attention in chapter vii, where much relevant evidence besides that of table 11 is examined.

Figure 3 shows, for 1946-active balance-sheet corporations, the complete age distribution in terms of total assets, as plotted from the percentages of line *f* of table 8.[34] The most striking fact about the curve of figure 3 is that, unlike that of figure 2, it does not show a generally downward course from a very high level at the left to a very low level at the right. (A direct comparison between the two curves appears in figure 1, where the curve of figure 3 appears as the heavy line.) The second most striking feature of figure 3 is the unmistakable peak for the period 1925–1929. The 1946-active balance-sheet corporations chartered in that period held greater total assets in 1946 than those chartered in any other five-year period; and, assuming (as the figure does) that the relevant incorporations in any period longer than one year are uniformly distributed among the years of such period, those chartered in each year 1925–1929 held greater total assets in 1946 than those chartered in any year outside—before or after—that period. Corporations chartered in each year after the 1925–1929 period, though more numerous than those chartered in each year 1925–1929, held less in assets in 1946 than did those chartered in each year 1925–1929.[35] At the right of the period 1925–1929—for periods before 1925—the curve shows a course generally downward to the right, with slight interruptions before 1910 and before 1870; but that section of the

total assets for any period rests upon a J-shaped size distribution (in terms of number of returns classified by amount of total assets); and the arithmetic mean of such a distribution is likely to be heavily influenced by a few cases, or even one case, of very large size. (Evidence on the shape of the size distribution of corporations by age periods appears in chap. iii.) The foregoing comment bears upon the two points discussed in the text above, but it manifestly has no bearing upon the main conclusion from table 11—the huge increase in average total assets from the youngest to the oldest corporations.

[34] As in fig. 2, the percentage for Before-1860 is not shown, and the percentage of any period longer than one year is converted before plotting to an annual average for such period. See nn. 24 and 25.

[35] This statement relies upon the same somewhat unrealistic assumption: that within each five-year period, the relevant incorporations are uniformly distributed over the five years. See nn. 24 and 25.

curve is somewhat less steeply downward than the corresponding section of the curve of figure 2. This less steep incline reflects the generally increasing average total assets (in 1946) per corporation as age increases.

Another way of pointing out the contrast shown in figure 1 between the distribution in terms of number and in terms of total assets is to observe the differences in area under the two curves for the left (after 1929) and the right (before 1930) sections of the figure. For the younger corporations—those chartered since 1929—

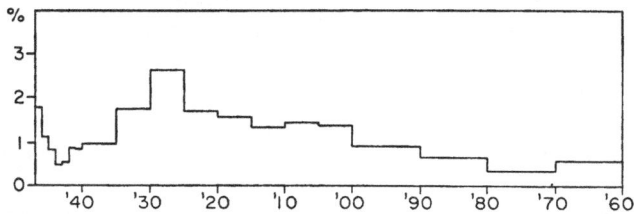

Fig. 3. Percentage distribution among periods of incorporation, of dated balance-sheet corporations active in 1946, in terms of estimated total assets held in 1946.
SOURCE: Data from line *f* of table 8. Percentage for Before-1860 not shown.

the area reflecting number of incorporations is vastly greater than that reflecting total assets. For the older corporations—those chartered before 1930—the reverse is true. The same comparison can be made from line *g* of tables 4 and 8. The younger corporations were 68.4 per cent of the total in terms of number but held only 19.9 per cent of the total assets. Similarly, the older corporations were 31.6 per cent in terms of number but held 80.1 per cent of the total assets.[36] All the foregoing facts confirm and emphasize the basic conclusion that the age of the corporate system is greater in terms of importance (total assets) than in terms of mere number. In terms of number, the system is dominated by its very young members; in terms of total assets held at the end of the most recent period (1946 or 1945)—which may be taken as a rough indicator of business importance—it is dominated by its older members.

[36] These comparisons, in this and the three preceding sentences are not strictly valid, because table 4 and fig. 2 apply to *all* active-dated corporations whereas table 8 and fig. 3 apply *only* to dated balance-sheet corporations; but this fact has slight bearing upon the contrast noted. See chap. iii.

CHAPTER **III**

Age Structure According to
Size of Corporation

THE PRECEDING CHAPTER examined the age structure of the corporate system as a whole, without regard to differences in size or in type of business of the corporations included in the system. Important differences in age structure appear among corporations of different sizes or different types of business. Such differences according to size are the subject of analysis in this chapter, and those according to type of business are examined in chapter iv. In both chapters the examination of age structures runs mainly in terms of the quartile ages, which are explained in section 7. For every class, according to size or to type of business, the basic analysis has been worked out by the procedure shown in table 4; and the quartile ages serve merely as a convenient summary of the age structure thus found.

11. *The combined list of balance-sheet corporations.*—As already indicated in section 2, the balance-sheet corporations, to which the classification of corporations according to size must be limited, do not afford complete coverage of the corporate system. Some corporate income-tax returns are not accompanied by balance sheets, or show balance sheets in which the data are fragmentary and are therefore not tabulated.[37] Although about 10 per cent of all 1946-active returns were not tabulated as balance-sheet returns, the deficiency in coverage of the corporate system by the balance-sheet returns was much smaller than 10 per cent in terms of any appropriate measure of importance.

We examine first the age distribution of all balance-sheet corporations, regardless of size, considered as a single group. Balance sheets were tabulated from 440,750 of the 491,152 active corporations for 1946, and from 374,950 of the 421,125 active corporations

---

[37] See comment in *1946 S. of I.,* p. 7.

TABLE 12

ANALYSIS OF DATE-OF-INCORPORATION STATISTICS OF ALL
BALANCE-SHEET CORPORATIONS FOR 1946*

a	All returns	1944	1935–1939	1910–1914	1870–1879
b	334,042	13,297	51,920	11,882	632
c	106,708	4,892	15,014	2,172	90
d	440,750	18,189	66,934	14,054	722
e	24.2	26.9	22.4	15.4	12.5
f	....	4.2	15.5	3.2	0.2
g	....	27.2	55.0	92.3	99.7
a	Date not stated	1943	1930–1934	1905–1909	1860–1869
b	5,572	9,153	45,972	11,294	671
c	2,523	3,388	11,221	1,984	78
d	8,095	12,541	57,193	13,278	749
e	31.2	27.0	19.6	14.9	10.4
f	....	2.9	13.2	3.1	0.2
g	....	30.2	68.2	95.4	99.9
a	All stated	1942	1925–1929	1900–1904	Before 1860
b	328,472	7,718	34,932	7,890	428
c	104,185	3,131	8,369	1,213	102
d	432,657	10,849	43,301	9,103	530
e	24.1	28.9	19.3	13.3	19.2
f	....	2.5	10.0	2.1	0.1
g	....	32.7	78.2	97.4	100.0
a	1946	1941	1920–1924	1890–1899	Quartiles
b	40,263	10,726	23,962	5,451	1944
c	24,415	3,770	4,967	851	1936
d	64,678	14,496	28,929	6,302	1926
e	38.8	26.0	17.2	13.5	3
f	15.0	3.4	6.7	1.5	11
g	15.0	36.0	84.9	98.9	21
a	1945	1940	1915–1919	1880–1889	Loss points
b	23,487	11,367	15,024	2,401	1.568
c	11,546	3,882	2,761	339	0.642
d	35,033	15,249	17,785	2,740	1860–1869
e	33.0	25.5	15.5	12.4	1940
f	8.1	3.5	4.1	0.6	1935
g	23.0	39.5	89.0	99.5	1940

* Description of items accompanies table 4.

TABLE 13

ANALYSIS OF DATE-OF-INCORPORATION STATISTICS OF ALL
BALANCE-SHEET CORPORATIONS FOR 1945*

a	All returns	1944	1935–1939	1910–1914	1870–1879
b	281,244	12,959	51,875	11,696	620
c	93,706	6,348	17,845	2,599	118
d	374,950	19,307	69,720	14,295	738
e	25.0	32.9	25.6	18.2	16.0
f	....	5.3	19.1	3.9	0.2
g	....	10.9	45.4	90.6	99.5

a	Date not stated	1943	1930–1934	1905–1909	1860–1869
b	6,683	9,825	45,339	11,180	665
c	2,980	3,755	13,285	2,308	82
d	9,663	13,580	58,624	13,488	747
e	30.8	27.7	22.7	17.1	11.0
f	....	3.7	16.0	3.7	0.2
g	....	14.6	61.4	94.3	99.7

a	All stated	1942	1925–1929	1900–1904	Before 1860
b	274,561	8,289	34,366	7,745	486
c	90,726	3,394	10,228	1,472	77
d	365,287	11,683	44,594	9,217	563
e	24.8	29.1	22.9	16.0	13.7
f	....	3.1	12.2	2.5	0.2
g	....	17.7	73.6	96.8	99.9

a	....	1941	1920–1924	1890–1899	Quartiles
b	....	10,894	23,597	5,403	1940
c	....	4,322	6,066	976	1933
d	....	15,216	29,663	6,379	1924
e	....	28.4	20.4	15.3	6
f	....	4.2	8.1	1.7	13
g	....	21.9	81.7	98.5	22

a	1945	1940	1915–1919	1880–1889	Loss points
b	10,793	11,468	14,977	2,384	1.907
c	9,685	4,442	3,326	398	0.734
d	20,478	15,910	18,303	2,782	1860–1869
e	47.3	27.9	18.2	14.3	1935–1939
f	5.6	4.4	5.0	0.8	1932
g	5.6	26.3	86.7	99.3	1936

* Description of items accompanies table 4.

TABLE 14

Period of incorporation	1946-active corporations			1945-active corporations		
	All	With balance sheets	Without balance sheets	All	With balance sheets	Without balance sheets
1946............	14.7	15.0	12.7	....	....	....
1945............	8.1	8.1	8.3	5.6	5.6	5.2
1944............	4.2	4.2	4.0	5.3	5.3	5.3
1943............	2.9	2.9	2.9	3.7	3.7	3.5
1942............	2.5	2.5	2.9	3.3	3.1	3.8
1941............	3.4	3.4	3.7	4.2	4.2	4.6
1940............	3.6	3.5	3.9	4.4	4.4	4.9
1935–1939......	15.6	15.5	17.1	19.2	19.1	20.6
1930–1934......	13.4	13.2	14.9	16.2	16.0	17.9
1925–1929......	10.0	10.0	10.4	12.2	12.2	12.2
1920–1924......	6.6	6.7	5.7	8.0	8.1	6.6
1915–1919......	4.1	4.1	3.7	4.9	5.0	4.1
1910–1914......	3.2	3.2	3.2	3.9	3.9	3.7
1905–1909......	3.1	3.1	2.9	3.7	3.7	3.4
1900–1904......	2.1	2.1	1.7	2.5	2.5	2.0
1890–1899......	1.4	1.5	1.2	1.7	1.7	1.3
1880–1889......	0.6	0.6	0.4	0.7	0.8	0.5
1870–1879......	0.2	0.2	0.1	0.2	0.2	0.1
1860–1869......	0.2	0.2	0.1	0.2	0.2	0.1
Before 1860.....	0.1	0.1	0.1	0.2	0.2	0.1
Quartile ages						
First.........	3	3	3	6	6	6
Second.......	11	11	11	13	13	12
Third........	21	21	20	22	22	20

* Data for "All" from line *f* of tables 4 and 5, for "With balance sheets" from line *f* of tables 12 and 13, for "without balance sheets" from analyses similar to tables 12 and 13.

for 1945; and these balance-sheet returns were classified according to date of incorporation, for the balance-sheet returns as a single group, for each of ten size classes specified in terms of amount of total assets, and for the active returns not showing balance sheets (50,402 for 1946, and 46,175 for 1945) as a single group.[38] The data are given separately in *S. of I.* for net and for no-net corporations; and these data, for the inclusive groups and for the size classes, have

[38] *1946 S. of I.*, pp. 26–27; *1945 S. of I.*, pp. 28–29. The specified boundaries of the size classes are shown below in table 15.

been analysed by the method described in section 5 and illustrated in table 4. The detailed analysis is shown in tables 12 and 13 for the inclusive balance-sheet group in 1946 and 1945. The results in line *f* of the 20 (19 for 1945) period blocks of these tables and in the Quartiles block are shown in table 14, in comparison with similar results for all active dated corporations (taken from tables 4 and 5) and for all active dated nonbalance-sheet corporations.

Table 14 shows, for both 1946 and 1945, a striking approach to identity in the results—the percentages for the various periods, and the quartile ages—for the dated balance-sheet corporations and for the somewhat more inclusive group of all active dated corporations. The identity is perfect in each year for the quartile ages. A somewhat less close approach to identity exists between the results for the dated nonbalance-sheet returns and those for all active dated returns, but the similarity is nevertheless fairly close. Thus, as evidence of shape of the age distribution, the nonbalance-sheet returns constitute a fairly dependable sample of all active returns. We may also conclude that failure to file a balance sheet is not associated with age (but see n. 40, below). The evidence of table 14 appears to justify the assumption that indications concerning age structure afforded by the data on balance-sheet corporations may be taken as valid for all corporations. The same assumption is, however, somewhat less clearly valid for indications drawn from the balance-sheet data for various size classes, particularly the smaller-size classes. We may fairly assume that balance-sheet data for large-size classes (and perhaps for medium-size classes) yield results which closely reflect the age structure of *all* active dated corporations in such size classes, but this assumption is somewhat lacking in foundation for the classes of very small size. The reason is that the balance-sheet coverage is probably close to complete for large-size classes, but is deficient for small-size classes.[30]

[30] We can obviously have no direct evidence on this point, for the very fact that nonbalance-sheet returns show no balance sheets precludes their classification according to size. The indirect evidence appears in a tabulation of all active returns and of all balance-sheet returns according to size of net income or deficit. Such tabulations—published in *1946 S. of I.*, p. 9, and *1945 S. of I.*, p. 10—show that the percentage coverage of all returns by balance-sheet returns rises from about 83 for returns with net income less than $1,000 to about 100 for returns with very large net income, and from about 74 for returns with deficit less than $1,000 to about 100 for returns with very large deficit. Although the amount of net income or deficit is not a very satisfactory measure of corporate size, because a very large corporation *can* have a small net income or small deficit, a strong presumption exists that most corporations showing small net income or deficit are small, and that almost every corporation showing a large net income or deficit is large. This presumption is supported by evidence published in *Statistics of Income* for two earlier years—*1936 S. of I.*, pp. 42–43, and *1937 S. of I.*, p. 188.

12. *Variation in age structure as size varies.*—The balance-sheet corporations are classified into ten size classes, specified in terms of the total assets shown on the balance sheet; and the lower boundary of each size class is shown (in thousands of dollars) among the line stubs of table 15. That table lists, separately for 1946 and 1945, the

TABLE 15

QUARTILE AGES, FOR 1946 AND 1945, FOR ALL ACTIVE DATED RETURNS, ALL ACTIVE DATED NONBALANCE-SHEET RETURNS, ALL DATED BALANCE-SHEET RETURNS, AND TEN SIZE CLASSES*

(in thousands of dollars)

	Quartile age					
	1946-active returns			1945-active returns		
	First	Second	Third	First	Second	Third
All active returns............	3	11	21	6	13	22
Those without balance sheets..	3	11	20	6	12	20
All balance-sheet returns.....	3	11	21	6	13	22
Balance-sheet returns by size classes (in thousands of dollars)						
0....................	2	8	16	5	10	17
50....................	3	10	19	6	13	21
100....................	4	12	22	8	15	24
250....................	7	16	27	10	18	29
500....................	10	20	32	12	21	34
1,000....................	15	25	40	16	26	40
5,000....................	18	31	47	18	30	46
10,000....................	19	31	49	18	31	49
50,000....................	21	35	53	20	34	54
100,000....................	24	41	64	23	40	63

* Figures in first three lines from same sources as in table 14. Figures in other lines derived by analyses similar to table 12. The size classes are specified by their lower boundaries.

quartile ages for every size class and also for the inclusive groups of all active returns, all balance-sheet returns, and all nonbalance-sheet returns.[40]

For each of the two years a noteworthy progression in each of the

[40] The quartiles apply, of course, only to the dated corporations in the various classes and in the inclusive groups: the Not-stated category of returns is ignored. As shown in sec. 2, the Not-stated category is a very small fraction of all balance-sheet returns: it is 1.84 per cent for 1946 and 2.58 per cent for 1945. For the nonbalance-sheet returns, the Not-stated category is much more important: 10.13 per cent for 1946, 13.52 per cent for 1945. Among the size classes, the percentage—of all balance-sheet returns in the class for which the date of incorporation is not stated—ranges markedly, and

three quartile ages runs from the smallest-size class to the largest-size class. The only interruptions in these steady progressions appear in the second quartile (median) age for 1946 at the $10,000,000 class, and in the first quartile age for 1945 at the $10,000,000 class; and each of these exceptions marks a mere halt in, and not a reversal of, the progression. The total progressions, from the smallest-size to the largest-size class, is very large for each quartile age for each year. The table affords emphatic evidence that most large corporations are older than most small corporations, and that very large corporations tend to have much greater age than very small corporations. This finding is, of course, not surprising, in view of the probability that most corporations are small at the beginning and that those which survive are likely to grow in size as time passes.[a] That such a finding should be so completely verified by the statistics with such striking regularity for the successive increases in size among the ten classes, is nevertheless remarkable.

The quartile ages, for 1946, of the two classes having total assets less than $100,000 are smaller than (in one instance, not greater than) those for all balance-sheet returns as a single group; and the reverse is true for all classes of more than $100,000. For 1945, only the smallest-size class has quartile ages clearly below the quartile ages for all balance-sheet returns; and, for 1945 as for 1946, all classes of more than $100,000 have quartile ages above those for the inclusive group. The quartile ages for the inclusive group of all balance-sheet corporations are "averages" of the corresponding quartile ages for the various size classes, and the reason why these averages correspond to class figures fairly near the bottom of the size scale is that the small corporations are so numerous as to dominate the averages.

generally declines as size increases, as shown by the following table (where the size classes are specified as in table 15).

Size	1946	1945	Size	1946	1945
0	2.23	3.26	1,000	1.49	2.02
50	1.77	2.42	5,000	1.06	1.60
100	1.60	1.89	10,000	0.75	1.25
250	1.19	1.48	50,000	0.43	1.41
500	1.02	1.57	100,000	0.56	0.74

Even for the small-size classes, however, the percentage is so small that we may fairly regard the dated corporations as a dependable sample of all balance-sheet corporations in each size class.

[a] That not all corporations are small at the beginning, and that not all old corporations are large in their old age, are points given more detailed attention in section 13.

In comparing a particular quartile age for 1946 with the corresponding figure for 1945, we might expect to find the former one year greater than the latter and be surprised to find many instances in which the 1946 figure is smaller than that for 1945. Although the

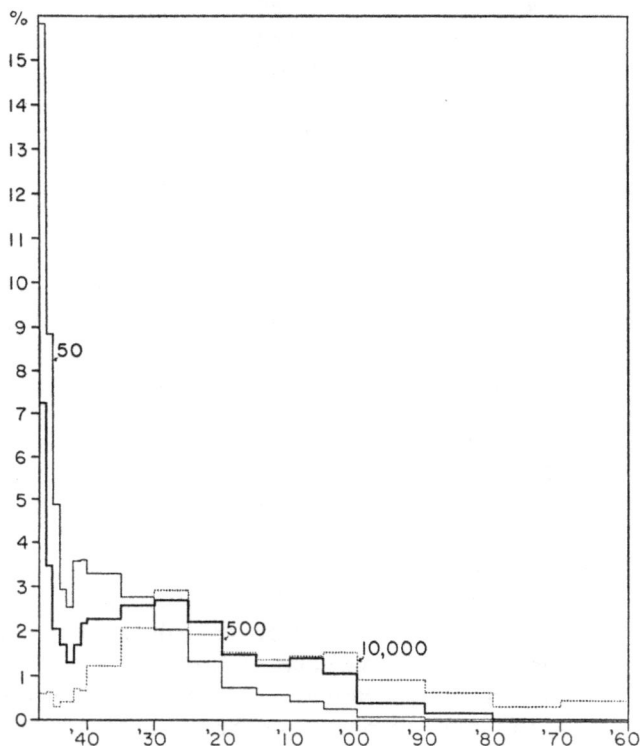

Fig. 4. Percentage distribution among periods of incorporation, of dated balance-sheet corporations active in 1946, in terms of number of such corporations, separately for three size classes—those with total assets of $50,000–$100,000, $500,000–$1,000,000, and $10,000,000–$50,000,000.

Source: Data derived by the process used in securing line *f* of table 4. Percentages for Before-1860 not shown.

1945-active corporations which survived as active in 1946 did become one year older, the list of 1946-active corporations includes also those chartered in 1946.[42] The great wave of incorporations which followed the end of the war introduced so large a number of

---

[42] Moreover, many corporations which were chartered in 1945 (and probably some corporations chartered in other recent years) were not active in 1945 but became active in 1946. See chap. vii.

very young companies into the system that such summary indicators of the age structure as the quartile ages were shifted downward. This effect is most clearly revealed for the smaller-size classes and in the first quartile age. Thus, for the two smallest-size classes, the first quartile age dropped from 5 to 2 and from 6 to 3—instead of rising from 5 to 6 and from 6 to 7, as would have been the case if no active corporations had entered or left these classes between 1945 and 1946.[43]

Although the quartile ages, as shown in table 15, give the essential facts about variation in age structure with size of corporation, a more detailed graphic comparison of entire age structures for selected size classes (for 1946) may be informing. Such a comparison appears in figure 4, wherein the curves are constructed by the method already described in reference to figure 2. Among the curves for the three selected classes ($50,000, $500,000, and $10,000,000), important differences appear. The first two are J-shaped, although the concentration in 1946 is much smaller for the $500,000 class than for the $50,000 class. The third curve is not J-shaped, but has a peak in the 1925–1929 period. Near the right side of the figure, the curves stand in the order of size of corporation—the greater the size, the higher the level of the curve—whereas near the left side of the chart, they stand in inverse order of size. These relative positions of the curves merely confirm the conclusion already reached: small corporations are predominantly young, and old corporations are predominantly large.

13. *Variation in size distribution as age varies.*—The relation between age structure and size can be helpfully viewed from another angle: as variations in size distribution with age. For example, of the 64,678 1946-active balance-sheet corporations chartered in 1946, 66.8 per cent were in the smallest-size class, and less than 1.3 per cent were in classes of more than $1,000,000; whereas, of the 9,103 chartered in 1900–1904, 17.7 per cent were in the smallest-size class, and almost 30 per cent were in classes of more than $1,000,000. Corresponding percentages, for every size class in each age period, are shown in table 16. The table also includes, for pur-

---

[43] We may remark that departures (through corporations being dissolved or otherwise becoming inactive) from the active list of corporations, as well as entries into that list, may cause shifts in the age structure; and the nature of such shifts depends upon the age of the departing corporations. Nevertheless, for a year like 1946, the new entrants have the major effect on the age structure; and, as new entrants are likely to be of small size, the effect is more manifest in small-size classes than in large. Notice, for example, that the largest-size class actually shows a one-year increase in each quartile age.

TABLE 16

PERCENTAGE SIZE DISTRIBUTION OF ALL 1946-ACTIVE BALANCE-SHEET CORPORATIONS, THOSE FOR WHICH DATE OF INCORPORATION WAS NOT STATED, THOSE FOR WHICH DATE WAS STATED, AND THOSE INCORPORATED IN EACH SPECIFIED PERIOD*

	Size class ($1,000 of total assets)									
	0	50	100	250	500	1,000	5,000	10,000	50,000	100,000
All corporations	45.3	17.4	17.4	7.8	4.7	5.6	0.96	0.76	0.105	0.120
Date not stated	54.7	16.9	15.2	5.1	2.6	4.5	0.55	0.31	0.025	0.037
All stated	44.9	17.4	17.4	7.8	4.7	5.6	0.97	0.76	0.106	0.122
1946	66.8	18.4	15.7	5.4	2.3	1.16	0.074	0.031	0.005	0.000
1945	57.8	19.0	14.6	4.9	2.0	1.30	0.114	0.060	0.003	0.003
1944	56.4	20.1	14.7	4.8	2.3	1.57	0.193	0.055	0.006	0.016
1943	55.8	17.6	15.9	5.9	2.8	1.75	0.192	0.104	0.008	0.000
1942	57.1	17.4	15.1	5.9	2.5	1.68	0.212	0.129	0.018	0.009
1941	55.6	18.6	15.6	5.6	2.4	1.81	0.221	0.166	0.000	0.021
1940	55.0	17.8	15.9	6.0	2.9	2.0	0.118	0.151	0.066	0.007
1940-1944	56.0	18.5	15.4	5.6	2.6	1.77	0.185	0.118	0.020	0.011
1935-1939	50.1	18.6	17.3	6.7	3.5	3.1	0.40	0.30	0.028	0.010
1930-1934	43.8	18.2	18.7	8.0	4.6	5.2	0.81	0.59	0.061	0.059
1925-1929	35.7	17.6	20.3	10.2	6.4	7.1	1.25	1.12	0.150	0.159
1920-1924	30.9	17.2	21.0	11.5	7.8	8.7	1.40	1.10	0.152	0.135
1915-1919	28.2	15.6	20.6	12.2	8.6	11.1	1.85	1.44	0.180	0.254
1910-1914	26.9	15.0	19.6	11.8	9.1	13.8	1.82	1.63	0.24	0.26
1905-1909	23.0	12.5	19.1	12.6	11.0	17.4	2.62	1.81	0.33	0.27
1900-1904	17.7	10.6	17.0	12.6	13.0	22.2	4.2	2.8	0.39	0.38
1890-1899	13.7	9.2	16.0	12.3	12.3	23.8	6.1	4.9	0.55	0.95
1880-1889	9.7	6.0	11.0	10.9	12.1	29.8	9.6	7.8	1.54	1.57
1870-1879	8.2	4.7	9.0	10.5	5.8	26.3	15.0	14.7	2.2	3.6
1860-1869	5.7	2.5	4.7	3.5	5.1	29.2	18.7	21.3	3.1	6.1
Before 1860	7.4	3.2	6.1	7.0	10.2	24.5	15.1	14.3	3.6	8.1

* Computed from *1946 S. of I.*, pp. 26-27 and 214-215.

poses of comparison, the percentages for the five-year period 1940–
1944, for all dated balance-sheet returns as a single group, for all
balance-sheet returns on which the date of incorporation was not
stated, and for the combined list of all balance-sheet returns.

Every line of this table shows a J-shaped frequency distribution: the percentage is high for the smallest-size class and tapers off
without interruption as size increases.[44] The schedule of percentages
is almost the same for all dated balance-sheet corporations as for all
balance-sheet corporations, the latter covering both dated and not-
dated returns.[45] The size distribution for 1946 is much more steeply
J-shaped than that for all dated balance-sheet corporations. The
distributions for the six years 1940–1945 are closely similar to each
other; all are less steeply J-shaped than that for 1946, but more
steeply J-shaped than that for all dated balance sheets. The average
shape for the five years 1940–1944 is shown in a separate summary
line and is closely similar to those of the five included years.

As we pass successively through the five-year periods from 1940–
1944 to 1900–1904 and the ten-year periods 1890–1899 to 1860–
1869, the steepness of the distribution is seen to decline without
interruption. This is evidenced most strikingly by the percentage
for the smallest-size class, which declines progressively from 56.0 to
5.7; but this progressive decline is interrupted for the period Before-
1860. Similarly, for a large-size class such as the $5,000,000 class, the
percentage rises steadily from 0.185 for 1940–1944 to 18.7 for 1860–
1869, but a reversal in this course likewise appears for Before-1860.
In general, these tendencies—for the percentage of a small-size class

---

[44] The "frequency" shown by the percentages is relative frequency: the sum of the
frequencies in every line is 100 per cent. This table does not in all cases clearly
reveal the uninterrupted J-shaped form—a steady decline in relative frequency as
size increases. In order to test the steadiness of decline, account must be taken of the
varying widths of the class intervals in terms of total assets. Thus, for all balance-sheet
returns, the percentage rises from 4.7 for the $500,000 class to 5.6 for the $1,000,000
class. But the latter class ($1,000,000–$5,000,000) is 8 times as wide as the former
($500,000–$1,000,000). Hence, to render the two percentages comparable for testing
the shape of the distribution, 5.6 should be divided by 8; and then no interruption to
the J-shaped form appears. Similar adjustments, to allow for differences in width of
interval, explain away the apparent interruptions to the steady decline, required by
the J-shaped size distribution, in all lines of table 16. (As the $100,000,000 class is
of unknown width, no test of shape is possible at that level.)

[45] The line for the not-dated group reveals a percentage substantially higher than
that for the more inclusive group in the smallest-size class, whereas its percentage in
each of the nine other size classes runs lower than that for all balance-sheet returns.
This may suggest that corporations for which date of charter was not stated were in
general younger corporations, because the percentages of the not-dated group are
fairly close to those for 1940–1944; but this evidence is not conclusive.

to decline, and that of a large-size class to rise, as the period becomes more remote from 1940–1944—appear in all size classes. Such exceptions as exist appear most frequently among the very-large-size classes, for which the percentages are somewhat lacking in significance as samples because of the small numbers of corporations on which they are based.

The over-all indication is emphatically clear: the size distribution is J-shaped for each period, and it becomes steadily less steeply J-shaped as the period becomes more remote from 1946.[46] For every period since 1890, small corporations (here including all with less than $500,000 of total assets as "small") predominate; but the degree to which they do so is exceptionally high for recent periods and declines steadily for the earlier periods as far back as 1890. All these findings concerning shape of the size distribution of corporations refer to dated balance-sheet corporations active in 1946. Hence, the line for any particular period, as presented in table 16, does not show the size distribution for all corporations chartered in that period but only for those among such corporations which survived as active dated balance-sheet corporations in 1946. For example, the percentages for the 1860–1869 line show the size distribution for 749 corporations which (1) were chartered in that ten-year period, (2) were active in 1946, and (3) stated the dates of incorporation and furnished balance sheets on their tax returns. Moreover, even for these 749 corporations, the size distribution shown is in terms of total assets in 1946, not total assets at time of incorporation. The same conclusion stated above would appear from the data for 1945-active corporations, which are not specifically examined in this section, except of course that the 1946 period would be missing.

The finding that the degree to which small corporations predominate, among corporations chartered in a period, declines as the period becomes more remote from 1946, admits of certain partial explanations. One might suppose that the size distribution, of the corporations chartered in some remote period such as 1870–1879, expressed in terms of total assets *at the end of that period* (1879) of such corporations then active, would be J-shaped and show a steepness comparable with that for the 1946-active corporations chartered in 1935–1939 or 1940–1944. Although only 722 dated balance-sheet corporations chartered in 1870–1879 were active in 1946, the number active in 1879 must have been much greater—perhaps

---

[46] The period Before-1860 is an exception, for which no explanation readily appears.

several times 722. Of this larger number, those which were small in 1879 were less likely to survive until 1946 than those which were large in 1879, and those among the small corporations of 1879 which did survive until 1946 were likely to become large—and perhaps very large—with the passage of many years. These are the main reasons why the size structure of corporations chartered in 1870–1879 is likely to be much less steeply J-shaped in 1946 than in 1879.[47]

The supposition that the size distribution in 1879 may have been similar in shape and steepness to that for 1946-active corporations chartered in some very recent period is, however, open to question; and no statistical facts are available for testing it. Some possibility exists that the corporate form of organization was less likely to be used for small enterprises in a remote period such as 1870–1879 than in 1935–1944. In the earlier years of the developing system of private corporations, the notion that the corporate device was peculiarly appropriate for large enterprises was widely prevalent. In those years also special legislative enactment of charters was being only gradually replaced by general incorporation laws, and therefore a major obstacle to the chartering of small corporations had not yet been fully removed. Another possible factor in the situation in those earlier years is that use of the corporate device may have been more nearly limited to certain lines of industry in which enterprises are not very small—such as the quasi-public enterprises of which banks and railroads are chief examples—than is true in later times. These factors, and perhaps others not mentioned, suggest the possibility that the 1879 size distribution (of corporations chartered in 1870–1879) may not have been as steeply J-shaped as the 1946 size distribution (of corporations chartered in 1935–1944). Even so, we may confidently hold that the steepness of the size distribution for corporations chartered in 1870–1879 which were active in 1879 was greater, and perhaps much greater, than that of such corporations which were active in 1946.

14. *Size variations among lines of industry.*--One of the factors noticed in the last preceding paragraph suggests that corporations tend, even at their creation, to be larger in some lines of industry than in others. We have no direct evidence on this point, but can examine evidence on a somewhat less narrow point. Does the size distribution of corporations, disregarding their date of incorpora-

[47] For each of the two years, the size distribution is in terms of the total assets for that year and is limited to the corporations (chartered in the stated period) active in that year.

TABLE 17

Class	Percentage	
	Low	High
Among 8* divisions		
Service..	9.1	
Mining and quarrying..............................		30.7
Among 5* mining and quarrying groups		
Nonmetallic mining and quarrying....................	24.8	
Metal mining......................................		46.1
Among 22* manufacturing groups		
Apparel and products made from fabrics...............	15.6	
Cotton manufactures...............................		71.6
Among 3 public utilities groups		
Communication....................................	15.4	
Other public utilities..............................		34.6
Among 2* trade groups		
Retail..	8.8	
Wholesale...		20.8
Among 2 wholesale trade subgroups		
Commission merchants.............................	10.9	
Other wholesalers.................................		22.4
Among 12* retail trade subgroups		
Package liquor stores..............................	1.6	
General merchandise...............................		23.3
Among 8* service groups		
Miscellaneous repair services, hand trades.............	1.5	
Hotels and other lodging places.....................		24.5
Among 4 finance, insurance, real estate, and lessors of real property groups		
Real estate, including lessors of buildings.............	14.0	
Finance...		57.2
Among 7* finance subgroups		
Other finance.....................................	9.9	
Banks and trust companies..........................		95.4
Among 2 insurance carriers, agents, etc., subgroups		
Insurance agents, brokers, etc.......................	6.0	
Insurance carriers.................................		78.0
Among 3 agriculture, forestry, and fishery groups		
Fishery...	9.8	
Forestry..		30.9

* The not-allocable division, groups, and subgroups are excluded from the reckoning of Low and High.

tion, vary among lines of industry? Such variations exist, and are very striking, as this section will show by summarizing size-distribution figures for 1946.[48] The 440,750 balance-sheet returns for 1946 have been classified according to line of industry into 9 divisions (including a Not-allocable class); each division, except construction and Not-allocable, has been subclassified into groups; and certain of the groups have been further classified into subgroups; and, for each such division, group, or subgroup, a size distribution in terms of total assets in 1946 is published in *Statistics of Income.*[49]

For the present purpose, analysis of these data can be confined to a very brief summary of certain results derived from the published figures. For all balance-sheet returns as a single class, and for each division, group, and subgroup, a single summary indicator of the size distribution has been calculated: the per cent of the number of corporations in the class which have total assets of more than $250,000. Thus, among the 440,750 balance-sheet returns, considered as a single class, 88,261 had assets of more than $250,000; and the summary indicator is therefore 20 per cent. The usefulness of such an indicator depends upon the fact that, for every line of industry, the size distribution is approximately J-shaped. Hence, if for any line of industry the indicator is substantially less than 20 per cent, we may conclude that the size distribution for that line is steeper—the concentration of small corporations is greater—than for the all-inclusive class. As between two lines of industry—two divisions, two groups, or two subgroups—a wide difference between the percentages is evidence of wide difference in the two size distributions, particularly in the steepness of such distributions and therefore in the degree to which the distribution is dominated by very small corporations.

A complete list of the summary indicators for all 85 divisions, groups, and subgroups is not presented at this point.[50] For the present purpose, which is to reveal the wide diversity in steepness of the size distribution among lines of industry, only certain pairs of high and low figures for the percentage need be given. In determining these high and low cases, the not-allocated division and all not-allocated groups and subgroups are ignored. Among the divisions, the summary indicator (percentage) ranges from 9.1 for

---

[48] The figures used are derived from *1946 S. of I.*, pp. 226–311.

[49] A more detailed description of the classification by line of industry, with comment upon imperfections in the classification, appears in chap. iv.

[50] The complete list is reported below, in chap. iv, where the percentages are used in another phase of the analysis.

Service to 30.7 for Mining and quarrying; in the former broad line
of industry, large corporations are relatively less numerous than in
the latter. Corresponding results, for the groups in each of seven
divisions, and for the subgroups in each of four groups, appear in
table 17. The range between low and high is in only one case less
than 100 per cent of the low, and in three cases the high is more than
10 times the low. Little doubt can remain that large corporations are
relatively much more numerous in some lines of industry than in
others. As the table shows the low and high percentages—among
the various divisions, or among the various groups in any one
division, or among the various subgroups in any one group—the
evidence gives merely an extreme indication of diversity in age
distribution. Between the high and low figures—for the 22 Manufacturing groups, for example—the percentage may take on a range
of values. Nevertheless, diversity is characteristic of the results:
the percentages for most divisions, groups, and subgroups depart
markedly from 20, the over-all average.

In view of these results, we may be tempted to infer that the differences in age structure according to size of corporation, mentioned
above in section 12, may be merely or largely a reflection of differences according to line of industry. If in certain lines of industry,
corporations tend to be large, and if corporations in such lines tend
also to be old, one might expect to find that large corporations tend
to be old. Further attention to this hypothesis can be deferred until
the evidence of chapter iv, concerning variations in age structure
among lines of industry, is in view. No adequate examination of
this point could, however, be made without a three-way tabulation
of corporations according to size (amount of total assets), line of
industry, and date of incorporation. Such tabulation was not included in *Statistics of Income* for 1945 or 1946.

CHAPTER **IV**

Age Structure According to
Type of Industry

THE AGE DISTRIBUTION of corporations may be studied not only for classes of corporations according to size, examined in the preceding chapter, but also for classes according to line of industry. We may also inquire whether the diversity in age structure among the size classes may in some degree be due to diversity among lines of industry, in view of the tendency for corporations of large size to appear more commonly in some lines of industry than in others.

15. *Description of the classification by line of industry.*—The statistics on date of incorporation here under study are classified by type or line of industry into nine divisions; and further classification appears in narrower groups for each division except Construction and Not-allocable, and in still narrower subgroups for two groups in the Trade division and for two groups in the Finance, insurance, real estate, and lessors of real property division. The total number of such divisions, groups, and subgroups is 85; and, of these, seven are described as Not-allocable and give therefore no clear indication of type of industry. The present chapter reports the age structure for each of these 85 classes and examines certain bodies of evidence bearing upon differences among such age structures. Some comments are ventured upon possible economic implications or explanations of some of the more striking statistical results, but no attempt at a systematic economic interpretation of the results is made. Such interpretation would require consideration of much information about the characteristics of particular industries and their historical backgrounds, and the collection of that information and the interpretation of the present results in relation thereto would disproportionately extend the scope of an examination which is only one of several aspects of the subject of present investigation. Any economic interpretation of the results of this

chapter will at best be obstructed by two important peculiarities of those results. The first, which has been mentioned before in these pages, is that the age structures here under study relate to corporations active in 1946 (or 1945) and not necessarily to the economic enterprises then under the control of such corporations. Although much of economic interest can undoubtedly be inferred from facts concerning the age of corporations, various important economic questions would surely be concerned rather with the age of enterprises (see chap. vi, for limited evidence on the enterprises predecessor to corporations). The second obstacle is that the classification according to line of industry is, as explained later in this section, not clear-cut. A particular corporation, especially if it is not very small, may be engaged in more than one type of activity; and yet it is counted in a single type more or less precisely determined with reference to the apportionment of its total receipts among its various activities. This blurring of the classification probably means that the results here shown for any particular line of industry are dependent in some degree upon conditions in some other lines.

The industrial classification in *Statistics of Income* rests upon information supplied in the corporate income-tax return. For example, page 3 of Form 1120 for 1946 (*1946 S. of I.*, p. 463) presents the instruction:

In answering the question, "Kind of business," on page 1, give a brief outline of your predominant business activity, and also from the following list give the serial number of the business group which corresponds to your predominant business.

The business group in which your predominant business falls is that which most nearly describes the activity accounting for the largest percentage of "total receipts." "Total receipts" means the sum of gross sales (where inventories are an income-determining factor); gross receipts (where inventories are not an income-determining factor); and income from other sources required to be included in gross income.

Use the appropriate business group under the heading "Finance" wherever over 50 per cent of "total receipts" consists of investment income.

Following this instruction, Form 1120 lists 197 line-of-business groups, in sections under various headings and subheadings.

From the information thus supplied, *Statistics of Income* constructs two classifications according to line of business. The first is the basis of the date-of-incorporation analysis in this chapter and also of several basic tables in *Statistics of Income* which present aggregates of accounting items compiled from tax returns (for example, *1946 S. of I.*, pp. 104–145, 146–179, and 226–311). This classification includes 74 mutually exclusive classes (of which seven are Not-allocable); and some of these are combined in various broader classes, and all classes are combined in a single over-all "class" covering all corporations. The second classification is into narrower classes and is the basis of one important *Statistics of Income* table presenting aggregates of a limited list of accounting items (*1946 S. of I.*, pp. 94–103). This classification includes 233 mutually exclusive classes; and some of these are combined in various broader classes, and all classes are combined in a single over-all "class" covering all corporations. The total number of classes, mutually exclusive classes and combinations, is 86 for the first scheme and 283 for the second scheme of classification.[51]

Although date-of-incorporation statistics are published only for the 86 classes of the first scheme of classification, certain information about the more elaborate second classification is useful in describing the makeup of the 86 (74 mutually exclusive) classes of the shorter list. Such information is brought together in table A of the Appendix (p. 165). The first serial number attached to any line of that table identifies the line with the item in the second (more detailed) classification as shown in *Statistics of Income*, and the second serial number (in parentheses) attached to certain lines identifies the line thus labeled with the item in the first, less detailed classification shown.[52] The table also shows certain statistics by which the relative importance of the various classes may be appraised: number of active returns, total compiled receipts, and (for the classes of the shorter list) total assets.[53]

As the date-of-incorporation statistics run only in terms of *numbers* of corporations chartered in the various periods, a primary criterion of relative importance—among the divisions, among the

---

[51] The first includes 7, and the second 36, Not-allocable "classes." Some corporation returns are not allocable even among the divisions, some are allocable within a division but not among the groups of that division, some are allocable within a group but not among the subgroups, and some are allocable within a subgroup but not among the sub-subgroups. See table A, in the Appendix, for a listing of all classes, including the Not-allocable classes. See also *1946 S. of I.*, pp. 76–90, for availability of tabulated information on the various classes.

[52] *1946 S. of I.*, pp. 94–102 for the second classification, pp. 18–19 for the first.

[53] The figures have been obtained by combining the data for net and no-net corporations: number of returns and total compiled receipts from pp. 94–103, and total assets from pp. 146–179, of *1946 S. of I.*

groups of a division, or among the subgroups of a group—is the number of corporations in a class. Thus, among the nine divisions (section A of the table), Trade has the largest number and Finance, etc. stands next.[54] Similarly, among the ten subgroups in the Food, etc. manufacturing group (section G of the table), Other food, including ice and flavoring sirups has the largest number, and Dairy products stands next. In the former case, this information is of slight importance, since we have date-of-incorporation statistics for each division separately. In the latter case, however, we have no such data for the separate Food, etc. subgroups. Hence, in studying the age structure for the Food, etc. *group,* we may be impressed by the fact that, of the 9842 (section F of the table) corporations in the Food, etc. group, 1734 fall in Dairy products and only 36 in Cereal preparations. The age structure for Dairy products can have substantial effect, that for Cereal preparations can have little effect, upon the age structure of the Food, etc. group as a whole.

Any attempt at economic interpretation would, however, require attention to the relative *economic* importance of the various classes; and such importance is indicated by the figures for total compiled receipts and total assets. Thus, any difference in age structure noted between the Manufacturing and the Trade divisions might be the object of economic interpretation, and such interpretation could be advanced by observing (section A of the table) that Manufacturing is more important than Trade in terms of total compiled receipts, and that the preponderance of Manufacturing is still greater in terms of total assets. Total compiled receipts is in some respects a less satisfactory test of economic importance than total assets, chiefly because the former is more susceptible to year-to-year variations than the latter. The figures on total compiled receipts are included in the table for two reasons. They are, in some respects, significant indications of economic importance. They are the only figures indicative of importance for the 197 classes of the second scheme of classification which do not appear in the first scheme (the items of the table for which a second serial number is not given). The figures in the table showing rank—among the divisions, within a division, within a group, or within a subgroup—are intended to show that relative importance as measured by total com-

---

[54] The presence, in table A or in the text of this chapter, of "etc." in any line title—except for the very few cases where the *S. of I.* title includes that symbol—indicates that the full title used in *S. of I.* has been condensed for purposes of the table or of citation in the text. The reader can find the full titles on the pages, of *1946 S. of I.,* cited in n. 53.

TABLE 18

ANALYSIS OF DATE-OF-INCORPORATION STATISTICS OF ALL MANUFAC-
TURING CORPORATIONS ACTIVE IN 1946*

a	All returns	1944	1935–1939	1910–1914	1870–1879
b	72,567	2,298	9,472	3,182	143
c	25,564	1,215	2,671	467	23
d	98,131	3,513	12,143	3,649	166
e	26.0	34.6	22.0	12.8	13.9
f	....	3.6	12.6	3.8	0.2
g	....	31.2	54.7	90.6	99.8

a	Date not stated	1943	1930–1934	1905–1909	1860–1869
b	969	1,515	8,636	2,970	89
c	644	873	1,836	444	6
d	1,613	2,388	10,472	3,414	95
e	39.9	36.6	17.5	13.0	6.3
f	....	2.5	10.8	3.5	0.1
g	....	33.7	65.5	94.1	99.9

a	All stated	1942	1925–1929	1900–1904	Before 1860
b	71,598	1,378	7,289	2,209	53
c	24,920	881	1,316	321	8
d	96,518	2,259	8,605	2,530	61
e	25.8	39.0	15.3	12.7	13.1
f	....	2.3	8.9	2.6	0.1
g	....	36.0	74.4	96.7	100.0

a	1946	1941	1920–1924	1890–1899	Quartiles
b	10,424	2,012	6,117	1,802	1945
c	7,911	876	973	221	1936
d	18,335	2,888	7,090	2,023	1924
e	43.2	30.3	13.7	10.9	2
f	19.0	3.0	7.4	2.1	11
g	19.0	39.0	81.8	98.8	23

a	1945	1940	1915–1919	1880–1889	Loss points
b	5,031	2,085	4,140	753	1.671
c	3,264	878	653	83	0.496
d	8,295	2,963	4,793	836	1860–1869
e	39.4	29.6	13.6	9.9	1940
f	8.6	3.1	5.0	0.9	1934
g	27.6	42.1	86.8	99.7	1943

* Description of items accompanies table 4.

TABLE 19

ANALYSIS OF DATE-OF-INCORPORATION STATISTICS OF ALL TRADE
CORPORATIONS ACTIVE IN 1946*

a	All returns	1944	1935–1939	1910–1914	1870–1879
b	122,132	4,683	19,111	3,498	27
c	29,379	1,395	4,133	342	6
d	151,511	6,078	23,244	3,840	33
e	19.4	23.0	17.8	8.9	18.2
f	....	4.1	15.8	2.6	0.0
g	....	32.2	59.8	95.1	100.0

a	Date not stated	1943	1930–1934	1905–1909	1860–1869
b	2,863	2,938	17,632	3,205	11
c	1,147	881	2,910	290	..
d	4,010	3,819	20,542	3,495	11
e	28.6	23.1	14.2	8.3	..
f	....	2.6	13.9	2.4	0.0
g	....	34.8	73.7	97.5	100.0

a	All stated	1942	1925–1929	1900–1904	Before 1860
b	119,269	2,484	11,670	1,945	10
c	28,232	776	1,446	144	6
d	147,501	3,260	13,116	2,089	16
e	19.1	23.8	11.0	6.9	37.5
f	....	2.2	8.9	1.4	0.0
g	....	37.0	82.6	98.9	100.0

a	1946	1941	1920–1924	1890–1899	Quartiles
b	19,467	3,783	8,131	1,155	1945
c	8,325	1,045	913	96	1938
d	27,792	4,828	9,044	1,251	1929
e	30.0	21.6	10.1	7.7	2
f	18.8	3.3	6.1	0.8	9
g	18.8	40.2	88.7	99.8	18

a	1945	1940	1915–1919	1880–1889	Loss points
b	9,729	4,406	5,127	257	1.565
c	3,838	1,134	535	17	0.466
d	13,567	5,540	5,662	274	1880–1889
e	28.3	20.5	9.4	6.2	1940
f	9.2	3.8	3.8	0.2	1936
g	28.0	44.0	92.5	100.0	1943

* Description of items accompanies table 4.

piled receipts does not differ markedly from the corresponding ranks in terms of total assets.

16. *Variations in age structure among lines of industry.*—The date-of-incorporation statistics, for 1946 and 1945, have been analyzed for each of 85 lines of industry (excluding the over-all "class," analyzed in chap. ii), by the method explained in section 5 and illustrated in table 4. Further illustrations—for 1946-active returns—are shown in table 18, for the Manufacturing division, and in table 19, for the Trade division.[55] Although various interesting similarities and differences might be noticed by comparing the complete age distributions for Manufacturing and Trade, as shown in line *f* (and cumulatively in line *g*) of the 20 period blocks of tables 18 and 19, the comparison among divisions—or other classes—in this chapter are confined mainly to the quartile ages.[56] On this basis, the Manufacturing division has a somewhat older age structure than the Trade division: quartile ages 2, 11, and 23 compared with 2, 9, and 18.[57]

---

[55] These tables are included not only as further illustrations of the method, but also to present the basic data and the complete age distribution for these two highly important divisions.

[56] The quartile ages, and likewise the detailed record of the age distribution, apply only to the dated corporations of the specified class (see n. 40). The Not-stated category of returns is ignored; and we may in general assume that, as the dated returns cover a very high percentage of all returns in each class, findings based upon the dated returns are approximately valid for all returns. The deficiency in coverage—measured by the percentage, of all returns of a class, for which date of incorporation is not stated—varies greatly among the classes (representing various lines of industry). Such percentages have been calculated for all classes; and those for the 74 mutually exclusive classes, separately for 1946-active and 1945-active corporations, have been arranged in the following frequency distribution according to size of the percentage.

Lower limit of percentage class	Number of industry classes		Lower limit of percentage class	Number of industry classes	
	1946	1945		1946	1945
0.........................	4	3	7.........................	..	1
1.........................	23	12	8.........................	1	2
2.........................	21	15	9.........................	..	1
3.........................	13	18	10........................	1	2
4.........................	5	12	11........................	..	..
5.........................	3	5	12........................	..	1
6.........................	3	2	Total..............	74	74

For each year, the bulk of the classes show small percentages; but, on the average, the percentages for 1946 run about one (unit of per cent) smaller than those for 1945. This may reflect a marked improvement, in 1946 compared with 1945, in reporting date of incorporation by corporations active in both years. It may also reflect nearly full reporting of the date by the many corporations chartered in 1946. In any case, deficiency in coverage is not seriously large except for a small number of the 74 classes.

[57] The derivation and significance of the quartile age are set forth in section 7. The

Age Structure of the Corporate System

Corresponding figures for each division and for all divisions combined, for 1946 and 1945 separately, appear in table 20. The Not-allocable "division" is included, though it is by definition not pertinent to any particular line of industry. The divisions are arranged in the table in the inverse order of size of the median (second quartile) age for 1946, ranging from 8 for Construction

TABLE 20

Quartile Ages, for 1946 and 1945, for All Divisions Combined
and for Each Division*

Division	Quartile age					
	1946-active returns			1945-active returns		
	First	Second	Third	First	Second	Third
1 All industrial divisions......	3	11	21	6	13	22
81 Construction..............	2	8	18	6	12	20
37 Trade...................	2	9	18	6	12	20
56 Service..................	3	10	18	5	11	19
9 Manufacturing...........	2	11	23	6	14	26
2 Mining and quarrying......	6	12	22	7	13	22
66 Finance, insurance, real estate, and lessors of real property..............	5	12	22	6	13	23
86 Not allocable.............	5	13	21	6	13	21
33 Public utilities...........	5	14	26	7	15	27
82 Agriculture, forestry, and fishery...............	6	14	23	8	15	24

* The serial numbers preceding the row titles correspond to those (in parentheses) of table A. The description of Quartile ages is given in section 7. Divisions are ranked by the second-quartile age for 1946.

to 14 for Agriculture, etc. Where two divisions have the same median age—Mining and quarrying, and Finance, etc.—they are arranged in the order followed in *S. of I.* tables. The order of arrangement would be somewhat different if it were based on the median age for 1945, and these differences in rank indicate that some shifts in comparative age structure occurred among the divisions between 1945 and 1946. Such shifts reflect mainly the disproportionate entrances of new corporations in certain divisions in 1946 (see section 17), but they depend to a limited degree also upon the disproportionate withdrawals in 1946 from the active-corporation list in cer-

second quartile age is of course the median age: if the median age of a class is 11, more than half of the corporations in that class are less than 11 years old, and more than half are more than ten years old.

tain divisions. The ranking would also be somewhat altered if it were based, not upon median age, but upon first-quartile age or third-quartile age for 1946 (or for 1945). Such differences in ranking indicate that the age distributions for the various divisions, all of which are J-shaped, differ from each other in other respects besides steepness. The median age has been chosen here as the basis of ranking because it is more likely to reflect differences in steepness (differences in concentration among young corporations) than any other readily obtainable summary number. The system of ranking used in table 20 has been followed below in tables 21 to 26, which show groups within certain divisions or subgroups within certain groups.

Table 20 indicates that moderate differences in age structure exist among the eight (excluding Not-allocable) divisions. The maximum range, in terms of median age in 1946, is from 8 to 14; and this is small compared to the range shown below for groups within each of several divisions. Construction corporations active in 1946 were on the average much younger than those in Agriculture, etc.: very young corporations were a larger share of the total in Construction than in Agriculture, etc. The range over which the median ages for 1945 vary is much narrower, from 11 to 15. This reflects mainly the fact that net additions to the active-corporation list in 1946 were disproportionately numerous in certain divisions, such as Construction, Trade, and Manufacturing. But, even for 1946, the range is not wide; and differences in age structure among the divisions were not strikingly large. Put another way, the quartile ages for each division differ only moderately from those for all divisions combined. This is partly accounted for by the fact, stated above, that the industrial classification of corporations is somewhat blurred: various corporations classified in any particular division may have economic activities in one or more other divisions. This tends to bring each division, in some degree, closer to the average for all divisions than it would otherwise be.

So far as the differences in age structure indicated by table 20 reflect true differences among lines of economic activity, they are not surprising. Construction, which had experienced a long slack period before the war and was under severe restrictions during the war, was in 1946 entering upon a vigorous boom. That numerous new construction corporations should come into existence was to be expected, and their entry increased greatly the concentration of young corporations in the Construction division. In the case of

Agriculture, etc., the opportunities for totally new enterprises were not numerous, and actually (see chap. vi) most of the corporations chartered in 1946 were successors to previously existing agricultural businesses. Moreover, the corporate form is comparatively rare in agriculture, and conditions encouraging the creation of new corporations in this line were not particularly likely to exist in 1946. The apparent differences in age structure between Trade or Manu-

TABLE 21

Quartile Ages, for 1946 and 1945, for the Mining and Quarrying Division and Each of Its Groups*

Group	Quartile age					
	1946-active returns			1945-active returns		
	First	Second	Third	First	Second	Third
2 Mining and quarrying......	6	12	22	7	13	22
4 Anthracite mining.........	3	7	13	5	9	15
5 Bituminous coal, lignite, peat, etc..............	4	11	25	3	11	25
6 Crude petroleum and natural gas production.......	7	12	19	8	12	19
3 Metal mining............	7	15	29	7	15	29
8 Not allocable............	5	15	30	7	17	29
7 Nonmetallic mining and quarrying.............	6	16	25	9	17	26

* The serial numbers preceding the row titles correspond to those (in parentheses) of table A. The description of Quartile ages is given in section 7. Groups are ranked by the second-quartile age for 1946.

facturing and Finance, etc. or Public utilities can best be interpreted in the light of details concerning the groups within these divisions presented below.

Table 21 shows corresponding figures for the groups of the Mining and quarrying division. Here again the range of variation, median ages running from 7 to 16 in 1946, is not strikingly wide; but the table indicates moderate differences in age structure among the groups. Here the ranking would be the same if based on 1945 median ages, and the 1945 range from low to high is about the same as that for 1946. Presumably, therefore, the net increases in the active-corporation list in 1946 were roughly proportional among the Mining and quarrying groups.

One may perhaps be surprised to find Anthracite mining as the youngest group, and Nonmetallic mining and quarrying—which, according to section E of table A, is dominated by stone, sand, and gravel production—as the oldest. The former industry, in which quasi-monopolistic conditions have long been assumed to exist, would not be expected to show the many new entries which would yield an exceptional concentration of young corporations. The latter, in view of the enlarged demand for its products resulting from the postwar construction boom and in view of the wide geographical shifts in the impact of that boom because of recent migrations of population, might be expected to have very many entries in 1945 and 1946, and hence to show a "young" age structure. An economic explanation of the actual situation revealed by table 21 does not readily appear.

A peculiarity in the range between first and third quartile ages for Bituminous coal, etc. is worthy of mention. For this group, the first quartile age is lower, and the third quartile age is higher, than that for the entire division. For one half of the corporations of the group, age is more than three years and less than twenty-five years; for one half of the corporations of the division, age is more than five years and less than twenty-two years. The "middle aged" section is spread over a range extending, in both directions, beyond the corresponding range for the division. This means that, for Bituminous coal, etc., an abnormal concentration of corporations exists both among the very young and among the very old members of the group. The opposite situation prevails for the Crude petroleum, etc. group: in this case an abnormal concentration exists among members which are neither very young nor very old. In instances of either sort, the shape of the age distribution for the group differs from that of the division not only in steepness (the general dominance of young members), but also in the relative frequency of incorporation during a "middle" period in which corporations neither very young nor very old were chartered. For Bituminous, etc. chartering was comparatively inactive, for Crude petroleum, etc. chartering was comparatively active, during such middle period.[58]

Table 22 shows the quartile ages for the 24 Manufacturing groups, and here the differences in age structure are much more noteworthy than those of tables 20 and 21. The range in median age is from 4 for Apparel, etc. to 21 for Cotton manufactures. That

---

[58] The terms middle-aged and middle period are here used in the special senses indicated: middle-aged does not refer to a zone midway in the life span of a corporation; and middle period does not refer to a zone midway between 1946 and some date before 1860.

TABLE 22

Group	1946-active returns			1945-active returns		
	First	Second	Third	First	Second	Third
9 Manufacturing............	2	11	23	6	14	26
15 Apparel and products made from fabrics............	1	4	12	3	8	15
31 Other manufacturing.......	1	5	16	4	11	20
32 Not allocable............	1	6	18	4	10	21
26 Nonferrous metals and their products..........	1	7	21	6	14	25
27 Electrical machinery and equipment.............	2	7	17	4	11	21
30 Transportation equipment, except automobiles......	3	7	19	4	9	19
16 Leather and products......	2	8	19	5	12	23
18 Lumber and timber basic products.............	1	9	23	6	15	28
14 Textile mill products, except cotton..........	2	10	21	6	13	24
19 Furniture and finished lumber products........	2	10	22	7	14	26
29 Automobiles and equipment, except electrical ...	2	10	21	8	14	23
11 Beverages...............	6	12	21	8	13	21
17 Rubber products.........	3	12	25	7	14	26
28 Machinery, except transportation equipment and electrical.............	2	12	27	6	16	29
22 Chemicals and allied products.............	5	13	25	7	15	25
23 Petroleum and coal products	7	13	21	8	13	21
10 Food and kindred products.	4	14	24	8	16	26
24 Stone, clay, and glass products.............	2	14	26	9	18	30
25 Iron, steel, and products...	3	14	28	8	18	30
20 Paper and allied products...	7	17	30	10	19	31
21 Printing and publishing industries.............	7	17	28	9	18	30
12 Tobacco manufactures.....	8	20	31	10	20	31
13 Cotton manufactures......	6	21	39	11	24	41

* The serial numbers preceding the row titles correspond to those (in parentheses) of table A. The description of Quartile ages is given in section 7. Groups are ranked by the second-quartile age for 1946.

Apparel, etc. should be exceptionally young is not surprising: this is an industry in which large requirements of fixed capital and similar obstacles to free entry do not exist and in which competition is notoriously keen. In Cotton manufactures, on the other hand, although capital requirements are not extraordinarily large and competition is vigorous, the role of large enterprises is much greater than in Apparel, etc., and the uncertainties of the market for cotton yarn and fabric tend to discourage new entry.

Although no systematic attempt is here made to comment upon the economic implications of the important differences in age shown in the table, I may remark that various factors need consideration. We might expect that large fixed-capital requirements, through making entry of new firms difficult, would result in the appearance of certain groups, such as Iron, etc. and Paper, etc., among those which are "old." But this factor is not conclusive: large fixed capital is characteristic of Electrical machinery, etc. and of Transportation equipment; but these groups are fairly young, perhaps because another factor—technical innovation—is dominant. I may remark also that general impressions of the fixed-capital requirements (or any other factor) for a group need to be tested for the constituents of that group. Thus, for Electrical machinery, etc., some branches of the industry may require very heavy installations of plant and equipment, whereas others may operate with very slight installations (see section V of table A for constituents of this group). Similarly, the parts and accessories subgroup in the Automobiles, etc. group may be subject to very different factors from the subgroup comprising makers of cars and trucks (see section X of table A). Various other factors may have important effects upon the age structure of a group, and these also need examination in reference to the constituents of the group.[59] The number of factors which should be considered, and the variety of ways in which such factors may impinge upon the constituents of any particular group, mean that an adequate economic interpretation of such results as appear in table 22 would require extensive and critical research. This is a primary reason for confining the comments on economic implications in this chapter to a limited number of remarks which are merely suggestive.

[59] Moreover, attention may need to be given to other indications of the age structure besides the median age. For example, in two groups—Beverages, and Petroleum and coal products—the "middle period" (between the first and third quartile ages) lies entirely within the middle period for the division. See the above discussion of Crude petroleum in the Mining and quarrying division, and n. 58.

TABLE 23

QUARTILE AGES, FOR 1946 AND 1945, FOR THE TRADE DIVISION AND ITS GROUPS, THE
WHOLESALE GROUP AND ITS SUBGROUPS, AND THE RETAIL GROUP AND ITS SUBGROUPS*

| Group or subgroup | Quartile age | | | | | |
| | 1946-active returns | | | 1945-active returns | | |
	First	Second	Third	First	Second	Third
37 Trade....................	2	9	18	6	12	20
38 Wholesale...............	2	8	18	6	12	21
41 Retail...................	2	10	18	6	12	20
55 Not allocable.............	2	10	20	6	13	22
38 Wholesale...............	2	8	18	6	12	21
39 Commission merchants.....	2	7	16	4	10	19
40 Other wholesalers.........	2	9	19	6	12	22
41 Retail...................	2	10	18	6	12	20
48 Eating and drinking places..	2	7	11	4	7	11
49 Automotive dealers........	1	7	15	6	12	18
44 Package liquor stores......	3	8	11	5	8	11
43 Food stores, including market milk dealers.........	2	9	16	5	10	16
46 Apparel and accessories....	3	9	16	5	11	16
47 Furniture and house furnishings...............	2	9	18	6	13	21
50 Filling stations............	4	11	17	7	12	16
53 Other retail trade..........	3	11	19	7	13	21
45 Drug stores...............	7	12	20	7	13	20
54 Not allocable.............	3	13	25	9	17	28
42 General merchandise.......	4	15	28	9	18	30
51 Hardware................	6	16	26	10	17	28
52 Building materials, fuel, and ice................	9	17	27	10	18	28

* The serial numbers preceding the row titles correspond to those (in parentheses) of table A. The description of Quartile ages is given in section 7. Groups and subgroups are ranked by the second-quartile age for 1946.

The Trade division is classified into two groups, other than Not-allocable; and each of these groups is classified into subgroups. The quartile ages for these classes appear in the three sections of table 23. Difference in age structure between the two groups, Wholesale and Retail, is slight; and this is also true for the two subgroups under Wholesale.

Among the subgroups under Retail, however, the differences are substantial: the 1946 median age ranges from 7 for Eating and drinking places and for Automotive dealers to 17 for Building materials, etc. That Eating and drinking places and Automotive dealers should appear as very young subgroups is not surprising: the former is notoriously a line of activity in which new, and particularly small, enterprises spring up; the latter might be expected to show many new entries at, and shortly after, the close of the war because of the resumption of a boom in motorcar selling after the severe restrictions of wartime. It might be expected that Building materials, etc. (disregarding the fact that the subgroup also includes fuel and ice) would not appear as an older subgroup, for here also a postwar boom in activity followed the restrictions of wartime; but the shortages of materials and price uncertainties immediately following the war may have prevented the impact of this boom upon the subgroup until after 1946. Similar remarks apply to another older subgroup, Hardware.

The groups within the Service division, table 24, also show substantial differences in age structure. That the youngest subgroup should be Miscellaneous repair, etc. might be expected, in view of the small fixed-capital requirements in comparison with Automotive repair, etc. and Hotels, etc. That Personal service, in which about half of the corporations are in the subgroup Laundries, cleaners, and dyers (see section KK of table A), should appear as an older group is somewhat surprising.

Table 25 shows quartile ages for the Finance, etc. division and its groups, and for the subgroups in the Finance and in the Insurance, etc. groups. Age variation among the groups is fairly sharp. The youngest group, Real estate, etc., is made up mainly (see section UU of table A) of the subgroup Owner operators and lessors of buildings, and one might expect it to appear as fairly young in comparison with other groups of the division. In comparison, however, with the younger groups in certain other divisions already examined, Real estate, etc. is not strikingly young. One of the two oldest groups of the division is Lessors of real property, except buildings; and nearly half of such (corporate) lessors are owners of mineral and oil properties (see section VV of table A).

The other "oldest" group is Finance, and available date-of-incorporation statistics for its subgroups are summarized in the quartile ages of the second section of table 25. The youngest subgroup, as might be expected, is Short-term credit agencies, except banks, which is dominated (see section PP of table A) by the sub-subgroups Sales finance and industrial credit and Personal credit.

The oldest subgroup is emphatically Banks and trust companies; and this is in fact the oldest class—its closest competitor being Cotton manufactures—for which separate date-of-incorporation statistics are available. That Banks and trust companies should have a strikingly old age structure is not surprising, in view of the effects of the great depression of the 'thirties in discouraging the subsequent entry of new companies into this field.

TABLE 24

QUARTILE AGES, FOR 1946 AND 1945, FOR THE SERVICE DIVISION AND ITS GROUPS*

Group	Quartile age					
	1946-active returns			1945-active returns		
	First	Second	Third	First	Second	Third
56 Service..................	3	10	18	5	11	19
61 Miscellaneous repair services, hand trades.........	2	6	16	3	9	18
65 Not allocable.............	2	6	14	4	8	14
63 Amusement, except motion pictures...............	2	7	15	5	10	16
57 Hotels and other lodging places.................	3	9	17	5	10	18
59 Business service..........	3	10	18	6	11	19
60 Automotive repair services and garages.............	2	10	17	6	12	18
62 Motion pictures..........	4	10	16	6	10	16
64 Other service, including schools................	2	10	20	5	12	21
58 Personal service..........	4	12	20	7	16	20

* The serial numbers preceding the row titles correspond to those (in parentheses) of table A. The description of Quartile ages is given in section 7. Groups are ranked by the second-quartile age for 1946.

Among the two subgroups of the Insurance, etc. group, shown in the third section of table 25, Insurance carriers is, as might be foreseen, much older than Insurance agents, etc. A surprising fact is that the latter subgroup does not appear even younger than its median and first-quartile ages (15, and 8, for 1946) would imply; but we must bear in mind that presumably many of the younger and smaller firms in this field are not incorporated, and the evidence from the corporation data may therefore not accord with our general impressions. This last point is pertinent for various classes examined in this chapter. In some lines of business, such as banking and railroad transportation and basic steel production, the cor-

TABLE 25

QUARTILE AGES, FOR 1946 AND 1945, FOR THE FINANCE, ETC. DIVISION AND ITS GROUPS, AND FOR SUBGROUPS OF TWO GROUPS*

Group or subgroup	Quartile age					
	1946-active returns			1945-active returns		
	First	Second	Third	First	Second	Third
66 Finance, insurance, real estate, and lessors of real property..............	5	12	22	6	13	23
79 Real estate, including lessors of buildings............	4	10	18	5	10	18
76 Insurance carriers, agents, etc....................	9	16	25	9	16	25
67 Finance.................	11	20	36	12	22	36
80 Lessors of real property, except buildings.........	10	20	35	11	20	34
67 Finance.................	11	20	36	12	22	36
70 Short-term credit agencies, except banks...........	4	11	19	6	11	18
73 Security and commodity-exchange brokers and dealers................	7	12	17	8	12	16
74 Other finance companies....	7	12	18	7	12	18
69 Long-term credit agencies, mortgage companies, except banks.............	7	13	21	7	14	22
75 Not allocable.............	7	14	24	8	15	24
71 Investment trusts and investment companies......	11	18	24	11	17	23
72 Other investment companies, including holding companies................	13	20	27	13	19	26
68 Banks and trust companies..	20	36	45	20	35	45
76 Insurance carriers, agents, etc....................	9	16	25	9	16	25
78 Insurance agents, brokers, etc....................	8	15	22	9	14	21
77 Insurance carriers..........	12	23	45	12	24	46

* The serial numbers preceding the row titles correspond to those (in parentheses) of table A. The description of Quartile ages is given in section 7. Groups and subgroups are ranked by the second-quartile age for 1946.

porate form is not only dominant but almost exclusively so; but, in such lines as retailing and personal service and agricultural production, the unincorporated form is very common or even dominant. The share under control of the corporate form varies widely among lines of business. The age statistics under examination in this book relate only to corporations; and, for any industrial class in which unincorporated forms are very common, the indications

TABLE 26

QUARTILE AGES, FOR 1946 AND 1945, FOR THE PUBLIC UTILITIES DIVISION AND ITS GROUPS, AND THE AGRICULTURE, ETC. DIVISION AND ITS GROUPS*

Group	Quartile age					
	1946-active returns			1945-active returns		
	First	Second	Third	First	Second	Third
33 Public utilities............	5	14	26	7	15	27
34 Transportation............	3	11	20	6	12	20
36 Other public utilities.......	13	24	41	13	24	41
35 Communication...........	11	25	40	13	27	39
82 Agriculture, forestry, and fishery................	6	14	23	8	15	24
85 Fishery.................	2	7	16	3	9	16
83 Agriculture and services....	6	14	23	8	15	24
84 Forestry.................	10	18	33	10	18	34

* The serial numbers preceding the row titles correspond to those (in parentheses) of table A. The description of Quartile ages is given in section 7. Groups are ranked by the second-quartile age for 1946.

of age structure here reported may not be representative of the age structure of all firms—corporate and unincorporated—in such class. For some classes of business, of course, the corporate section may be a good sample—so far as measuring age structure is concerned— of all firms in the class, but this point would need separate examination in all cases except those in which the corporate form is almost completely in control.

Three divisions (not counting Not-allocable) have not yet been surveyed in terms of the age structure of the groups included in such divisions. For one, Construction, no date-of-incorporation statistics are available for the groups (listed in section WW of table A); and comment on the division as a whole appears above. The other two, Public utilities and Agriculture, etc., despite their lack of relation to each other, are shown together in table 26.

Transportation is much younger than the two other Public utilities groups, though it is far from young in comparison with several groups in other divisions. If we think of transportation in terms of railroads and ocean shipping, we might expect the group to run older than appears from the table. Actually, however, the group is dominated (in terms of number of corporations) by the subgroup Highway freight transportation, etc. (see section AA of table A);

TABLE 27

NUMBER OF MUTUALLY EXCLUSIVE LINE-OF-INDUSTRY CLASSES
SHOWING SPECIFIED MEDIAN AGES IN 1946*

Median age	Number of classes	Median age	Number of classes
4	1	17	3
5	1	18	2
6	1	19	..
7	9	20	3
8	3	21	1
9	6	22	..
10	8	23	1
11	5	24	1
12	8	25	1
13	3	..	
14	4	..	
15	3	36	1
16	2		
		Total	67

* The lowest median age is for the Manufacturing group, Apparel and products made from fabrics; and the highest is for the Finance subgroup, Banks and trust companies.

and this is a line of activity which we should expect to appear young. Examination of the subgroups (listed in section BB and CC of table A) of the two other groups, Communication and Other public utilities, renders the relatively greater age of these groups readily understandable.

Although the differences in age structure among the three groups of the Agriculture, etc. division are marked, the Forestry and Fishery groups are of minor importance in the division (see section XX of table A). For all three groups, the corporate form of organization is much less common than are unincorporated forms; and the remarks above, concerning inferences as to age structure of all enterprises in the class from facts as to age structure of corporations, are here especially pertinent.

Examination of tables 20–26 has brought out great diversity in age structure among various lines of industry. The extent of such diversity may be more clearly seen from a summarization in terms of median age. Such a summarization appears in table 27, where 67 line-of-industry classes are arranged according to median age for 1946-active dated corporations. The 67 classes tabulated exclude, from the 86 classes shown in tables 20–26, all Not-allocable classes and also all classes which are combinations of more finely divided classes. The 67 classes are therefore mutually exclusive, and they exclude those "classes" (Not-allocable) which have no significance as representing specific lines of industry.[60] Half of the classes have median ages ranging from 9 to 15 years, and even this range reflects important diversity. Still stronger evidences of diversity appear at the ends of the frequency distribution in table 27: nearly one quarter of the classes have median ages less than 9, and nearly one quarter are more than 15. We must conclude that the age structure for the entire corporate system, discussed in chapter ii, is not characteristic of many line-of-industry classes, so far as median age is concerned. But the *shape* of the over-all age distribution—a J-shape, with heavy concentration among young corporations—is characteristic of nearly all classes, although the degree of concentration among young corporations varies widely from class to class.

Figure 5 illustrates the difference between the age structures of the two extreme cases of table 27, the Apparel, etc. group in Manufacturing (median age for 1946, 4), and the Banks and trust companies subgroup in the Finance group (median age, 36). Apparel, etc. is clearly J-shaped, with an exceptionally high concentration (compared with figure 2, for all corporations, regardless of line of industry) among very young corporations. The Banks, etc. subgroup is not even J-shaped, but has a modal peak in the period 1904–1909; and, in this case, very young corporations are not numerous.

Similarly, figure 6 shows the difference in age structure for two subgroups of the Retail group, Food stores, etc. and General merchandise. The 1946 median ages for these two subgroups are 9 and 15; and these are the approximate first and third quartiles of table 27, since about one quarter of the 67 median ages are less than 9, and about one quarter are greater than 15. Both curves of the chart

---

[60] Even the 67 mutually exclusive classes do not precisely represent specific lines of industry, for two reasons. In some lines, the corporate form is so uncommon that corporation data on age do not adequately represent the entire industry. And, as already stated, the line-of-business classification assigns a particular corporation to one class, though its activities may reach into several classes.

are J-shaped; but that for Food stores, etc., which has the smaller median age, is more steeply J-shaped than that for General merchandise. About one half of the 67 mutually exclusive classes tabulated in table 27 have age distributions which are J-shaped curves ranging in steepness from that of Food stores, etc. to that

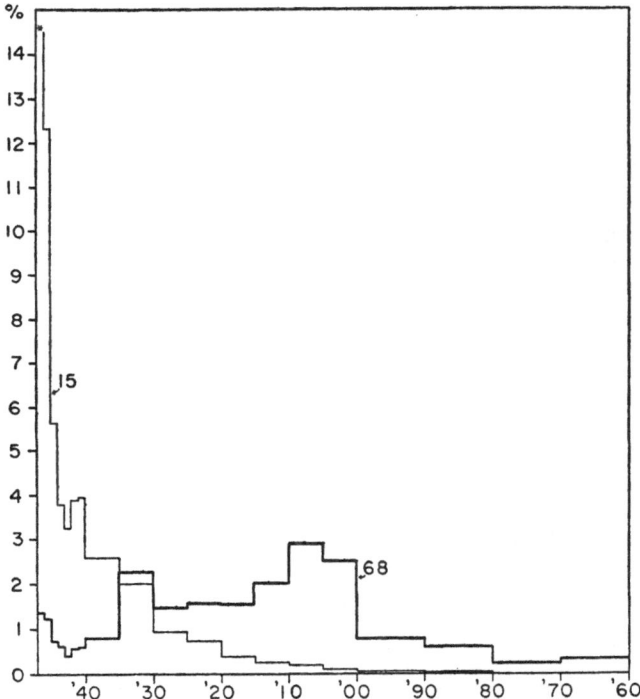

Fig. 5. Percentage distribution among periods of incorporation, of dated corporations active in 1946, in terms of number of such corporations, separately for two line-of-industry groups—Apparel and products made from fabrics (15), and Banks and trust companies (68).

SOURCE: Data derived by the process used in securing line *f* of table 4. Percentages for Before-1860 not shown. The percentage for 1946 runs off the figure, to 31.5 per cent.

of General merchandise. The 15 classes for which median age ranges from 4 to 8 have J-shaped curves which are steeper than that for Food stores, etc.; and the steepest of these is that for Apparel, etc., shown in figure 5. The 15 classes for which median age ranges from 16 to 36 are mainly J-shaped with steepness less than that of General merchandise; but a small number of these classes have age-

distribution curves which are not J-shaped but instead show a modal
peak (usually in some period close to 1930), and the extreme case
of this sort is the Banks and trust companies curve of figure 5.

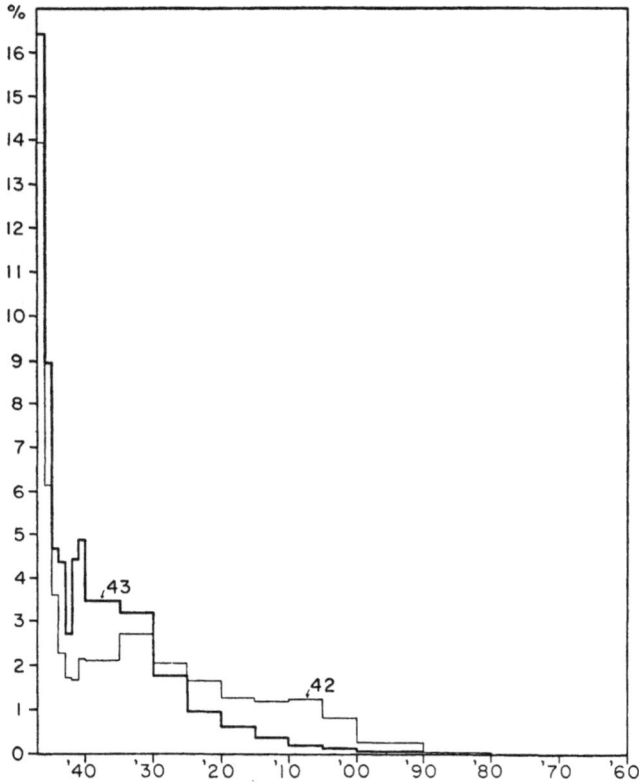

Fig. 6. Percentage distribution among periods of incorporation, of dated corporations active in 1946, in terms of number of such corporations, separately for two subgroups of the Retail trade group—General merchandise (42), and Food stores including
market milk dealers (43).

SOURCE: Data derived by the process used in securing line *f* of table 4. Percentages for
Before-1860 not shown.

17. *Variations in number of incorporations among lines of industry*.—Comments on the age structures in various lines of business
in section 16 refer to exceptional activity in chartering new corporations in such lines in 1946. A great wave of incorporation
developed after the war, but activity in chartering was by no means
uniformly distributed among the various industrial classes. Table

28 shows this lack of uniformity and clearly indicates that activity in chartering new corporations was exceptionally high in a limited number of lines.

The comparison in the table is between the distribution among lines of industry, of incorporations in 1946 (or 1945) and that before 1946 (or 1945).[61] Section A of the table shows that, among the eight divisions (not counting Not-allocable), chartering activity in 1946 was abnormally high in Trade, Manufacturing, and Construction, and abnormally low in Finance, etc. and Mining and quarrying, with minor departures from normal for the other divisions. Chartering activity in 1945 departed from normal for each division in the same direction as in 1946; but the departures were in all cases less noteworthy, and for Manufacturing it was almost negligible. Not only was the postwar wave of incorporations much less clearly revealed in 1945 than in 1946, but the differential impact of that wave upon different lines of industry was much less fully developed in 1945 than in 1946.

Comparison of these results with those in table 20 shows that divisions in which chartering activity in 1946 was exceptionally high are "young" divisions, and that those in which activity was exceptionally low are "old."[62] This close correlation between the two sets of results is to be expected: excessively high or excessively low incorporations in 1946 were a dominant factor determining median age for certain divisions. For any division, the median age depends upon a variety of factors, bound up in the history of incorporations in that division during the various age periods and in the disappearances of such corporations from the 1946-active list. When, however, the volume of incorporation in 1946 was extraordinarily large, or small, this fact alone could result in a marked shift in median age from the position determined by the multiplicity of other factors.

Sections B to L of table 28 show corresponding indications of differential chartering activity in 1946 (or 1945) among the groups

[61] Strictly, the distribution of incorporations before 1946 (or 1945) is not indicated by the percentages in the second (or fourth) column; for the figures apply only to dated corporations active in 1946 (or 1945), and actual incorporations in earlier years had included an unknown number of corporations which had become inactive by the most recent year. Nevertheless, the percentages for before 1946 (or 1945), as shown in the table, may probably be regarded as roughly indicative of differences in chartering activity among lines of business in the years before 1946 (or 1945).

[62] Similar comparisons for 1945 show less close correlation, presumably because differential impact of chartering activity in 1945 was not strong enough to dominate the various other factors controlling median age.

TABLE 28

Per Cent Distribution, Among the Nine Divisions, Among the Groups in Each Specified Division, and Among the Subgroups in Each Specified Group, of the 1946-active Corporations Chartered in 1946 and Before 1946 and the 1945-active Corporations Chartered in 1945 and Before 1945

Class	1946-active corporations chartered		1945-active corporations chartered	
	In 1946	Before 1946	In 1945	Before 1945
A. *Among 9 divisions*				
2 Mining and quarrying..............	.88	1.67	1.12	1.77
9 Manufacturing....................	26.03	19.19	19.93	19.03
33 Public utilities...................	3.06	4.61	3.63	4.67
37 Trade...........................	39.45	29.38	33.49	28.41
56 Service..........................	8.15	7.99	9.32	8.21
66 Finance, etc......................	15.68	31.71	26.57	32.47
81 Construction.....................	5.12	2.92	3.45	2.79
82 Agriculture, etc..................	0.90	1.40	1.02	1.45
86 Not allocable.....................	0.74	1.13	1.47	1.20
B. *Among mining and quarrying groups*				
3 Metal mining.....................	6.80	11.48	11.86	11.63
4 Anthracite mining.................	3.72	2.20	3.95	1.98
5 Bituminous, etc...................	24.43	20.91	29.25	20.95
6 Crude petroleum, etc..............	38.03	45.36	36.36	45.62
7 Nonmetallic mining and quarrying....	23.79	17.34	15.02	17.52
8 Not allocable.....................	3.24	2.70	3.56	2.29
C. *Among manufacturing groups*				
10 Food and kindred products...........	7.07	10.59	7.64	11.08
11 Beverages........................	1.72	3.19	1.67	3.35
12 Tobacco manufactures..............	0.08	0.25	0.24	0.27
13 Cotton manufactures...............	0.65	1.03	0.49	1.08
14 Textile-mill products, except cotton...	5.22	4.59	4.34	4.59
15 Apparel, etc......................	19.84	10.11	15.49	9.34
16 Leather and products..............	3.37	2.80	3.32	2.60
17 Rubber products..................	0.44	0.62	0.62	0.58
18 Lumber, etc......................	4.25	2.78	2.74	2.93
19 Furniture, etc....................	5.99	5.09	5.57	4.92
20 Paper and allied products...........	1.33	2.68	1.45	2.74
21 Printing and publishing industries.....	5.42	12.45	7.03	12.92
22 Chemicals and allied products........	4.27	7.58	6.30	7.88
23 Petroleum and coal products........	0.20	0.57	0.31	0.58
24 Stone, clay, and glass products........	3.73	3.70	2.54	3.56
25 Iron, steel, and products.............	6.63	8.22	6.50	8.43
26 Nonferrous metals, etc..............	5.05	3.22	4.45	3.02
27 Electrical machinery, etc.............	2.90	2.54	3.38	2.32
28 Machinery, except transportation equipment and electrical..........	6.95	7.83	8.77	7.81

TABLE 28—*Continued*

Class	1946-active corporations chartered		1945-active corporations chartered	
	In 1946	Before 1946	In 1945	Before 1945
29 Automobiles, etc....................	1.11	0.88	0.73	0.79
30 Transportation equipment, except automobiles.....................	0.74	1.12	1.47	1.40
31 Other manufacturing..............	8.14	5.06	8.77	4.80
32 Not allocable.....................	4.89	3.11	6.17	3.01
D. Among public utilities groups				
34 Transportation....................	89.96	68.16	88.77	67.04
35 Communication...................	7.70	17.09	5.37	17.44
36 Other public utilities.............	3.34	14.74	5.86	15.52
E. Among trade groups				
38 Wholesale.......................	36.70	30.67	33.69	29.73
41 Retail...........................	49.42	57.22	52.01	58.93
55 Not allocable....................	13.89	12.11	14.31	11.34
F. Among wholesale subgroups				
39 Commission merchants.............	14.35	14.17	20.84	14.35
40 Other wholesalers.................	85.65	85.83	79.16	85.65
G. Among retail subgroups				
42 General merchandise..............	5.60	6.93	5.20	7.28
43 Food stores, etc....................	7.47	7.63	9.35	7.72
44 Package liquor stores..............	2.11	2.49	2.65	2.44
45 Drug stores......................	2.86	5.40	3.36	5.83
46 Apparel and accessories............	13.16	14.66	11.77	14.80
47 Furniture, etc.....................	9.02	7.35	9.70	6.70
48 Eating and drinking places.........	12.65	13.45	19.94	13.34
49 Automotive dealers................	23.61	12.28	16.38	10.89
50 Filling stations...................	1.85	2.23	2.11	2.41
51 Hardware........................	2.42	3.00	2.24	3.10
52 Building materials, etc.............	5.19	9.92	4.23	10.28
53 Other retail trade.................	10.00	9.64	8.97	10.04
54 Not allocable.....................	4.04	5.02	4.10	5.18
H. Among service groups				
57 Hotels, etc........................	11.98	12.30	12.81	12.17
58 Personal service..................	18.83	23.09	17.10	23.12
59 Business service..................	18.25	18.99	18.19	19.08
60 Automotive repair, etc.............	8.67	7.75	8.52	8.59
61 Miscellaneous repair, etc...........	6.90	3.87	8.14	4.02
62 Motion pictures...................	7.26	11.66	7.95	11.72
63 Amusement, except motion pictures...	14.60	10.73	12.95	10.16
64 Other service, etc.................	12.28	10.96	13.38	10.64
65 Not allocable	1.22	.66	.95	.51

TABLE 28—*Concluded*

Class	1946-active corporations chartered		1945-active corporations chartered	
	In 1946	Before 1946	In 1945	Before 1945
I. Among finance, etc., groups				
67 Finance........................	11.01	25.27	10.87	24.79
76 Insurance, etc....................	3.49	5.65	2.82	5.71
79 Real estate, etc..................	83.22	64.74	83.79	64.86
80 Lessors of real property, except build-				
ings...........................	2.28	4.34	2.52	4.64
J. Among finance subgroups				
68 Banks and trust companies...........	16.12	43.52	19.20	45.27
69 Long-term credit agencies, etc........	9.87	7.79	10.45	8.95
70 Short-term credit agencies, etc........	28.21	10.53	28.26	9.70
71 Investment trusts, etc..............	9.21	10.61	8.60	10.58
72 Other investment companies, etc......	5.18	5.67	4.15	5.78
73 Security brokers, etc...............	9.62	3.66	7.07	3.79
74 Other finance companies.............	4.77	3.82	4.76	3.97
75 Not allocable.....................	17.02	14.39	17.51	11.96
K. Among insurance, etc., subgroups				
77 Insurance carriers..................	14.03	26.64	21.30	26.16
78 Insurance agents, brokers, etc........	85.97	73.36	78.70	73.84
L. Among agriculture, etc., groups				
83 Agriculture and services............	90.81	90.49	83.98	91.73
84 Forestry........................	2.22	5.19	2.16	4.39
85 Fishery.........................	6.97	4.32	13.85	3.88

of several divisions and the subgroups of several groups. The over-all indication is of wide diversity in 1946: for some groups and subgroups, activity was extraordinarily high; for others, extraordinarily low. In 1945, diversity among the classes is less marked, and the departure of activity in any one class from normal is in most cases less emphatic than in 1946.

Without commenting in detail upon the evidence in sections B to L of the table, brief mention may be made of the more striking instances (for 1946) among classes within certain divisions or groups. In the Manufacturing division, chartering activity was exceptionally high for the Apparel, etc. group and exceptionally low for the Printing, etc. group. In the Public utilities division, chartering was exceptionally active in Transportation and exceptionally inactive in Communication and in Other public utilities. In the Retail group, chartering was exceptionally active in Automotive dealers, exceptionally inactive in Drug stores. In the Service division, chartering was exceptionally active in Miscellaneous repair, etc., exceptionally inactive in Motion pictures. In the Finance, etc. division, chartering was exceptionally active in Real estate, etc., exceptionally inactive in Finance. These, and other contrasts which can be discovered in the table, confirm and emphasize the wide diversity in chartering activity in 1946. Comparison of the results of sections B to L of the table with relevant results in tables 21 to 26 shows some correlation between chartering activity in 1946 and median age—an inverse correlation, because high activity tends to lower the median age—but this correlation is generally less close than that between section A of table 28 and table 20.

18. *Size distribution of corporations as a partial cause of line-of-industry differences in age.*—Wide differences, among lines of industry, in the size distribution of corporations have been noticed in section 14. Section 12 showed a remarkable correlation between age and size: a systematic shift toward older age structures as size of corporation increases. May not the differences in age structure among lines of industry, discussed in this chapter, be largely a reflection of differences in size distribution among lines of industry? Evidence on this question is presented in table 29, which is confined to the 67 mutually exclusive line-of-industry classes, for 1946-active dated corporations. As in section 14, the criterion of size for any line-of-industry class is the percentage, of all balance-sheet corporations in the class, showing total assets of more than $250,000. Median age is taken as a summary indicator of the age of the class. The size criterion applies to all 1946-active balance-sheet corporations in the class; the age criterion applies to all 1946-active dated corporations of the class, whether or not they furnished balance sheets. The differences in coverage for the two criteria are negligible for purposes of the present comparison, for reasons set forth in section 11.

Table 29 clearly indicates some tendency for high median ages to be associated with a high percentage of corporations with more than $250,000 of total assets, but the association is far from complete and systematic. If the 67 pairs of statistics are arranged in a correlation scatter diagram, as in figure 7, the relationship—and incompleteness thereof—between the two criteria is more clearly revealed. A general tendency for the size percentage to increase as median

TABLE 29

COMPARISON OF THE AGE DISTRIBUTION WITH THE SIZE DISTRIBUTION, FOR 1946-ACTIVE
CORPORATIONS IN 67 MUTUALLY EXCLUSIVE LINE-OF-INDUSTRY CLASSES*

Class		Median age	Per cent with total assets more than $250,000
81	Construction	8	26.9
4	Anthracite mining	7	42.8
5	Bituminous coal, lignite, peat, etc.	11	38.4
6	Crude petroleum and natural gas production	12	25.8
3	Metal mining	15	46.1
7	Nonmetallic mining and quarrying	16	24.8
15	Apparel and products made from fabrics	4	15.6
31	Other manufacturing	5	17.4
26	Nonferrous metals and their products	7	22.3
27	Electrical machinery and equipment	7	34.3
30	Transporation equipment, except automobiles	7	38.4
16	Leather and products	8	27.0
18	Lumber and timber basic products	9	33.4
14	Textile mill products, except cotton	10	38.9
19	Furniture and finished lumber products	10	41.0
29	Automobiles and equipment, except electrical	10	39.6
11	Beverages	12	31.6
17	Rubber products	12	43.6
28	Machinery, except transportation equipment and electrical	12	35.7
22	Chemicals and allied products	13	27.3
23	Petroleum and coal products	13	50.5
10	Food and kindred products	14	31.4
24	Stone, clay, and glass products	14	25.6
25	Iron, steel, and products	14	36.8
20	Paper and allied products	17	43.3
21	Printing and publishing industries	17	15.8
12	Tobacco manufactures	20	47.2
13	Cotton manufactures	21	71.6
39	Commission merchants	7	10.9
40	Other wholesalers	9	22.4
48	Eating and drinking places	7	2.6
49	Automotive dealers	7	9.1
44	Package liquor stores	8	1.6
43	Food stores, including market milk dealers	9	10.2
46	Apparel and accessories	9	8.9
47	Furniture and house furnishings	9	12.7
50	Filling stations	11	2.3
53	Other retail trade	11	8.4
45	Drug stores	12	3.7
42	General merchandise	15	23.3
51	Hardware	16	3.7
52	Building materials, fuel, and ice	17	10.5
61	Miscellaneous repair services, hand trades	6	1.5

TABLE 29—*Continued*

Class	Median age	Per cent with total assets more than $250,000
63 Amusement, except motion pictures..................	7	8.0
57 Hotels and other lodging places......................	9	24.5
59 Business service...................................	10	7.4
60 Automotive repair services and garages...............	10	3.8
62 Motion pictures....................................	10	13.2
64 Other service, including schools.....................	10	6.5
58 Personal service...................................	12	5.2
79 Real estate, including lessors of buildings.............	10	14.0
80 Lessors of real property, except buildings.............	20	20.1
70 Short-term credit agencies, except banks.............	11	27.4
73 Security and commodity-exchange brokers and dealers....	12	26.2
74 Other finance companies...........................	12	9.9
69 Long-term credit agencies, mortgage companies, except banks..	13	25.0
71 Investment trusts and investment companies...........	18	37.9
72 Other investment companies, including holding companies.	20	63.8
68 Banks and trust companies..........................	36	95.4
78 Insurance agents, brokers, etc.......................	15	6.0
77 Insurance carriers.................................	23	78.0
34 Transportation....................................	11	18.0
36 Other public utilities..............................	24	34.6
35 Communication....................................	25	15.4
85 Fishery...	7	9.8
83 Agriculture and services...........................	14	19.4
84 Forestry..	18	30.9

* Classes are arranged in the order in which they appear in tables 20 to 26, from which the median-age figures are taken. The percentage figures are calculated by the method described in section 14.

age increases appears from the chart, and this tendency is summarized by the moderately inclined line of regression.[63] But the clustering of the points about this line is by no means close, and this implies that the relationship indicated by the line is far from precise.

[63] This is the line of regression of the size percentage on median age, fitted to the scatter diagram by the Pearsonian method. The relevant correlation coefficient is 0.61. The moderately high correlation, shown by the figure and by the coefficient 0.61, is misleading. Actually, if the points in the figure representing four lines of industry—cotton manufactures, banks and trust companies, insurance carriers, and other investment companies—are excluded, correlation among the remaining points would be so slight as to be almost insignificant. Mr. A. C. Rosander, of the Bureau of Internal Revenue, called my attention to this fact; and I am also grateful to him for certain other suggested improvements in the manuscript.

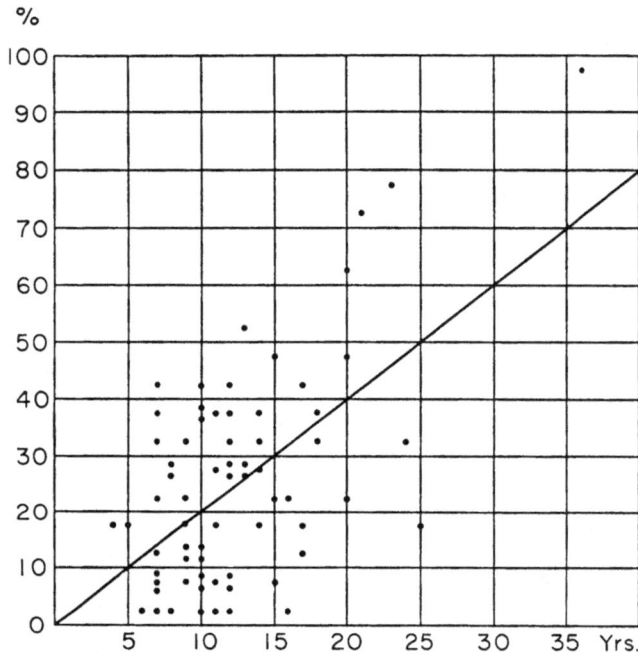

Fig. 7. Correlation, for 67 mutually exclusive line-of-industry classes, of per cent of corporations in the class having total assets more than $250,000 with median age of the class in years, for 1946.

SOURCE: Data from table 29. The inclined line of regression of size on age is described in the accompanying text.

We are forced to conclude that, though median age and the size percentage are in some degree interdependent, they are also in important degree independent. In other words, though the relation between age and size found in section 12 may *partly* account for that between age and line of industry found in section 16 (or vice versa), these two relations are in important degree independent of each other. Neither relation fully, or even largely, "explains" the other.

CHAPTER V

Age and Profitability

THE PURPOSE of this chapter is to examine the relation of the age of corporations to their profitability. Are older corporations more or less likely to be profitable in a particular year, such as 1946 or 1945, and to what extent? How do the observed differences, according to age, in chance of profit vary among lines of industry and among corporations classified by size? Examination of these questions is at once restricted by the fact that the date-of-incorporation statistics run solely in terms of *numbers* of corporations, and not in terms of aggregates of accounting items relevant to determination of the amount or rate of profit.

19. *Loss points as indirect indicators of profitability.*—Among the 491,152 1946-active corporations, 359,310 showed net income, and 131,842 showed no net income.[64] These figures alone afford some insight into profitability in 1946: we may say that, if we chose any one of the 491,152 corporations at random, the chance of its showing a net income in 1946 is 359,310 out of 491,152, or about 73.2 out of 100. Likewise, the chance of its showing a deficit is 131,842 out of 491,152, or about 26.8 out of 100. Ratios of this second sort—ratios such as the 26.8 per cent—are the backbone of the analysis of profitability in this chapter. Such a ratio is, of course, an indirect indicator of profitability: it indicates directly the chance of *not* showing profit.

Much more informing indicators of profitability could be derived from various accounting items. One example would be a mere comparison of the aggregate amounts of net income and of deficit. Thus, the 359,310 net corporations had aggregate net income of $27,185,-000,000 in 1946, and the 131,842 no-net corporations had aggregate

[64] *1946 S. of I.,* pp. 118 and 132, for these figures and those of the following paragraph. Net income is defined in terms of a figure pertinent to calculation of Federal income tax, and is not necessarily equal to what is called net income for business-accounting purposes. It is the difference between total income and total deductions (except the net-operating loss deduction), as reported on the tax return.

deficit of $1,992,000,000. A somewhat more satisfactory comparison of this sort is between compiled net profit after tax for the net corporations and the compiled net loss for the no-net corporations: between $18,510,000,000 and $1,986,000,000.[65] Either pair of figures suggests that the importance of the no-net category of corporations may be much smaller than the above 26.8 per cent implies. Another example of a comparison drawn from accounting items runs in terms of total compiled receipts: $265,597,000,000 for net corporations, and $23,357,000,000 for no-net corporations in 1946. Of the total compiled receipts for both categories combined, $288,954,-000,000, about 8.1 per cent was reported by the no-net corporations: and this also suggests that the original 26.8 per cent overstates the importance of the no-net category.

As further examples, we may consider the 440,750 1946-active corporations which filed balance sheets: 334,042 of these showed net income, and 106,708 showed deficit.[66] The percentage showing deficit is 24.2; and this is very close to the 26.8 for all corporations, as is to be expected because the deficiency in coverage by the balance-sheet returns is small. The total assets reported on balance-sheet returns were: $416,844,000,000 for the net corporations, $37,861,-000,000 for the no-net corporations, and $454,705,000,000 for both categories combined. About 8.3 per cent of aggregate total assets was held by the no-net corporations, and this figure also suggests that the mere ratio of *number* of no-net corporations to number of all corporations overstates the importance of the no-net category.[67]

A final example, of more detailed information as to profitability than is available in the date-of-incorporation statistics, is a classification of corporations according to the size of net income or deficit. Such a classification has been carried in many annual issues of

---

[65] Compiled net profit (or compiled net loss) differs from net income (or deficit) by its inclusion of wholly tax-exempt interest on certain government obligations, which is not part of net income for tax purposes.

[66] *1946 S. of I.*, pp. 214–219, for these and other figures of this paragraph.

[67] Other tests of the significance of the no-net category, in comparison with the net category or both combined, can be worked out in terms of rate of profit (or loss). Thus, for all active corporations (regardless of the inclusion or exclusion of balance-sheet information on the return), the rate of profit (or loss) after taxes on total compiled receipts shows: for net corporations in 1946, about 7 per cent; for no-net corporations, about – 8.5 per cent; for both categories combined, about 5.7 per cent. Although these figures show a high negative rate of "profit" for the no-net category, they show that the over-all rate for both categories combined was a substantial positive figure. Somewhat similar results would be found, for the balance-sheet corporations, by comparing the rate of profit (or loss) after taxes on the equity as a base, for the net and no-net categories and both combined.

Statistics of Income, and shows for 17 size classes of net income, ranging from net income less than $1,000 to net income more than $10,000,000, the number of returns and the aggregate net income in the class, with 17 similar size classes of deficit. Although such a classification does not include any other accounting item than amount of net income (or deficit), which might be taken as a measure of importance, it does give a passable basis for the inference not only that net corporations are far more important than no-net corporations, but also that returns with large net income vastly outweigh returns with large deficit.[68]

None of the more precise tests of profitability indicated in the foregoing examples is available for corporations classified by date of incorporation. In studying the relation between age and profitability, we must therefore be content with such an imperfect indicator of profitability as the ratio of the *number* of no-net corporations to the number of net and no-net corporations combined. This indicator is highly useful, particularly if we interpret it along the lines suggested above—as the chance that a corporation chosen at random, from the entire list or from a particular age class, showed a deficit. Moreover, we may have confidence that comparisons of such ratios for two or more age classes has high significance: if the ratio is clearly higher for corporations chartered in 1946 than for those chartered in 1925–1929, we may fairly conclude that corporations of the older class were less likely to show deficit (in 1946) than those of the younger class. We may even have moderate confidence that, in cases where the comparison shows a large disparity between the ratios for two age classes, more precise measures of profitability, by some of the devices suggested in the foregoing examples, would yield disparities pointing in the same direction. Despite the defects in our chosen indirect measure of profitability, therefore, we may hold that the many comparisons between age and profitability set forth in this chapter are of high significance.

The ratios, of number of no-net corporations to number of net and no-net combined, appear in line *e* of tables 30 and 31, for 1946-active corporations in two divisions of industry.[69] For the Public

[68] Such classifications, for the years here under study, appear in *1946 S. of I.,* p. 13, and *1945 S. of I.,* p. 14.

[69] These two tables, together with tables 18 and 19 for Manufacturing and Trade, complete the presentation of the full analysis—along the lines of table 4—of 1946 date-of-incorporation statistics for the four divisions of industry most important in terms of total compiled receipts or of total assets. In terms of number of corporations, the Service division is more important than Public utilities; but the full analysis for Service is not shown.

Age Structure of the Corporate System

TABLE 30

a	All returns	1944	1935–1939	1910–1914	1870–1879
b	14,395	478	2,104	610	72
c	7,428	311	878	242	17
d	21,823	789	2,982	852	89
e	34.0	39.4	29.4	28.4	19.1
f	....	3.8	14.2	4.1	0.4
g	....	20.7	46.4	85.8	99.5
a	Date not stated	1943	1930–1934	1905–1909	1860–1869
b	336	363	2,084	705	31
c	541	188	749	377	13
d	877	551	2,833	1,082	44
e	61.7	34.1	26.4	34.8	29.6
f	....	2.6	13.5	5.2	0.2
g	....	23.3	59.9	91.0	99.7
a	All stated	1942	1925–1929	1900–1904	Before 1860
b	14,059	333	1,731	586	46
c	6,887	198	609	249	20
d	20,946	531	2,340	835	66
e	32.9	37.3	26.0	29.8	30.3
f	....	2.5	11.2	4.0	0.3
g	....	25.8	71.1	95.0	100.0
a	1946	1941	1920–1924	1890–1899	Quartiles
b	951	426	1,021	420	1942
c	1,205	209	309	143	1933
d	2,156	635	1,330	563	1921
e	55.9	32.9	23.2	25.4	5
f	10.3	3.0	6.4	2.7	14
g	10.3	28.9	77.4	97.7	26
a	1945	1940	1915–1919	1880–1889	Loss points
b	744	442	687	225	1.700
c	643	244	220	63	0.864
d	1,387	686	907	288	1870–1879
e	46.4	35.6	24.3	21.9	1940
f	6.6	3.3	4.3	1.4	1932
g	16.9	32.2	81.8	99.1	1937

* Description of items accompanies table 4.

TABLE 31

ANALYSIS OF DATE-OF-INCORPORATION STATISTICS OF ALL FINANCE, INSURANCE, REAL
ESTATE, AND LESSORS OF REAL PROPERTY CORPORATIONS ACTIVE IN 1946*

a	All returns	1944	1935–1939	1910–1914	1870–1879
b	102,278	4,930	17,139	3,927	409
c	42,095	1,680	6,902	1,201	51
d	146,373	6,610	24,041	5,128	460
e	28.8	25.4	28.7	23.4	11.1
f	....	4.7	17.1	3.7	0.3
g	....	19.4	50.5	90.1	99.3

a	Date not stated	1943	1930–1934	1905–1909	1860–1869
b	2,232	3,806	13,873	4,090	571
c	1,868	1,266	5,787	1,037	64
d	4,100	5,072	19,660	5,127	635
e	45.6	25.0	29.4	20.2	10.1
f	....	3.6	14.0	3.7	0.4
g	....	23.1	64.5	93.7	99.7

a	All stated	1942	1925–1929	1900–1904	Before 1860
b	100,046	2,999	10,913	2,948	334
c	40,227	1,129	4,956	581	73
d	140,273	4,128	15,869	3,529	407
e	28.7	27.4	31.2	16.5	17.9
f	....	2.9	11.3	2.5	0.3
g	....	26.0	75.8	96.2	100.0

a	1946	1941	1920–1924	1890–1899	Quartiles
b	6,203	3,733	6,658	1,981	1942
c	4,843	1,450	2,756	459	1935
d	11,046	5,183	9,414	2,440	1925
e	43.8	28.0	29.3	18.8	5
f	7.9	3.7	6.7	1.7	12
g	7.9	29.7	82.5	98.0	22

a	1945	1940	1915–1919	1880–1889	Loss points
b	6,643	3,652	4,101	1,136	1.529
c	2,993	1,486	1,315	198	0.817
d	9,636	5,138	5,416	1,334	1860–1869
e	31.1	28.9	24.3	14.8	1945
f	6.9	3.7	3.9	1.0	1934
g	14.7	33.4	86.4	98.9	1936

* Description of items accompanies table 4.

utilities division, the ratio is higher for 1946, 1945, and 1944 than for any earlier period of incorporation: Public utilities corporations chartered in 1944–1946 were much more likely to show a deficit in 1946 than those chartered before 1944. Very young corporations in this division were much more likely to show a deficit in 1946 than were older corporations. This conclusion is in line with the general expectation that new corporations may experience one or more years of loss before they become firmly established, and the conclusion will be repeatedly confirmed in the examination below of various lines of industry.

Examination of the ratios for successively earlier periods, before 1944, shows a general tendency for the ratio to decline as the period becomes more remote from 1946; but such decline is not rapid in passing to periods before 1944, and is frequently interrupted by moderate advances in the ratio (a very large advance for 1860–1869). The course of the ratio in line *e* of table 31 is likewise generally downward from 1946 to the more remote periods, but here also several interruptions in the decline appear. Thus, although the ratio is emphatically higher in both divisions for 1946 than for any earlier period, and it tends to decline as the period becomes remote from 1946, it does not invariably decline from one period to an earlier period. Hence, although *very* young corporations are emphatically more liable to deficit than older corporations, we may not conclude that the liability to deficit (in 1946) always declines as age increases.

For studying the relation of age to profitability for a large number of line-of-industry and size classes of corporations, some summarization of such ratios as those of line *e* in table 30 is needed. For this purpose, lines *b* to *e* of the Loss-points block of the table have been prepared. Line *b* of that block is the ratio of line *e* for the 1946 block to line *e* for the All-stated block. The 1.700 in line *b* of the Loss-points block of table 30 indicates that 1946-active Public-utilities corporations chartered in 1946 were 1.7 times as likely to show a deficit (in 1946) as were all dated Public-utilities corporations active in 1946. Similarly, line *c* of the Loss-points block is the ratio of line *e* of the 1910–1914 block to line *e* of the All-stated block: the figure entered in line *c* means that 1946-active Public-utilities corporations chartered in 1910–1914 were 0.864 times as likely (a little less than ⅞ as likely) to show a deficit in 1946 as were all dated Public-utilities corporations active in 1946. The selection of the 1910–1914 period for this Loss point is aimed to make the comparison for fairly old corporations, and yet avoid choosing a still earlier period for which, in various line-of-industry classes (though not in Public utilities) the number of incorporations is so small as to render the ratio in line *e* somewhat erratic. The disparity between lines *b* and *c* of the Loss-points block is, accordingly, an indication of the difference in risk of deficit between very young and fairly old corporations.

Line *d* of the Loss-points block names the period for which the ratio in line *e* is minimum; and, as in the cases shown in tables 30 and 31, this period generally falls far back in the record—it represents corporations of great age.[70] Line *e* of the Loss-points block names a period such that for that period and all more recent periods line *e* is at least as high as line *e* of the All-stated block. Thus, for Public utilities, the chance of deficit in 1946 is for all corporations (active in 1946) chartered from 1940 to 1946 *inclusive* higher than (or at least as high as) the chance of deficit for all dated corporations of the class which were active in 1946. For Public utilities, the chance of deficit in 1946 was, for corporations chartered in every year from 1946 back to 1940, at or above the over-all average: not until corporations became more than seven years old did their chance of showing deficit drop below the over-all average.

The two remaining Loss points, lines *f* and *g*, are not summaries of the line *e* ratios of the period blocks, but are summaries of the separate age distributions for net and no-net corporations: line *f* is the median year for the net category, line *g* for the no-net category. They are obtained in the same manner as line *c* of the Quartiles block. Line *c* of the Quartiles block is the year in which the median (second quartile) date falls for the combined list of net and no-net corporations: it is a year such that half of all dated corporations active in 1946 (20,946 for table 30) were chartered after some date in that year, and half were chartered before that date. The process of determining this median year, and the corresponding median age (14, for Public utilities), has been set forth in section 7. By an exactly similar process, the median year for the 14,059 dated net corporations for Public utilities has been determined as 1932; and that for the 6,887 no-net corporations as 1937. The corresponding median ages are: net, 15; no-net, 10.

In general, for any line-of-industry or size class of corporations, the median age is higher for the net than for the no-net category:

---

[70] Where two or more periods show the minimum figure in line *e* of their respective blocks, the most recent period is named in line *d* of the Loss-points block.

corporations which show net income are on the average older than corporations which show deficit. The disparity between lines *f* and *g* of the Loss-points block is an indicator of the degree of difference between the age structure for net and that for no-net corporations.

The full picture of the two age structures could be presented by showing, for each date-of-incorporation period, two additional percentages corresponding to line *f* of the 20 period blocks of table 30. One such percentage would be the ratio of line *b* of the period block to line *b* of All stated; the other ratio would be based similarly on line *c*. Such percentages, for all 1946-active dated corporations (basic data in table 4, lines *b* and *c*), appear in the first two columns of table 32, and the last two columns show these figures cumulated from 1946 backward to Before-1860.[71]

The first two columns of the table show that the period ratios for no-net corporations exceed those for net corporations in all periods from 1946 to 1940, and that the reverse is true for all periods before 1940 (it is true even for Before-1860, if the ratio is stated in hundredths of 1 per cent). This is emphatic evidence that the age distribution is more steeply J-shaped—the concentration among young corporations is greater—for the no-net than for the net category. The cumulative percentages show that the median year for no-net corporations is 1940 and that for net corporations is in the period 1935–1939. Actually, the latter median year is identified, by a method identical with that used in table 4 to determine the second-quartile year, as 1935. The median ages are accordingly: 12 for net corporations; 7 for no-net corporations. The corporations showing deficit are on the average (median) five years younger than those showing net income.

For purposes of the analyses in this chapter, the full schedule of the net and no-net age distributions, such as those shown in table 32, need not be presented and examined in detail. Instead, the quartile ages, derived from the quartile years as listed in the Loss-points block, are taken as sufficient bases for a summary comparison of the two—net and no-net—age structures. The six Loss points are taken together as indicators of differences in profitability between net and no-net corporations. In nearly all cases studied below, these six indicators generally agree in support of a single conclusion—

[71] As in table 4, and certain similar tables, the cumulative figures are rounded to tenths of 1 per cent after first being calculated from the original percentages of the first two columns carried to hundredths of 1 per cent; and the cumulations shown in table 32 do not therefore check exactly in all cases as cumulations of the percentages in the first two columns.

that young corporations are more likely to show deficit than old corporations, or, stated differently, that no-net corporations are on the average younger than net corporations.

20. *Limitations on the significance of Loss points.*—The relation between age and profitability, as indicated by the Loss points, has

TABLE 32

PERCENTAGE DISTRIBUTION AMONG PERIODS OF INCORPORATION, OF THE DATED CORPORATIONS ACTIVE IN 1946, SEPARATELY FOR NET AND NO-NET CATEGORIES; AND CUMULATIVE PERCENTAGES*

Period of incorporation	Per cent of total		Cumulative per cent	
	Net	No-net	Net	No-net
1946	12.1	22.0	12.1	22.0
1945	7.2	10.6	19.3	32.7
1944	4.0	4.6	23.4	37.3
1943	2.8	3.2	26.2	40.4
1942	2.4	3.0	28.6	43.4
1941	3.3	3.6	31.9	47.0
1940	3.5	3.8	35.3	50.8
1935–1939	15.9	14.8	51.3	65.6
1930–1934	14.1	11.4	65.4	77.0
1925–1929	10.6	8.4	76.0	85.4
1920–1924	7.2	4.9	83.2	90.3
1915–1919	4.5	2.8	87.7	93.0
1910–1914	3.6	2.2	91.3	95.3
1905–1909	3.4	2.0	94.8	97.3
1900–1904	2.4	1.3	97.1	98.6
1890–1899	1.6	0.9	98.7	99.5
1880–1889	0.7	0.3	99.4	99.8
1870–1879	0.2	0.1	99.6	99.9
1860–1869	0.2	0.1	99.8	99.9
Before 1860	0.1	0.1	100.0	100.0

* Derived from data in lines *b* and *c* of table 4.

been worked out for various size classes (section 21) and for various lines of industry (section 22, below), separately for 1946-active and 1945-active corporations. Although both the 1946 and the 1945 Loss points are presented in the remaining tables of this chapter, those for 1946-active corporations are presumably more indicative of the true relation between age and profitability. The year 1945 is peculiarly unsatisfactory for separating corporations between the net and no-net categories, since conditions that might determine whether a particular corporation would show a profit in 1945 were

far from normal. The termination of war contracts and the recon-
version to civilian production affected the actual operating conditions and reported earnings of many corporations. The beginnings
of the postwar struggles over governmental control of the economy
and over the establishment of new wage levels were already in evidence. Acute shortages of certain materials obstructed production
and encouraged speculation in commodities. The excess-profits tax,
with its important but immeasurable effects upon incentives influencing output and costs, was still in force. The wartime allowance
of an abnormal rate of depreciation for certain facilities was still
in effect; and the distortions on this account were exaggerated by
the presidential proclamation of September, 1945, as a result of
which the remaining cost could be written off in a single charge.
On these various grounds, and perhaps others, many corporations
which might have shown a profit (loss) in a more normal year—and
normal here is not intended to mean a year free from ordinary
cyclical influences—showed instead a loss (profit) in 1945.

One may fairly hold that 1946 was not entirely free from some of
the influences listed above, and that it may also have been abnormal
on other counts. In particular, 1946 was abnormal in the sense that
new incorporations were at an unprecedented level; and this out-
burst of chartering has a direct bearing upon the results for certain
Loss points. Nevertheless, 1946 is almost certainly a better year
than 1945 for the sort of analysis presented in this chapter; and,
so far as comments are made below upon the implications of the
Loss points, they are confined mainly to the record for 1946-active
corporations. I may remark that study of the relation between age
and profitability on the basis of indications from data for *any* single
year must be somewhat unsatisfactory. Certain broad inferences
concerning the relation, as derived from data for one year (such as
1946) and particularly if largely confirmed by data of another year
(such as 1945), may indeed be stated with moderate confidence. But
any precise formulation of the relation between age and profitability
should rest upon data for a number of years in which the influences
affecting the showing of profit take on various forms and intensities.

Furthermore, many corporations active in 1946 (or 1945) had
lived through several years when the economy was disturbed by
war, and many of these had earlier lived through the most severe
depression of recorded history. These abnormal conditions had not
only affected the earning capacity of such corporations during the
years of war and severe depression, but they had also influenced, to

a degree which is important but unknown, the capacity of such corporations to earn a profit in 1946 (or 1945). In addition, these abnormal conditions had an undoubted effect, though we cannot measure it, upon the creation of new corporations and the demise of old corporations, with a resultant effect upon the age structure of corporations—and various classes thereof, including the net and no-net categories—which survived as active in 1946 (or 1945). The various Loss points, for the several classes of corporations, are accordingly the resultants of an intricate complex of historical influences, as well as a reflection in some degree of actual conditions in 1946 (or 1945).

Finally, we may remark that the various influences mentioned above may have had impact in varying degrees upon different classes, according to size or line of industry, of corporations. Hence, differences in the schedule of Loss points among classes of corporations may to some extent reflect such influences, rather than a fundamental variation among classes in the relation between age and profitability.

21. *Relation between age and profitability: variations among size classes of corporations.*—Table 33 shows a summary of the six Loss points, for 1946-active and 1945-active corporations, by size classes and for all active dated corporations and those without and those with balance sheets.[72] The results for all returns and all balance-sheet returns are nearly identical, as might have been expected in view of the nearly complete coverage of the total list by the balance-sheet list. In both cases, and for both 1946 and 1945, all the Loss points support the conclusion that the no-net corporations have a younger age structure than the net corporations. In each case and for both years, column I, which gives the ratios of risk of loss for corporations chartered in 1946, (1945, for the second line of the pair) to the general average, is sharply above one; and column II, which gives the corresponding ratio for a selected group of older corporations—those chartered in 1910–1914—is sharply below one. Column III shows in each case 1860–1869—the next to "oldest" period of incorporation in the record—as that for which

[72] In this table and in tables 34 and 35, the fourth Loss point, corresponding to line *e* in the Loss-points block of table 30, is entered as the number of years ending in 1946 (or 1945) rather than as a date. Thus, the entry 7 in the first line of table 33 means that the risk of loss (in 1946) was greater for corporations chartered in *each* of the seven years ending in 1946 than the average for all dated corporations. Where the fourth Loss point is a five-year period, as in the $500,000 class, the number of years is calculated from the middle of that period.

TABLE 33

SUMMARY OF LOSS POINTS, FOR ALL ACTIVE DATED CORPORATIONS, THOSE WITHOUT BALANCE SHEETS, THOSE WITH BALANCE SHEETS, AND SIZE CLASSES AMONG THE BALANCE-SHEET RETURNS*

	I	II	III	IV	V	VI
All corporation returns	*1.495*	*0.685*	*1860–1869*	*7*	*12*	*7*
	1.785	.764	1860–1869	9	14	11
Returns without balance sheets	*1.204*	*.901*	*1860–1869*	*3*	*12*	*9*
	1.281	.921	Before 1860	5	13	12
All balance-sheet returns	*1.568*	*.642*	*1860–1869*	*7*	*12*	*7*
	1.907	.734	1860–1869	9	14	10
Size classes (lower limit in $1,000)						
0	*1.361*	*.893*	*1930–1934*	*2*	*9*	*6*
	1.470	.907	1915–1919	2	10	9
50	*1.484*	*.810*	*1915–1919*	*2*	*11*	*7*
	1.904	.909	1930–1934	5	13	11
100	*1.456*	*.665*	*1910–1914*	*7*	*13*	*9*
	2.139	.824	1915–1919	6	15	13
250	*1.348*	*.680*	*Before 1860*	*7*	*17*	*11*
	2.818	.846	1890–1899	9	19	15
500	*1.642*	*.657*	*1905–1909*	*10*	*21*	*14*
	3.137	.718	1905–1909	9	22	17
1,000	*2.809*	*.583*	*1900–1904*	*10*	*26*	*18*
	4.438	0.652	1880–1889	9	26	20
5,000	*2.355*	*1.164*	*1905–1909*	*5*	*31*	*25*
	5.970	1.030	1900–1904	24	30	23
10,000	*4.222*	*.527*	*1870–1879*	*10*	*32*	*28*
	2.306	.500	1910–1914	1	31	27
50,000	*3.749*	*1.022*	*1930–1934*	*1*	*35*	*38*
	0	1.754	1920–1924	0	33	45
100,000	.....	*1.000*	*1880–1889*	..	42	*34*
	.....	.482	1860–1869	..	40	46

* In each pair of rows, italic type refers to 1946-active, ordinary type to 1945-active, corporations. Significance of columns:
I and II show ratios of risk of loss (in 1946, for top row, in 1945 for bottom row, of each pair), for corporations chartered in 1946 (or 1945) and in 1910–1914 respectively, to the average risk of loss for those chartered in all periods.
III Period for which risk of loss (in 1946, or 1945), of corporations chartered in that period, was minimum. If more than one period shows the minimum, the most recent is listed.
IV Number of years, ending in 1946 (italic type) or 1945 (ordinary type), for which risk of loss (in 1946, or 1945) of corporations chartered in those years was continuously at or above the average for all periods.
V and VI are median ages for net and no-net corporations, respectively.

such ratio is minimum. The entry 7 (9, for 1945-active corporations) in each case for column IV indicates that the stretch of recent years for each of which the ratio was constantly above the general average was fairly long. Columns V and VI show that, in each case and for both years, the median age was lower for no-net corporations than for net corporations—the no-net corporations were on the average younger. Without exception, these points support the stated conclusion, for all returns and for all balance-sheet returns.

Examination of the records for the several size classes reveals support, with some exceptions, for a similar conclusion applicable to corporations of each size class. The only exception in column I is in the $50,000,000 class, for which one entry is zero: the "risk of loss" in 1945, of corporations chartered in this size class in that year, was not only far below the general average (5.7 per cent) for all dated corporations of the size class, but was actually zero.[73] Although several entries in column II are above one, three of them are emphatically below the corresponding entries of column I, and therefore constitute no exceptions to the general rule that risk of loss is smaller for older corporations (chartered in 1910–1914) than for the very young corporations. The 1.754 for 1945-active corporations in the $50,000,000 class is an exception to the rule, since it is above the corresponding zero of column I. The exceptions in column III are fairly numerous: they are cases in which the risk of loss is minimum, not for very old corporations, but for those chartered in more recent periods—1930–1934 in three cases, and somewhat less recent periods in several other cases. The three very low figures for two large-size classes in column IV are exceptions to the general rule: in these cases the span of very recent years for which risk of loss exceeds the general average is exceedingly brief— zero or one year.[74] The exceptions in columns V and VI appear in

[73] The term "risk of loss" is used here in the narrow sense indicated in section 19. Strictly, any corporation, chartered in any particular year, faces a risk of loss in that year and in each subsequent year in which it remains active. The result shown in the table, for corporations of the $50,000,000 class chartered in 1945, is simply explained: only one such corporation was chartered (unless one or more others may be concealed in the group for which date of incorporation was not stated), and it showed net income. The fact that the number chartered in 1945 (or 1946) in this and several other large-size classes was very small means that the ratios of column I are somewhat untrustworthy bases for generalization about these classes of very large size. The dashes for both years in column I (and likewise in column IV) for the largest-size class mean that *no* corporation (again ignoring the Not-stated group) of that size was chartered in 1946 or 1945.

[74] The low figure, 2, for two small-size classes is not similarly significant. For such classes (the smallest-size class for both years, and the next larger class for 1946) the

those instances for which median age is smaller for net corporations (column V) than for no-net corporations (column VI). Three such instances appear, and all are in the two largest-size classes. For those classes, the total number of dated corporations in the no-net category is small; and, hence, the determination of the median year, and from it the median age, is somewhat erratic and the results are not trustworthy bases for generalization.[75]

The indicated relation between age and profitability—that risk of loss generally decreases with age—is clearly established, in spite of the exceptions listed above, for the various size classes. Further examination of the table indicates that, to some extent, the tendency for young corporations to show exceptionally high risk of loss increases as size increases. Such increasing tendency clearly does not persist to the largest-size classes, and it is by no means consistently supported by all the Loss points for the small-size and medium-size classes. For both years, the entries in column I rise somewhat irregularly from the smallest-size class to the $10,000,000 class ($5,000,000, for 1945), and similarly the entries of column II decline somewhat irregularly from the smallest-size class to the $1,000,000 class. These two opposite directions of change with increasing size indicate that, up to a fairly high level of size, the disparity in risk of loss between very young corporations and those chartered in 1910–1914 widens as size increases. A similar inference can be drawn from the entries in column III: the period showing minimum risk of loss becomes, with some irregularities, increasingly remote from 1946 (or 1945) as size increases up to the $10,000,000 class. Further confirmation appears from column IV and from a comparison of columns V and VI, again with various irregularities and with the course of change with increasing size interrupted for the very large classes. We may fairly conclude that, for small-size and medium-size classes, the tendency, for risk of loss to be greater for young corporations than for old corporations, becomes more marked as size increases. This conclusion is, however, by no means as emphatic or as consistently

---

J-shaped distribution is so very steep that the over-all ratio is dominated by corporations chartered in the latest year or two and cannot run below the specified ratios of more than the last two years.

[75] One may, on the same ground, hold that the 42 to 34 comparison of median ages for 1946-active corporations in the largest-size class is not a trustworthy confirmation of the general conclusion that no-net corporations are on the average younger than net corporations. The numbers of dated no-net corporations involved in the largest-size class are: 44 for 1946; 30 for 1945. For the next class ($50,000,000), they are: 41 for 1946; 24 for 1945. Fortunately, the numbers are markedly larger for the next smaller class ($10,000,000), and increase rapidly as size declines.

supported by the evidence as the conclusion in chapter iii concerning the relation of age structure to size of corporations.

22. *Relation between age and profitability: variations among lines of industry.*—Corresponding summaries of Loss points, for

TABLE 34

Summary of Loss Points, for All Active Corporations, and for Each Line-of-industry Division*

		I	II	III	IV	V	VI
1	All divisions combined...	*1.495*	*.685*	*1860–1869*	*7*	*12*	*7*
		1.785	.764	1860–1869	9	14	11
2	Mining and quarrying...	*1.282*	*.804*	*1880–1889*	*3*	*14*	*11*
		1.449	.833	Before 1860	9	15	11
9	Manufacturing........	*1.671*	*.496*	*1860–1869*	*7*	*13*	*4*
		2.472	.671	Before 1860	6	16	9
33	Public utilities.........	*1.700*	*.864*	*1870–1879*	*7*	*15*	*10*
		1.242	.855	Before 1860	9	16	13
37	Trade...............	*1.565*	*.466*	*1880–1889*	*7*	*11*	*4*
		2.205	.595	Before 1860	9	13	9
56	Service...............	*1.549*	*.726*	*1870–1879*	*3*	*11*	*6*
		1.689	.751	Before 1860	6	12	9
66	Finance, insurance, real	*1.529*	*.817*	*1860–1869*	*2*	*13*	*11*
	estate, and lessors of real	1.437	.844	1860–1869	2	14	12
	property						
81	Construction..........	*1.415*	*.808*	*1900–1904*	*7*	*10*	*5*
		1.632	.769	1900–1904	9	13	10
82	Agriculture, forestry,	*1.492*	*.585*	*1880–1889*	*7*	*16*	*9*
	and fishery...........	1.582	.843	1880–1889	9	16	13
86	Not allocable.........	*1.186*	*.845*	*1920–1924*	*5*	*15*	*16*
		1.254	.901	1915–1919	9	15	12

* In each pair of rows, italic type refers to 1946-active, ordinary type to 1945-active, corporations. Significance of columns:

I and II show ratios of risk of loss (in 1946, for top row, in 1945 for bottom row, of each pair), for corporations chartered in 1946 (or 1945) and in 1910–1914 respectively, to the average risk of loss for those chartered in all periods.

III Period for which risk of loss (in 1946, or 1945), of corporations chartered in that period, was minimum. If more than one period shows the minimum, the most recent is listed.

IV Number of years, ending in 1946 (italic type) or 1945 (ordinary type), for which risk of loss (in 1946, or 1945) of corporations chartered in those years was continuously at or above the average for all periods.

V and VI are median ages for net and no-net corporations, respectively.

1946-active and 1945-active corporations, by divisions of industry, appear in table 34. Here, with the single exception of the column III item of Not-allocable for 1946, all the Loss points support the general conclusion about the relation of age to profitability. For every division, young corporations are clearly and emphatically more likely to show loss (in 1946, or 1945) than older corporations. Moreover, though some variation exists in each column, among the

TABLE 35

		I	II	III	IV	V	VI
	Section A						
2	Mining and quarrying...	1.282	0.804	1880–1889	3	14	11
		1.449	0.833	Before 1860	9	15	11
3	Metal mining.........	1.210	0.959	1943	3	15	15
		1.102	0.985	1933	1	16	14
4	Anthracite mining......	1.438	.....	1915–1919	4	9	5
		1.220	1.220	1905–1909	2	9	8
5	Bituminous coal, etc....	1.392	0.770	1880–1889	3	12	8
		1.707	0.692	1890–1899	6	13	8
6	Crude petroleum, etc....	1.293	0.678	1880–1889	7	14	11
		1.513	0.637	1890–1899	9	14	11
7	Nonmetallic mining and quarrying.............	1.624	0.735	1890–1899	3	18	11
		1.483	0.846	1890–1899	9	19	14
8	Not allocable..........	.980	1.153	1920–1924	..	16	14
		1.163	.930	1943	1	14	17
	Section B						
9	Manufacturing.........	1.671	0.496	1860–1869	7	13	4
		2.472	0.671	Before 1860	6	16	9
10	Food and kindred products..............	1.817	0.441	1910–1914	7	16	6
		2.437	0.699	1905–1909	5	17	13
11	Beverages.............	2.209	0.299	1900–1904	2	14	8
		2.694	0.285	1910–1914	9	14	9
12	Tobacco manufactures..	.836	0.196	1910–1914	..	23	11
		5.049	0.410	1925–1929	6	21	5
13	Cotton manufactures...	3.388	1.238	1925–1929	5	22	2
		6.594	1.261	1900–1904	2	25	14
14	Textile-mill products, except cotton.........	1.973	0.474	1890–1899	5	11	2
		3.042	0.585	1890–1899	2	14	8
15	Apparel, etc............	1.419	0.397	1890–1899	5	5	2
		2.358	0.642	1920–1924	2	9	5
16	Leather and products...	1.950	0.282	1905–1909	5	10	2
		3.551	0.804	1890–1899	3	13	6
17	Rubber products.......	1.746	0.697	1905–1909	7	15	1
		2.707	0.758	1900–1904	5	16	14
18	Lumber and timber basic products..............	1.771	0.363	1905–1909	2	12	2
		2.213	0.672	1890–1899	4	18	9
19	Furniture and finished lumber products........	1.886	0.432	1880–1889	5	13	2
		2.706	0.843	1880–1889	4	16	9
20	Paper and allied products	2.232	0.438	1880–1889	10	19	1
		3.673	0.496	1915–1919	9	20	11
21	Printing and publishing industries..............	2.181	0.527	1900–1904	7	19	7
		2.760	0.704	1870–1879	9	19	12
22	Chemicals and allied products..............	1.720	0.522	1880–1889	7	16	7
		2.253	0.598	1870–1879	9	17	10

TABLE 35—*Continued*

		I	II	III	IV	V	VI
23	Petroleum and coal products.............	*1.957*	*0.503*	*1900–1904*	*4*	*12*	*8*
		2.664	.....	1920–1924	4	14	10
24	Stone, clay, and glass products.............	*2.201*	*0.370*	*1890–1899*	*5*	*18*	*2*
		2.110	0.715	1880–1889	6	19	16
25	Iron, steel, and products	*1.655*	*0.571*	*1860–1869*	*7*	*18*	*3*
		2.670	0.710	1870–1879	9	20	11
26	Nonferrous metals and their products.........	*1.512*	*0.644*	*1890–1899*	*7*	*12*	*2*
		2.679	0.468	1880–1889	9	16	7
27	Electrical machinery and equipment............	*1.407*	*0.392*	*1910–1914*	*2*	*11*	*3*
		2.329	1.040	1905–1909	9	13	6
28	Machinery, except transportation equipment and electrical.............	*1.445* / 2.269	*0.677* / 0.686	*1870–1879* / 1860–1869	*7* / 9	*18* / 18	*5* / 9
29	Automobiles and equipment, except electrical...	*1.419*	*0.817*	*1941*	*5*	*12*	*4*
		3.206	0.704	1920–1924	2	16	9
30	Transportation equipment, except automobiles	*1.138*	*0.794*	*1880–1889*	*1*	*10*	*6*
		1.905	0.847	1900–1904	5	10	5
31	Other manufacturing....	*1.507*	*0.334*	*1910–1914*	*5*	*10*	*2*
		2.167	0.564	1890–1899	6	13	5
32	Not allocable..........	*1.379*	*0.433*	*1880–1889*	*5*	*10*	*2*
		1.893	0.430	1890–1899	6	13	5
	Section C						
33	Public utilities.........	*1.700*	*0.864*	*1870–1879*	*7*	*15*	*10*
		1.242	0.855	Before 1860	9	16	13
34	Transportation.........	*1.635*	*0.724*	*1915–1919*	*5*	*12*	*7*
		1.716	0.721	1915–1919	6	13	10
35	Communication........	*1.862*	*1.146*	*1890–1899*	*3*	*25*	*24*
		2.054	1.172	1890–1899	2	26	29
36	Other public utilities....	*2.645*	*0.434*	*1910–1914*	*5*	*26*	*18*
		1.939	0.707	Before 1860	3	26	19
	Section D						
37	Trade.................	*1.565*	*0.466*	*1880–1889*	*7*	*11*	*4*
		2.205	0.595	Before 1860	9	13	9
38	Wholesale.............	*1.498*	*0.528*	*1880–1889*	*7*	*10*	*3*
		2.069	0.704	1880–1889	6	13	8
41	Retail.................	*1.607*	*0.456*	*1900–1904*	*7*	*11*	*5*
		2.316	0.567	1900–1904	9	13	9
55	Not allocable..........	*1.587*	*0.380*	*1880–1889*	*7*	*11*	*3*
		2.067	0.486	1880–1889	9	14	9
	Section E						
38	Wholesale.............	*1.498*	*0.528*	*1880–1889*	*7*	*10*	*3*
		2.069	0.704	1880–1889	6	13	8
39	Commission merchants..	*1.341*	*0.846*	*1900–1904*	*3*	*8*	*3*
		1.416	0.996	1880–1889	2	11	9
40	Other wholesalers.......	*1.539*	*0.462*	*1880–1889*	*7*	*10*	*3*
		2.246	0.651	1880–1889	6	13	8

TABLE 35—*Continued*

		I	II	III	IV	V	VI
	Section F						
41	Retail...............	*1.607*	*0.456*	*1900–1904*	*7*	*11*	*5*
		2.316	0.567	1900–1904	9	13	9
42	General merchandise....	*1.996*	*0.460*	*1890–1899*	*2*	*16*	*7*
		2.835	0.669	1890–1899	9	18	13
43	Food stores, etc........	*1.524*	*0.565*	*1890–1899*	*3*	*10*	*6*
		1.720	0.715	1905–1909	2	11	8
44	Package liquor stores...	*1.322*	.....	*1925–1929*	*3*	*8*	*7*
		2.258	.....	1925–1929	4	8	6
45	Drug stores...........	*1.727*	*0.782*	*1900–1904*	*2*	*13*	*10*
		2.195	0.414	1890–1899	5	13	11
46	Apparel and accessories..	*1.723*	*0.405*	*1900–1904*	*6*	*10*	*5*
		2.523	0.550	1900–1904	2	11	8
47	Furniture and house furnishings...........	*1.709*	*0.430*	*1890–1899*	*2*	*11*	*2*
		2.570	0.597	1910–1914	2	14	9
48	Eating and drinking places...............	*1.458*	*0.198*	*1910–1914*	*2*	*7*	*5*
		1.805	0.376	1910–1914	2	8	6
49	Automotive dealers.....	*1.759*	*0.294*	*1905–1909*	*2*	*8*	*2*
		2.636	0.859	1915–1919	3	12	8
50	Filling stations........	*1.736*	*0.735*	*1925–1929*	*2*	*12*	*8*
		1.606	1.057	1920–1924	9	12	10
51	Hardware............	2.213	*0.374*	*1940*	*2*	*16*	*8*
		2.679	0.906	1915–1919	2	18	14
52	Building materials, fuel, and ice...............	*1.631*	*0.846*	*1900–1904*	*2*	*18*	*13*
		1.549	0.720	1890–1899	14	19	15
53	Other retail trade.......	*1.751*	*0.429*	*1890–1899*	*2*	*12*	*5*
		2.268	0.715	1900–1904	9	14	10
54	Not allocable.........	*1.962*	*0.524*	*1900–1904*	*5*	*14*	*5*
		2.577	0.514	1890–1899	14	18	11
	Section G						
56	Service...............	*1.549*	*0.726*	*1870–1879*	*3*	*11*	*6*
		1.689	0.751	Before 1860	6	12	9
57	Hotels and other lodging places...............	*1.793*	*0.547*	*1910–1914*	*3*	*10*	*5*
		1.925	0.561	1900–1904	6	11	8
58	Personal service........	*1.681*	*0.823*	*1890–1899*	*2*	*13*	*8*
		1.883	0.765	1880–1889	3	14	11
59	Business service........	*1.420*	*0.662*	*1880–1889*	*3*	*11*	*8*
		1.537	0.788	1890–1899	2	12	10
60	Automotive repair, etc...	*1.503*	*0.412*	*1910–1914*	*2*	*11*	*7*
		1.709	0.948	1905–1909	2	12	10
61	Miscellaneous repair, etc.	*1.341*	*0.770*	*1920–1924*	*5*	*8*	*3*
		1.715	0.855	1920–1924	4	11	6
62	Motion pictures........	2.271	0.776	*1915–1919*	*5*	*11*	*5*
		2.703	0.262	1915–1919	6	11	7
63	Amusement, except motion pictures...........	*1.360*	*0.747*	*1905–1909*	*3*	*9*	*5*
		1.334	0.788	1860–1869	6	10	8

TABLE 35—*Continued*

		I	II	III	IV	V	VI
64	Other service, including	*1.289*	*0.682*	*1890–1899*	*5*	*12*	*7*
	schools.............	1.317	0.744	1860–1869	3	14	10
65	Not allocable.........	*1.197*	*0.419*	*1920–1924*	*5*	*7*	*4*
		0.813	0.339	1905–1909	..	8	8
	Section H						
66	Finance, etc...........	*1.529*	*0.817*	*1860–1869*	*2*	*13*	*11*
		1.437	0.844	1860–1869	2	14	12
67	Finance..............	*2.380*	*0.661*	*Before 1860*	*20*	*22*	*14*
		2.408	0.739	Before 1860	24	22	15
76	Insurance carriers,	*1.668*	*0.824*	*1900–1904*	*7*	*17*	*14*
	agents, etc...........	1.708	0.835	Before 1860	14	17	14
79	Real estate, including	*1.381*	*0.955*	*1943*	*1*	*10*	*10*
	lessors of buildings......	1.255	0.970	1943	1	10	11
80	Lessors of real property,	*1.363*	*0.939*	*Before 1860*	*4*	*21*	*19*
	except buildings........	1.443	0.937	Before 1860	3	21	19
	Section I						
67	Finance..............	*2.380*	*0.661*	*Before 1860*	*20*	*22*	*14*
		2.408	0.739	Before 1860	24	22	15
68	Banks and trust com-	*16.176*	*0.992*	*1940*	*6*	*36*	*24*
	panies..............	12.500	1.063	1930–1934	5	35	33
69	Long-term credit	*1.149*	*1.339*	*1943*	*2*	*12*	*14*
	agencies, etc..........	1.413	1.123	1880–1889	1	13	15
70	Short-term credit agen-	*1.885*	*0.652*	*1905–1909*	*2*	*12*	*9*
	cies, except banks......	1.773	0.621	1910–1914	2	11	11
71	Investment trusts, etc...	*1.507*	*0.896*	*1860–1869*	*3*	*18*	*17*
		1.764	0.983	1941	4	17	18
72	Other investment com-	*1.913*	*1.269*	*1915–1919*	*5*	*20*	*18*
	panies, etc...........	1.359	1.359	1880–1889	14	19	18
73	Security and commodity-	*1.727*	*1.578*	*1890–1899*	*2*	*13*	*10*
	exchange brokers and	1.459	2.345	1942	3	13	11
	dealers..............						
74	Other finance com-	*1.280*	*0.644*	*1905–1909*	*4*	*12*	*11*
	panies...............	1.376	0.967	1905–1909	5	10	11
75	Not allocable.........	*1.168*	*0.973*	*1860–1869*	*1*	*14*	*16*
		1.125	1.095	1940	1	14	15
	Section J						
76	Insurance, etc.........	*1.668*	*0.824*	*1900–1904*	*7*	*17*	*14*
		1.708	0.835	Before 1860	14	17	14
77	Insurance carriers......	*2.314*	*0.534*	*1905–1909*	*2*	*25*	*18*
		2.732	0.208	1910–1914	19	26	17
78	Insurance agents,	*1.545*	*0.941*	*1900–1904*	*7*	*15*	*13*
	brokers, etc...........	1.495	1.034	1920–1924	14	15	13

TABLE 35—*Concluded*

		I	II	III	IV	V	VI
	Section K						
82	Agriculture, forestry,	*1.492*	*0.585*	*1880–1889*	*7*	*16*	*9*
	and fishery............	1.582	0.843	1880–1889	9	16	13
83	Agriculture and services.	*1.475*	*0.570*	*1880–1889*	*7*	*16*	*11*
		1.666	0.819	1880–1889	9	16	13
84	Forestry..............	*1.545*	*0.901*	*1944*	*2*	*17*	*21*
		1.370	1.285	1940	1	16	21
85	Fishery..............	*1.495*	*0.443*	*1920–1924*	*1*	*10*	*4*
		1.098	0.717	1925–1929	3	11	6

* In each pair of rows, italic type refers to 1946-active, ordinary type to 1945-active, corporations.
Significance of columns:
 I and II show ratios of risk of loss (in 1946, for top row, in 1945 for bottom row, of each pair), for corporations chartered in 1946 (or 1945) and in 1910–1914 respectively, to the average risk of loss for those chartered in all periods.
 III Period for which risk of loss (in 1946, or 1945), of corporations chartered in that period, was minimum. If more than one period shows the minimum, the most recent is listed.
 IV Number of years, ending in 1946 (italic type) or 1945 (ordinary type), for which risk of loss (in 1946, or 1945) of corporations chartered in those years was continuously at or above the average for all periods.
 V and VI are median ages for net and no-net corporations, respectively.

1946 figures and among those for 1945, the relation between age and profitability does not vary greatly among the divisions. The relation indicated by the six Loss points, for each year, for each division is fairly close to that for all divisions combined. No such sharp diversity appears in this table as that among the size classes of table 33.

Table 35 shows similar figures, in its sections A to K, for the groups in certain divisions and the subgroups in certain groups. Although no detailed comments are presented on the results for various groups and subgroups, a broad view of each section of the table shows that—ignoring the few exceptions, which can, in most cases, be ascribed to erratic Loss points based upon very small numbers of corporations—the general tendency for young corporations to have greater risk of loss than older corporations is borne out for the various groups and subgroups.

The detailed record in tables 34 and 35 of Loss points for the 1946-active and 1945-active corporations in each separate line of industry can furnish many interesting inferences concerning the comparative liability to loss of younger and older corporations in each industrial class, but no attempt is made here to draw those inferences. Because of the many differences in detail, an over-all view of the two tables is somewhat bewildering; and some summarization of the mass of detail can helpfully supplement such a view.

For this purpose, five pairs of frequency distributions of the relevant data in tables 34 and 35 were prepared for the 67 mutually exclusive classes—classes which exclude all groupings of more finely divided classes and exclude also all Not-allocable classes. One distribution of each pair refers to 1946-active corporations, the other to 1945-active corporations. The first four pairs summarize the data in columns I to IV, respectively; and the fifth pair summarizes the excess of the column V entry over that of column VI.

Thus, arrangement of the 67 *italicized* (1946) items of column I according to size shows that they range from 0.8 to 16.2 and what is more significant, that more than half of them are above 1.5. Similarly, the 1945 items range from 1.1 to 12.5, and more than half of them are above 2. The majority of the 67 mutually exclusive classes show, in both years, a substantially greater risk of loss for corporations chartered in the final year than the average risk for all corporations of the class regardless of date of incorporation. This excess of risk is indicated by the ratio 1.5 for 1946 and by 2 for 1945: for a majority of the 67 classes, corporations chartered in 1946 were at least 50 per cent more likely to show loss than the general average of corporations active in 1946, and the corresponding percentage for 1945 is 100.

A similar analysis of the data in column II shows: for 1946-active corporations, an outside range from 0.15 to 1.58, with the majority of the 65 classes (2 classes with indeterminate entries are ignored), having percentages below 0.65; and for 1945-active corporations, an outside range from 0.20 to 2.35, with the majority falling below 0.75. For both years, in the majority of classes (not necessarily the same classes in each year), corporations chartered in 1910–1914 were much less likely—less than 0.65 as likely for 1946, 0.75 for 1945—to show loss than were all corporations of the class on the average.

Frequency distributions of the entries in column III, separately for 1946 and 1945, by periods of incorporation show: for 1946-active corporations, an outside range from Before-1860 to 1944, with a majority falling in periods before 1905; for 1945-active corporations, an outside range from Before-1860 to 1943, with the majority also falling in periods before 1905. Thus, for each year, a majority of the 67 classes show minimum risk of loss for fairly old corporations—those chartered in some period before 1905.[78]

---

[78] For 1946, three quarters of the classes show the minimum period before 1915; for 1945, before 1920. One may need to be reminded that the risk of loss here in question pertains to loss in 1946 (or 1945) and not to loss during the specified period of incorporation.

Arrangement of the entries of column IV according to size shows: for 1946, an outside range from 0 to 10, with half of the 67 entries running at least as large as 4; for 1945, an outside range from 1 to 19, with half of the entries running at least as high as 4. The item of column IV is the number of years ending in 1946 (in 1945, for 1945-active corporations) during which the risk of loss is continuously greater than the average for all dated corporations of the class. Thus, for half of the 67 mutually exclusive classes, corporations chartered in each of the four most recent years were more likely to show loss in the final year than were all dated corporations of the class regardless of the date of incorporation. Moreover, for one quarter of the classes, this stretch of years was at least 5 for 1946 and at least 9 for 1945. These facts emphatically support the widely held opinion that new corporations may have to live through several precarious years before they begin to show a profit. This record is the more impressive when account is taken of general economic conditions in 1945 and 1946. Although both years were somewhat abnormal, they were assuredly not years of depression. Even in a fairly prosperous phase of the business cycle, youth is the dangerous period in the life span of the typical corporation. Records of failures and financial embarrassments indicate that a corporation may encounter crisis at any age, but the early years are more likely to be critical for large numbers of corporations.

Subtraction of an item of column VI from the corresponding item of column V gives the excess of the median age of net corporations over that of no-net corporations, of the particular class. The magnitude of that excess indicates the degree to which the age distribution is more steeply J-shaped for the no-net than for the net category—the degree to which concentration among younger corporations is greater for no-net than for net corporations. Frequency distributions of the excess thus calculated have been prepared for the 67 classes, and they show: for 1946, an outside range from – 4 to 20, with half of the cases at least as high as 5; for 1945, an outside range from – 5 to 16, with half of the cases at least as high as 4. For the majority of the 67 classes, median age of net corporations exceeds that of no-net corporations by at least 5 years (4 for 1945-active corporations), and this lends further support to the conclusion that the age structure is younger for no-net than for net corporations.[77]

---

[77] For only 4 classes in 1946 and 7 in 1945 is the excess (of median age of net corporations over that of no-net corporations) zero or negative. Only for these few classes is the age structure apparently not younger for no-net than for net corporations.

The foregoing survey of the frequency distributions, for 67 mutually exclusive classes, of the items in tables 34 and 35, is believed to show overwhelming support for the conclusions that young corporations are more liable to suffer deficits than older corporations, and that the age structure of corporations showing a deficit is younger—more steeply J-shaped—than that of corporations showing a profit. These conclusions are applicable, with almost negligible exceptions and despite numerous minor differences reflected by specific Loss points, to every line-of-industry class. The finding of such conclusions for the entire combined list of corporations regardless of line of industry might alone be impressive confirmation of ideas which have long been held in qualitative terms. When examination of a large number of separate lines of industry, for corporations reporting as active in two different years, leads to the same conclusions in nearly every case, the evidence in support of these ideas becomes well-nigh overwhelming.

CHAPTER VI

Incorporations of New and Previously Existing Enterprises

ATTENTION has been called in previous pages to the fact that date-of-incorporation statistics yield information about the age of corporations but not necessarily about the age of enterprises controlled and operated by corporations. Although many important inferences can be drawn from data on the age of corporations, various significant economic questions might be answered more satisfactorily if data were available on the entire life span to date of enterprises, whether or not each such enterprise had operated under the corporate form throughout its life.

23. *The background of corporations chartered in 1946 and 1945.*—Such data are not available in the *S. of I.* tables under study here; and they are not available, on any comprehensive basis, in any other source known to me. The date-of-incorporation tables in *S. of I.* do, however, include a section classifying 1946-active dated corporations chartered in 1946 and 1945-active dated corporations chartered in 1945 among those which were and those which were not completely new enterprises; and those which were successors are further classified according to the type of predecessor organization. Such data are the subject of analysis in this chapter. They do not, of course, answer the above questions involving the entire age of enterprises, as distinct from the age of corporations, but they do indicate that a very substantial fraction of incorporations represents completely new enterprises, and for such corporations corporate age is identical with enterprise age. In addition, these data are the basis for important findings concerning the types of organization of predecessor enterprises and concerning the comparative profitability of corporations which were completely new enterprises and those which took over enterprises previously operating under various types of organization.

The form in which the data appear in *S. of I.* is indicated, for 1946-active corporations, by columns I and II of table 36; and other columns of the table show the various calculations used in the basic analyses of this chapter.[78] Each line of column III combines the corresponding figures of columns I and II. In column IV, lines *b*

TABLE 36

ANALYSIS OF 1946-ACTIVE CORPORATIONS CHARTERED IN 1946, CLASSIFIED BETWEEN NEW
ENTERPRISES AND SUCCESSORS, AND BY TYPE OF PREDECESSOR*

	Number of active corporations chartered in 1946				
	With net income in 1946	With deficit in 1946	Net and no-net combined	Per cent by classes	Per cent no-net
	(I)	(II)	(III)	(IV)	(V)
a Active corporations chartered in 1946.................	42,666	27,781	70,447	....	39.4
b Whether new or successor not stated...................	4,499	3,984	8,483	12.0	47.0
c Whether new or successor stated....................	38,167	23,797	61,964	88.0	38.4
d New enterprises..............	17,513	17,312	34,825	56.2	49.7
e Successors to previous enterprises....................	20,654	6,485	27,139	43.8	23.9
f Type of predecessor not stated.	1,442	600	2,042	7.5	29.4
g Type of predecessor stated.....	19,212	5,885	25,097	92.5	23.4
Predecessors					
h Corporation.................	1,502	799	2,301	9.2	34.7
i Partnership.................	10,344	2,676	13,020	51.9	20.6
j Sole proprietorship..........	7,124	2,329	9,453	37.7	24.6
k Other type.................	242	81	323	1.3	25.1

* Columns I and II (except for *c* and *g*) transcribed from *1946 S. of I.*, pp. 28 and 30. Column III is sum of I and II. Column IV is percentage allocation of items in column III. Column V is ratio of II to III.

and *c* are the ratios of lines *b* and *c* to line *a* of column III, lines *d* and *e* are the ratios of lines *d* and *e* to line *c* of column III, lines *f* and *g* are the ratios of lines *f* and *g* to line *e* of column III, and lines *h–k* are the ratios of lines *h–k* to line *g* of column III. Column V gives the ratio of the corresponding figure in column II to that in column III. Lines *b* and *f* of column IV show the importance of the Not-stated categories, and they show that failure to state whether

[78] The basic data appear in *1946 S. of I.*, pp. 28–33, and in *1945 S. of I.*, pp. 31–35. Both issues of *S. of I.* include data of the sort shown in columns I and II of table 36 for active corporations classified by line of industry, and the 1946 issue includes also data for balance-sheet corporations classified by size.

a corporation was a completely new enterprise or a successor was relatively more common than failure of a successor corporation to state the type of predecessor.[79] Lines *d* and *e* of column IV show the comparative importance of corporations which were new enterprises and those which were successors; and this comparison is given further attention below, in section 24. Lines *h–k* of column IV show the relative importance of different types of predecessor, and these distinctions are the subject of section 25. Column V is an indirect indicator of profitability, and distinctions in profitability between new corporate enterprises (lines *d* and *e*) and among successors of various types of predecessor (lines *h–k*) are discussed in section 26.

Analytical tables similar to table 36 have been worked out for the various line-of-industry classes, separately for 1946-active dated corporations chartered in 1946 and for 1945-active dated corporations chartered in 1945, and for the various size classes of 1946-active dated balance-sheet corporations chartered in 1946. The relevant results are shown below in full for the size classes and for the nine industrial divisions, but are merely summarized for the industrial groups and subgroups in connection with the discussion in sections 24–6.

24. *Completely new enterprises and successors.*—Table 37 shows separately for 1946 and 1945 the fraction, of the newly chartered dated corporations which were completely new enterprises, for each industrial division and all divisions combined.[80] Table 38 (below, p. 110) presents, for 1946, corresponding figures for all dated balance-sheet corporations chartered in 1946, and the various size classes of such corporations.

Table 37 shows that the percentage varies over a wide range for both 1946 and 1945, and is lower in 1946 than in 1945 for each division as well as for all divisions combined. The number of active dated corporations chartered was very much greater in 1946 than in 1945: 70,447 compared with 22,543. Of these, 61,964 for 1946, and 17,303 for 1945, stated whether they were new enterprises or successors—about 3.6 times as many in 1946 as in 1945. Of the latter, the percentage reported as new enterprises was 56.2 for 1946, 76.2 for 1945, and the corresponding percentage reported as successors was 43.8 for 1946, 23.8 for 1945. The great wave of postwar incor-

---

[79] See section 4, n. 16.

[80] The percentage, corresponding to line *d* of column IV of table 36, is a fraction of only those corporations which stated whether they were new or successors. No basis exists for an assumption that the Not-stated class was in actuality apportioned similarly between new and successor corporate enterprises.

porations, already started in 1945 but much more fully developed in 1946, was marked by an emphatic tendency for successor corporations to increase more rapidly than corporations undertaking new enterprises. Between 1945 and 1946, the former increased to more than sixfold, the latter increased to less than threefold. This development may have been due to various causes, including the tax consideration which is noted in section 25.

TABLE 37

PERCENTAGE, OF NEWLY CHARTERED CORPORATIONS STATING WHETHER THEY WERE NEW ENTERPRISES OR SUCCESSORS TO PREVIOUS ENTERPRISES, WHICH WERE ENTIRELY NEW ENTERPRISES—FOR ALL ACTIVE CORPORATIONS AND BY INDUSTRIAL DIVISIONS*

Division	1946	1945
All divisions combined.	56.2	76.2
Mining and quarrying.	60.4	73.6
Manufacturing.	49.5	71.6
Public utilities.	61.8	68.2
Trade.	49.1	70.7
Service.	57.0	69.2
Finance, etc.	84.3	89.9
Construction.	57.9	78.2
Agriculture, etc.	48.0	66.8
Not allocable.	77.8	85.3

* Figures derived as in line *d* of column IV in table 36.

In 1946, the percentage in table 37 is more than 50 for most divisions, and becomes less than 50 only for three divisions, and in those cases only slightly. In 1945, the fraction representing new enterprises becomes less than two-thirds for no division, and is nearly nine-tenths for Finance, etc. The percentage is maximum, among the divisions, for Finance, etc., in both years; and the high figures for this division conceal wide diversity among its groups, ranging in 1946 from less than 47 for Insurance, etc., to more than 89 for Lessors of real property except buildings, and in 1945 from 70 to 91 for the same groups. The minimum percentage in each year is for Agriculture, etc., and the group percentages for this division range from 46 to 92 in 1946 and from 50 to 85 in 1945.[81] In general, examination of the percentages for the groups or sub-

[81] The figure 50 is not very dependable: it is for the Forestry group in which the total number of 1945 charters was very small.

groups in the several divisions shows more diversity than appears among the division figures.

Without presenting the percentages for the several groups and subgroups in detail, we may obtain a sufficient indication of their diversity by studying a frequency distribution, of 67 mutually exclusive line-of-industry classes, according to size of the percentage.[82] Such distributions, for 1946 and 1945, show very wide varia-

TABLE 38

Percentage, of Newly Chartered 1946 Corporations Stating Whether They Were New Enterprises or Successors to Previous Enterprises, Which Were Entirely New Enterprises—for All Active Corporations, Those Which Did Not and Those Which Did File Balance Sheets, and Size Classes Among Balance-sheet Corporations*

All active corporations	56.2
Those without balance sheets	66.6
All balance-sheet corporations	55.3
Size classes having lower limit ($1,000 of total assets)	
0	67.2
50	47.2
100	37.4
250	30.7
500	30.9
1,000	32.8
5,000	28.6
10,000	33.3
50,000	Zero

* Figures derived as in line *d* of column IV in table 36. The size class with total assets more than $100,000,000 is omitted. No dated corporation of that size was chartered in 1946.

tion among the 67 classes, with the percentages ranging from 14 to 92 for 1946 and from 36 to 91 for 1945.[83] Within this wide outside

[82] The mutually exclusive classes exclude all Not-allocable classes and all classes which are combinations of other classes. They include the Construction division, and 66 groups and subgroups in other divisions. They exclude, in the list given in *1946 S. of I.* on pp. 18 and 19, classes having serial numbers 1, 2, 8, 9, 32, 33, 37, 38, 41, 54, 55, 56, 65, 66, 67, 75, 76, 82, and 86. The excluded classes are marked with the same serial numbers, in parentheses, in table A of the appendix.

[83] The four classes (serial numbers as in *S. of I.* source listed in n. 82) for which the percentage is at or closest to the extreme for 1946 are: 12 Tobacco manufactures, 14.3; 45 Drug stores, 24.9; 10 Food and kindred products, 36.6; 44 Package liquor stores, 37.9; 84 Forestry, 92.2; 71 Investment trusts, etc., 90.6; 80 Lessors of real property, 89.7; 72 Other investment companies, etc., 88.5. For 1945, they are: 45 Drug stores, 36.2; 18 Lumber, etc., 37.4; 35 Communication, 42.4; 4 Anthracite mining, 42.9; 80 Lessors of real property, etc., 91.4; 79 Real estate, etc., 91.3; 71 Investment trusts, etc., 89.8; 77 Insurance carriers, 89.5.

range of variation, the percentages are somewhat thinly scattered; but slightly more than half of them range from 44 to 65 in 1946, and from 60 to 80 in 1945.

Slightly more than three-quarters of the 67 classes show percentages of 44 or greater in 1946, of 60 or greater in 1945. For 1946, 41 classes, and for 1945, 61 classes show percentages of 50 or more. Thus, for these two years, substantially more than half (very much more for 1945) of the mutually exclusive classes show at least half of the corporations chartered in those years as representing totally new enterprises. Although this does not imply that the analysis of corporate age by line of industry in chapter iv gives dependable evidence on enterprise age even for these lines of industry, it does suggest that the results of such analysis are not entirely lacking in significance with respect to enterprise age. This suggestion could be given greater weight if our evidence, concerning the fraction of new corporations representing entirely new enterprises, were not confined to two years such as 1946 and 1945, and if much ground did not exist for suspecting that those two years are abnormal.

Table 38 indicates that the percentage of 1946 charters which represented wholly new enterprises was nearly as high for all balance-sheet dated corporations as for all active dated corporations. The small difference reflects the fact that the percentage for non-balance-sheet corporations is much above the figure for all active corporations.[84] Among the balance-sheet corporations, the percentage is noticeably higher for the smallest-size class than for any other class; and a steady decline in the percentage occurs from the smallest-size class to the $250,000 class. For all the larger-size classes, the percentage remains close to that of the $250,000 class.[85] The evidence is emphatic that corporations newly chartered in 1946 were far more likely to represent new enterprises if they were small, particularly if they had total assets less than $100,000, than if they were large. This is not a surprising conclusion, but it has a significant bearing upon the interpretation of the analysis in chapter iii. There, a clear-cut relation was found between the age structure and the size of corporations. The evidence of table 38 suggests that such

[84] That the percentage for nonbalance-sheet corporations is close to that for the smallest-size class is not surprising. Notice is taken elsewhere in this study of evidence that the corporations which fail to file balance sheets are generally small.

[85] The zero figure for the $50,000,000 class is ignored. In that class only 3 dated corporations were chartered in 1946, and none of these was a new enterprise. The percentage rests upon too small a number of cases to afford any trustworthy basis for generalization.

finding can yield, except for the smallest-size classes, little or no insight into the relation between the age structure and the size of *enterprises*. We may suspect, on the basis of various general and vague considerations, that the relation between age and size for enterprises is similar to that for corporations, but so important a share (close to 70 per cent) of large corporations appears as successors of previously existing enterprises that the evidence of chapter iii cannot be depended upon to establish even approximately the relation between age and size of enterprises.

25. *Types of predecessor.*—Among the 1946-active dated corporations chartered in 1946 which reported that they were successors to previously existing enterprises (line *e* of table 36), 92.5 per cent specified the type of predecessor organization.[86] These are allocated according to four types of predecessor organization: corporation, partnership, sole proprietorship, and other. The last of these is of slight importance (line *k* of column IV of table 36); and, though it is listed in the various tables herein, receives no attention in the discussion of this section.[87] Table 39 shows in its first line the percentage distribution, as taken from lines *h–k* of column IV of table 36, for all 1946-active dated corporations chartered in 1946 which specified type of predecessor. Other lines of the table similarly classify those among such corporations which did not supply balance sheets, those which did supply balance sheets, and the various size classes of balance-sheet corporations.

The first and third lines of the table indicate that, both for all active corporations and for all balance-sheet corporations, the predecessor was a partnership in more than half the cases, a sole proprietorship in somewhat less than two-fifths of the cases, and a corporation in less than one-tenth of the cases. Clearly, in 1946 incorporations, the predecessor was an unincorporated enterprise in the great bulk of the cases and was another corporation in com-

---

[86] The percentage not specifying, 7.5, was small and it was small also for each class according to size or to line of industry in 1946; and the corresponding percentage was 1.7 for 1945-active dated corporations chartered in 1945, and was similarly small for every line-of-industry class in 1945. No reason readily appears for the fact that the Not-stated percentage runs higher for 1946 than for 1945; but we may observe that not only did the number of charters greatly increase from 1945 to 1946, but also the percentage which were successors greatly increased. Hence, the increase in number of successors—from 4,124 to 27,139—was very large. In any case, the percentage not stating type of predecessor is negligibly small for both years, so far as analysis in the text is concerned.

[87] The makeup of this category is not entirely clear, but it probably includes such organizations as fiduciaries, coöperatives, and possibly nonprofit corporations.

paratively few cases. That the situation for 1945 was markedly different is indicated below (in connection with table 40), where tentative explanations of the differences are suggested. The percentage distribution for the nonbalance-sheet corporations specifying type of predecessor (only 1,453 cases, out of the 25,097 for all corporations) was very different, but even here the percentage unincorporated runs more than 80.

TABLE 39

PERCENTAGE DISTRIBUTION, ACCORDING TO TYPE OF PREDECESSOR, OF SUCCESSOR CORPORATIONS CHARTERED IN 1946 WHICH SPECIFIED TYPE OF PREDECESSOR, FOR ALL CORPORATIONS, THOSE WITHOUT AND THOSE WITH BALANCE SHEETS, AND SIZE CLASSES OF THE LATTER*

	Corporation	Partnership	Sole proprietorship	Other
All corporations................	9.2	51.9	37.7	1.3
Those without balance sheets...	14.7	41.4	41.6	2.3
All balance-sheet corporations..	8.8	52.5	37.4	1.2
Size classes with lower limit ($1,000 of total assets)				
0.....................	10.1	43.5	45.1	1.3
50.....................	7.7	50.8	40.3	1.2
100.....................	7.0	59.5	32.2	1.4
250.....................	6.9	69.1	23.2	0.7
500.....................	8.0	73.9	16.7	1.5
1,000.....................	21.5	67.4	11.1	0.0
5,000.....................	73.3	23.3	3.3	0.0
10,000.....................	77.8	22.2	0.0	0.0
50,000.....................	100.0	0.0	0.0	0.0

* Figures derived as in lines *h–k* of column IV of table 36. The size class with total assets more than $100,000,000 is omitted, as it included no cases.

For the various size classes shown in table 39, important shifts in the various percentages as size increases are apparent. The percentage reporting corporate predecessors remains low up to the $500,000 class but then rises rapidly to 100 for the $50,000,000 class. Correspondingly, the percentage unincorporated remains steady at about 90 for the five smaller-size classes and then declines rapidly to zero as size rises to more than $50,000,000. The course of change, with increasing size, differs markedly between the two unincorporated types. The percentage reporting sole proprietorships as predecessors declines steadily from the smallest-size class to the largest; whereas, that for partnerships rises sharply from the smallest-size class to the $500,000 class, and thereafter declines to zero. For the three middle-size classes ($250,000 class to $1,000,000 class), partnerships constitute more than two-thirds of the reported predecessors. This difference in course of change with increasing size, between partnerships and sole proprietorships, is probably due in some degree to the fact that partnerships are, for financial and other reasons, more capable of handling moderately large enterprises than are sole properietorships.

Table 40 shows corresponding figures for the 9 industrial divisions, separately for 1946 returns (*italic* type) and 1945 returns (ordinary type). A first noteworthy indication of the table is that, for all divisions combined, the percentage for corporate predecessors is much higher for 1945 than for 1946; and this contrast appears also for each division.[88] Stated inversely, the percentage reporting unincorporated predecessors was noticeably higher for 1946 than for 1945. Why was the tendency of unincorporated enterprises to assume the corporate form greater in 1946 than in 1945? In any year, various considerations—such as the advantages of limited liability, the supposedly greater ease of securing additional capital funds under the corporate form, the desire to avoid the costs and annoyances incident to the death or withdrawal of a partner, and the comparative tax burdens of the corporate and unincorporated forms—may determine whether an unincorporated enterprise will shift to the corporate form. Perhaps any of these considerations might have had greater force in 1946 than in 1945, and thus have led to an increase between the two years in the rate of shift to the corporate form. But one consideration unmistakably did change in force between 1945 and 1946: the elimination of the excess-profits tax and certain less important changes in Federal taxes levied on corporations sharply reduced the corporate tax burdens. As a result, heads of unincorporated business firms who might not have seen

---

[88] Conceivably, some shift in this percentage from one year to another *might* occur because of a change in the frequency of corporate reorganizations following failure. In a typical case of such reorganization, a new corporation is chartered to take over the business of the bankrupt corporation; and such new corporation would presumably be reported in the *S. of I.* tables as a successor having a corporate predecessor, though it might be reported under "other" (the other type of organization being receivers or trustees in bankruptcy). No evidence exists for assuming any such decline in the rate of reorganizations between 1945 and 1946 as would account for the important change in percentage shown in table 40, and that change seems more likely to be explained by the inverse analysis in the text. We may remark that various other reasons, besides reorganization, probably account for the bulk of the corporate predecessors covered by the table.

a tax advantage in a shift to the corporate form in 1945 might in numerous cases have reached the opposite conclusion in 1946.[89] In my opinion, a substantial part of the disparity between 1946 and 1945 in the figures of the first column of table 40 reflects this tax change.

TABLE 40

PERCENTAGE DISTRIBUTION, ACCORDING TO TYPE OF PREDECESSOR, OF SUCCESSOR COR-
PORATIONS CHARTERED IN 1946 (ITALIC TYPE) AND IN 1945 (ORDINARY TYPE)
WHICH SPECIFIED TYPE OF PREDECESSOR, FOR ALL CORPORATIONS AND FOR EACH
DIVISION*

	Corporation	Partnership	Sole proprietorship	Other
All divisions................	*9.2*	*51.9*	*37.7*	*1.3*
	26.2	31.3	39.3	2.9
Mining and quarrying.........	*16.4*	*54.9*	*28.7*	*0.0*
	42.6	40.7	13.0	3.7
Manufacturing..............	*8.4*	*61.8*	*28.8*	*1.0*
	24.1	37.9	36.4	1.5
Public utilities..............	*16.4*	*40.9*	*40.8*	*2.0*
	27.6	27.1	42.3	3.0
Trade.....................	*7.8*	*50.3*	*41.0*	*1.0*
	22.8	30.2	44.6	2.5
Service...................	*13.2*	*41.1*	*43.6*	*2.1*
	29.5	29.9	37.6	2.6
Finance, etc................	*18.6*	*37.7*	*38.8*	*4.8*
	40.7	21.6	27.9	9.7
Construction...............	*5.8*	*45.2*	*48.2*	*0.8*
	16.3	36.2	45.5	2.1
Agriculture, etc.............	*8.9*	*47.8*	*41.5*	*1.9*
	25.4	29.1	43.6	1.8
Not allocable..............	*11.6*	*43.0*	*44.2*	*1.2*
	22.2	41.7	30.6	5.5

* Figures derived as in lines *h–k* column IV of table 36.

Comparisons among the divisions in table 40, separately for 1946 and 1945, show marked variations in the percentages reflecting the importance of the three main types of predecessor. The 1946 corporation percentage ranges from 5.8 for Construction to 18.6 for Finance, etc.; that for 1945 ranges from 16.3 for Construction to 42.6 for Mining and quarrying. The 1946 percentage for partner-

[89] Contrariwise, in certain earlier years when the corporate tax burden was sharply increased, suggestions have been made that various corporations gave up their charters and assumed the partnership or other unincorporated form in order to avoid taxes; but I know of no systematic tabulation of evidence on this point.

ships ranges from 37.7 for Finance, etc., to 61.8 for Manufacturing;
that for 1945 ranges from 21.6 for Finance, etc., to 40.7 for Mining
and quarrying (the Not-allocable class being ignored). The 1946
percentage for sole proprietorships ranges from 28.7 for Mining and
quarrying to 48.2 for Construction; that for 1945 ranges from 13.0
for Mining and quarrying to 45.5 for Construction. These ranges
are fairly wide: in no case is the maximum less than 160 per cent
of the minimum, and in two cases the maximum is more than three
times the minimum. Differences among the divisions, in the distribution of successor corporations according to type of predecessor,
are therefore large. To some extent, these differences may reflect
differences in average size of enterprise among the divisions. In Construction, for example, the typical enterprise may start out very
small and unincorporated and shift to the corporate form as it
becomes larger; whereas, in Finance, etc., a new enterprise may be
more likely to start out as a corporation.[90] This contrast is borne
out by observing, in table 37, that the percentage of incorporations
which were totally new enterprises is much higher for Finance, etc.
than for Construction. Nevertheless, general comparison of table
37 with table 40 indicates that the above explanation is by no means
complete. Any full explanation of the differences among divisions
disclosed by table 40 must probably be sought by studying in detail
the groups and subgroups which constitute the several divisions;
since, in nearly every division, the corporations included are in such
widely diverse lines of activity and differ so greatly among them-
selves in other relevant respects that one should not expect the
percentage distribution of the division to be ascribable to any
simple cause. No such detailed study of the groups and subgroups
is undertaken here.

Without reporting the percentage distributions, derived as in
lines *h–k* of column IV of table 36, separately for each group and
subgroup or discussing each division in terms of its groups or subgroups, we may get some idea of the diversity among such percentage distributions for the 67 mutually exclusive line-of-industry

[90] Much interesting information on the types of organization of the entire business
population, and various classes thereof, appears in "The business population by legal
form of organization," *Survey of Current Business*, June, 1951, pp. 9–14 and 24. Table
2 of that article shows, as of March 31, 1947, 78.2 per cent of the firms in Construction
and 54.3 per cent of the firms in Finance, etc., as sole proprietorships. These percentages refer to firms in existence at that date, and do not necessarily imply similar
figures for newly created firms. Table 5 of the article gives basic figures for new
firms established in the third quarter of 1950. The percentage of such firms taking
the sole-proprietorship type was 74 for Construction, 58 for Finance, etc.

classes in 1946. For these 67 classes, three frequency distributions according to size of the percentage (for 1946-active successors) have been prepared, one each for the percentage showing corporations, partnerships, and sole proprietorships as predecessors (percentages corresponding, respectively, to lines *h–j* of column IV of table 36).

The percentage for corporate predecessors ranges from 4 to 67; but half of the percentages are less than 12, and one quarter are less than 8. The percentage for partnership predecessors ranges from 12 to 88; but half of the percentages are more than 47, and one quarter are more than 60. The percentage for sole-proprietorship predecessors ranges from 0 to 59; but half of the percentages are less than 34, and one quarter are less than 27. The 33 classes which make up the "half," and the 17 which make up "one quarter," are not necessarily identical in the three cases.[91] For a large number of classes, the corporate predecessors are uncommon, sole-proprietorship predecessors are much more common, and partnership predecessors are most common. Considering the entire list of 67 classes, however, we find extraordinary diversity. For some classes, far more than half of the predecessors are corporations, and the two other types of predecessor are correspondingly unimportant. For some classes, far more than half of the predecessors are partnerships, with correspondingly poor representation of the two other types. For some classes, sole proprietorships are the most numerous predecessors, but in no class do they constitute more than 50 per cent.

Whatever the considerations which lead existing enterprises to take out new corporate charters, those considerations may have different weight according as the existing enterprise is in the corporate, partnership, or sole-proprietorship form. To be sure, as indirectly suggested above, the differences among the three percentages for any one class may largely reflect mere differences in the numbers of enterprises of the three types which already exist and are capable of taking out corporate charters. But differences in weight of the decision-controlling considerations are almost surely a cause of the differences among the three percentages for any one class. The observed wide diversity among the groups of three percentages for the 67 classes may be due chiefly to the same two causes. The mere fact that the number of existing firms in a particular line-of-industry class is made up predominantly by one

---

[91] For any one class, of course, the three percentages must total nearly 100—missing 100 merely by the very small percentage reflecting "other" types of predecessor organization.

type of organization—such as partnerships—may tend to render the percentage of successor corporations having that type (partnership) of predecessor organization high for that class. But here also the other cause may be at work: considerations leading to the taking of a new corporate charter may not only have different weight according as the existing enterprise is a corporation or partnership or sole proprietorship, but these differences in weight may vary widely among the line-of-industry classes. This matter is not pursued further herein, but I suggest that the wide diversity mentioned above may require intensive study of conditions in numerous lines of industry in order to reach an acceptable explanation.[92]

26. *Profitability and previous business background.*—Each line of column V of table 36 gives the percentage ratio of the figure in column II to that in column III. It is the risk-of-loss ratio which forms the basis of the discussion of profitability in chapter v—the number of chances out of a hundred that any particular corporation in the class showed a deficit in 1946. Such ratios, for corporations which are entirely new enterprises (line *d*) or successors (line *e*), and for successors which have various types of predecessor (lines *h–k*), are the subject of analysis and discussion in this section.[93] These ratios, for all 1946-active dated corporations chartered in 1946, regardless of size or line of industry, are shown in the first line of table 41, to which they have been carried from column V of table 36.

The risk of loss, shown in the first line of the table, is markedly greater for corporations which were entirely new enterprises than for successors. In fact, as the ratio of 49.7 to 23.9 is 2.08, the new enterprises were more than twice as likely to show loss as were the successors. This excess of risk for the new enterprises is indicated in every line of the table except that for the $10,000,000 class, in which the risk for successors is much higher than that for new enterprises, and that for the $50,000,000 class, which is indetermi-

---

[92] Frequency distributions of the 67 classes for 1945-active corporations, similar to those for 1946 cited above, are not here reported. They also show great diversity, but differ in important respects from those for 1946.

[93] The ratios for the "other" category of predecessor (line *k*) are shown in the accompanying tables but are not discussed, because this category is of minor significance. The ratios in lines *a, b, c, f,* and *g* have been calculated and examined, but are not reported herein (the ratio in line *a* has already received attention in chap. v). Corresponding ratios for 1945-active corporations have been calculated and examined; but only the results for 1946-active corporations are here reported (except in table 43), because—as indicated in chap. v—1946 is considered a less abnormal year than 1945 for testing profitability.

nate.[94] Ignoring these two classes, the ratio of the figure for new enterprises to that for successors ranges from 1.25 for the $5,000,000 class and 1.49 for the smallest-size class to 4.77 for the $500,000 class and 4.96 for the $1,000,000 class. For nearly all sizes of corporation, then, the risk of loss is very much higher for new enterprises than for successors.

TABLE 41

PERCENTAGE RATIOS INDICATING RISK OF LOSS IN 1946, FOR NEWLY CHARTERED CORPORATIONS WHICH WERE ENTIRELY NEW ENTERPRISES OR SUCCESSORS, AND FOR SUCCESSORS OF VARIOUS TYPES OF PREDECESSOR, FOR ALL ACTIVE RETURNS, THOSE WITHOUT AND THOSE WITH BALANCE SHEETS, AND SIZE CLASSES OF THE LATTER*

	New enterprises	Successors	Successors for which predecessors were			
			Corporations	Partnerships	Sole proprietorships	Other
All corporations............	49.7	23.9	34.7	20.6	24.6	25.1
Those without balance sheets..	62.8	46.2	56.6	40.4	47.7	33.3
All with balance sheets.......	48.4	22.5	32.5	19.6	23.1	24.1
Size classes having lower limit ($1,000)						
0...................	53.8	36.0	42.3	35.0	34.8	30.2
50...................	37.6	16.9	24.8	17.3	14.0	17.7
100...................	35.4	11.6	23.2	10.7	10.1	16.4
250...................	33.3	9.1	23.8	7.5	7.7	20.0
500...................	40.6	8.6	21.1	6.7	9.5	15.4
1,000...................	52.1	10.5	26.9	4.8	12.5	a
5,000...................	41.7	33.3	45.5	0.0	0.0	a
10,000...................	16.7	41.7	71.4	0.0	a	a
50,000...................	a	33.3	33.3	a	a	a

* Derived as in column V of table 36. The size class with total assets more than $100,000,000 had no cases. Entries marked a are for categories in which no cases appeared.

A corresponding contrast between new enterprises and successors is shown in the first two columns of table 42, which presents the risk-of-loss ratios for industrial divisions. The risk is greater for new enterprises in every division; and the degree to which it is greater is indicated by the ratio of the figure in the first column to that in the second, ranging from 1.61 for Public utilities to 2.32 for Trade.

The conclusion that corporations representing totally new enterprises are more in danger of loss in their first year than successors is not surprising. The successor has the advantage that its predeces-

[94] The 16.7 figure in the $10,000,000 class is based upon 6 cases, one of which showed loss. The number of cases may be too small to afford a dependable result.

sor has already undergone, perhaps years ago, the excessive initial
risks which confront a new enterprise. However, as is shown below
(p. 122), the disparity in the tables may be somewhat exaggerated
by an exceptional tendency for successor corporations having unincorporated predecessors to be chartered in precisely those cases
which do show a profit. This argument could not possibly apply,
however, in the case of successors of previously existing corpora-

TABLE 42

PERCENTAGE RATIOS INDICATING RISK OF LOSS IN 1946, FOR NEWLY CHARTERED COR-
PORATIONS WHICH WERE ENTIRELY NEW ENTERPRISES OR SUCCESSORS, AND FOR
SUCCESSORS OF VARIOUS TYPES OF PREDECESSOR, FOR ALL ACTIVE RETURNS AND
EACH INDUSTRIAL DIVISION*

	New enterprises	Successors	Successors for which predecessors were			
			Corporations	Partnerships	Sole proprietorships	Other
All divisions combined........	49.7	23.9	34.7	20.6	24.6	25.1
Mining and quarrying........	70.2	37.9	43.8	37.4	35.7	a
Manufacturing..............	57.2	27.2	37.3	24.7	28.3	23.4
Public utilities.............	63.8	39.6	54.2	33.5	38.0	53.8
Trade.....................	40.7	17.6	28.0	14.1	19.1	20.4
Service....................	63.1	34.5	40.0	29.5	36.9	26.8
Finance, etc................	45.9	29.8	38.5	25.8	28.5	28.6
Construction...............	52.3	23.8	20.5	23.0	24.6	10.0
Agriculture, etc.............	63.9	39.1	58.3	36.4	35.7	60.0
Not allocable...............	75.9	41.2	60.0	32.4	44.7	0.0

* Derived as in column V of table 36. Entry marked a is for a category in which no cases appeared.

tions, and the figure for new enterprises (first column) exceeds that
for successors of corporations (third column) in every line of table
42 and in every line of table 41 except those for the three largest-
size classes.

We must conclude, therefore, that the risk of loss in the first year
is emphatically greater for entirely new enterprises than for successors. Chapter v has already presented overwhelming evidence
that corporations are more in danger of showing loss in their first
year than in any subsequent year. But the evidence of that chapter
rested upon a comparison of risk of loss with age of *corporation*.
Although the evidence of tables 41 and 42 does not permit a correlation between risk of loss and age of *enterprise*, it does supplement

the finding of chapter v in one highly important respect. It shows that, if a corporation is an entirely new enterprise, its risk of loss in the first year is markedly greater than the already high average risk found in chapter v for all newly chartered corporations.

Before leaving this point, we may examine the relevant evidence for a finer breakdown by line of industry than that shown in table 42. The details for the groups and subgroups in the various divisions are not presented, but instead, certain summary results are shown for the 67 mutually exclusive line-of-industry classes. For each such class, the risk-of-loss ratio for entirely new enterprises and for successors (lines *d* and *e* of table 36) has been calculated, and the two sets of 67 ratios were arranged in two frequency distributions according to size of ratio. The ratios for new enterprises range from 25 per cent to 100 per cent, and three-quarters of them are more than 46 per cent. The ratios for successors range from 0 to 75 per cent, and three-quarters of them are less than 36 per cent.

The ratio of the new-enterprise percentage to the successor percentage (corresponding to the figure 2.08, cited above for all corporations) was calculated for each of the 67 classes, and these ratios were arranged in a frequency distribution. These ratios in percentage form range from 100 (equal risk for new enterprises and successors) to about 1,200 (risk 12 times as great for new enterprises as for successors). Half of the ratios are at least as high as 200, and three-quarters are at least as high as 160 per cent. For a majority of the 67 classes, risk of loss is at least twice as high for new enterprises as for successors; and for three quarters, at least 1.6 times as high. For none of the 67 classes is the risk greater for successors than for new enterprises.

These findings, for the 67 classes, lend additional and emphatic support to the conclusion stated above. In nearly every line of industry, risk of loss is clearly higher for new enterprises than for successors; and for many lines it is very much higher. Any new corporation is in greater danger of showing loss than an older corporation, as shown in chapter v; but a new corporation which is also a new enterprise is in still greater danger of showing loss in its initial year.

The third, fourth, and fifth columns of tables 41 and 42 show the percentage risk of loss for successor corporations according as their predecessors were corporations, partnerships, or sole proprietorships. In every line of table 41, except those which are indeterminate because of missing data, and in every line of table 42, except that for Construction, the ratio for corporate predecessors is higher than the two ratios for unincorporated predecessors. Some possibility exists that the corporation-predecessor ratio is high because of the inclusion of various successor corporations chartered to take over the business of unsuccessful or embarrassed corporations, but these cases are not likely to be sufficiently numerous to account for the disparity noted.

A more probable explanation has to do with tax incentives. Notice was taken in section 25 of the probability that the chartering

TABLE 43

PERCENTAGE RATIOS INDICATING RISK OF LOSS IN 1945, OF NEWLY CHARTERED SUCCESSOR CORPORATIONS HAVING VARIOUS TYPES OF PREDECESSOR*

	Corporation	Partnership	Sole proprietorship	Other
All divisions combined.........	40.3	40.2	41.1	38.3
Mining and quarrying.........	65.2	50.0	57.1	100.0
Manufacturing..............	42.5	50.0	46.5	53.3
Public utilities.............	53.6	60.0	54.7	83.3
Trade.....................	32.3	29.4	35.4	26.8
Service....................	44.8	47.0	47.6	46.2
Finance, etc................	41.4	30.2	36.3	27.9
Construction...............	39.1	45.1	43.7	66.7
Agriculture, etc.............	42.9	43.7	41.6	0.0
Not allocable..............	75.0	40.0	54.7	50.0

* Figures derived as in column V of table 36.

in 1946 of various corporations which had operated before as unincorporated enterprises reflected consideration of the comparative tax burdens of the corporate and unincorporated forms, and that changes in the tax law late in 1945 shifted this comparative burden somewhat in favor of corporations. We may now suggest that the unincorporated enterprises most likely to be impelled to take a corporate charter in 1946 because of this consideration were precisely those then showing, or expecting to show, a profit. Partnerships or sole proprietorships operating, or expecting to operate, at a loss in 1946 would see no tax advantage in an immediate shift to the corporate form. Further evidence in support of this view appears in the record for 1945-active newly chartered successor corporations, since the tax changes were not in effect for 1945. The relevant risk-of-loss percentages for 1945, by industrial divisions, appear in table 43. For all divisions combined, the ratio is almost identical for successors having corporations, partnerships, and sole proprietorships as predecessors. For several divisions the corpora- tion-predecessor percentage is lower than any of the other percent- ages, and for only two divisions (ignoring Not-allocable) is the corporation percentage higher than the percentages for both part- nerships and sole proprietorships. Unless some other explanation can be found for this striking difference between the 1945 record in table 43 and the 1946 record in table 42, the tax explanation discussed above must apparently be accepted as valid.

The results, for 1946-active newly chartered successors according to type of predecessor, for the 67 mutually exclusive line-of-industry classes can now be summarized in reference to frequency distribu- tions of the risk-of-loss percentages for the three main types of predecessors. The corporate-predecessor percentages for 66 classes (one class is missing because it contains no cases) range from zero to 100, but one-half of them are at least as high as 36, and three- quarters are at least as high as 25. The partnership percentages for 65 classes (2 classes have no cases) range from zero to 100, but one- half of them are less than 23, and three-quarters are less than 34. The sole-proprietorship percentages for 65 classes (2 classes have no cases) range from zero to 100, but one-half of them are less than 29, and three-quarters are less than 39. Although these summary facts do not conclusively establish that the corporation percentage runs higher than the two other percentages in every class, they clearly indicate that the corporation percentage is likely to run higher than the other two for any particular class. Specific examina- tion of the separate classes shows the partnership percentage less than (and in many cases much less than) the corporation percentage for all except 13 classes, and the sole-proprietorship percentage less than the corporation percentage for all except 17 classes. These facts indicate that the contrasts observed in table 42 are widely prevalent among the 67 more finely classified lines of industry.

The 1946 differences in loss experience of newly chartered suc- cessors, according to type of predecessor, therefore appear in most lines of industry. That they can apparently be ascribed largely to tax changes which became effective in 1946 implies that they are not normal and would not be likely to appear in a year unaffected by important changes in the comparative tax burdens of corporate and unincorporated enterprises. On the other hand, the difference in risk of loss as between corporations which represent entirely new enterprises and those which are successors is more fundamental and may be expected to appear in any year. That a small part of that difference noticed for 1946 is probably due also to the tax factor may be conceded, but the major part reflects the hard fact that a truly new enterprise typically faces its greatest danger of loss in its initial year.

CHAPTER **VII**

Corporate Births and Deaths

THE FORTUNATE FACT that *Statistics of Income* presents date-of-incorporation statistics for two successive years, 1945 and 1946, makes possible the derivation of important though limited information about births and deaths within the corporate system. Some of these derivations, those presented in sections 28 and 29, rest mainly upon direct calculations from *S. of I.* data and are dependent only in moderate degree upon assumptions which are debatable. Others, those presented in sections 30 and 31, rest upon a more tenuous foundation because, as is indicated at the relevant points below, the assumptions which bear decisively upon the analysis are seriously open to question. All the derivations in this chapter must be confined to the entire list of corporations, without regard to size or line of industry. This is because these derivations rest initially upon the subtraction of 1946 figures from 1945 figures, in order to find how many corporations disappeared from the active list in 1946. As a particular corporation may, between two years, shift from one size class to another or from one line-of-industry class to another, such subtractions have no clear significance for the separate classes.

27. *The Age Structure for All Active Corporations in 1945 and 1946.*—Suppose we seek the number of corporations chartered in the period 1935–1939 which disappeared from the active list in 1946.[95] Table 4 shows in line *d* that 74,669 dated corporations chartered in 1935–1939 were active in 1946, and table 5 similarly shows that 77,955 such corporations were active in 1945. Hence, by subtraction, 3,286 of the dated corporations chartered in 1935–1939 became inactive in 1946. This result is, however, only a tentative first approximation to the answer to the initial question for the following reason. The figures cited refer only to *dated* corporations,

---

[95] Here 1946 means the taxable year and may, for certain corporations, differ from the calendar year. See section 3.

those which specified the date of incorporation. Presumably some of the corporations actually chartered in 1935–1939 which were active in 1946 were in the Not-stated group—did not specify their date of incorporation. Presumably the same is true for certain corporations active in 1945; and, unfortunately, the Not-stated groups for the two reporting years probably do not consist entirely of identical corporations. This is partly because some corporations of the Not-stated group which were active in 1945 may have become inactive in 1946; but it is probably also a consequence of differences in reporting in the two years—certain corporations which in one year stated the date of incorporation may not have done so in the other year.

A more nearly precise answer to the question raised above must therefore rest, not upon the age distributions of *dated* corporations as given in tables 4 and 5, but upon the age distributions of *all* corporations active in 1946 and those active in 1945. For this purpose, the Not-stated group must be allocated for both years according to estimated date of incorporation. The remainder of this section is devoted to such allocation.

Among the 491,152 corporations active in 1946, 13,203 did not specify date of incorporation. An allocation of these 13,203 cases among the 20 age periods from 1946 to Before-1860 implies an estimate of the dates of incorporation for these corporations. The 477,949 corporations which did specify date of incorporation are already distributed by age periods as shown in line *d* of the 20 period blocks of table 4. An obviously possible device for allocating the Not-stated group of 13,203 cases consists in distributing them among the 20 age periods in the same proportions as the dated corporations are distributed. This amounts to multiplying 13,203 by the 20 ratios in line *f* of table 4. Such a crude device does not, however, yield a sufficiently close approximation to the desired result.

One reason for this is that the 13,203 cases are in part net and in part no-net corporations, and chapter v has shown that these two categories have very different age distributions. Another reason is that these cases include corporations of various sizes, and chapter iii has shown that the age distributions differ noticeably among the size classes.[98] Accordingly, an allocation was made, separately for net

[98] One might suggest further that the 13,203 cases include corporations from various lines of industry, which are shown in chap. iv to have differing age distributions. As, however, the *S. of I.* date-of-incorporation statistics do not give a double classification according to both size and line of industry, allowances—such as shown below in the text—cannot satisfactorily be made for both sorts of classification. If the allowances

TABLE 44

METHOD OF ALLOCATION, TO AGE PERIODS, OF THE NOT-STATED GROUP OF 1946-ACTIVE
CORPORATIONS, ILLUSTRATED FOR PERIOD 1935–1939*

Lower limit of size class ($1,000)		Number of returns in class		Ratio II/I	Number of dated returns in period	Estimate of not-stated in period
		Dated	Not stated			
		(I)	(II)	(III)	(IV)	(V)
0	N	125,077	2,532	0.02024	23,106	467.7
	D	69,561	1,906	.02740	10,408	285.2
50	N	61,517	1,084	.01762	10,493	184.9
	D	13,939	281	.02016	1,914	38.6
100	N	64,284	1,001	.01557	10,103	157.3
	D	11,078	229	.02067	1,479	30.6
250	N	29,511	350	.01186	3,953	46.9
	D	4,344	59	.01358	562	7.6
500	N	18,190	185	.01017	1,975	20.1
	D	2,401	27	.01125	339	3.8
1,000	N	22,047	345	.01565	1,838	28.8
	D	2,205	21	.00952	264	2.5
5,000	N	3,899	45	.01154	247	2.9
	D	297	.....	......	23	.....
10,000	N	3,041	25	.00822	183	1.5
	D	275	.....	......	21	.....
50,000	N	420	2	.00476	17	0.1
	D	41	.....	......	2	.....
100,000	N	484	3	.00620	5	0.0
	D	44	.....	......	2	.....
Nonbalance- sheet returns	N	23,345	1,914	.08196	4,111	336.9
	D	21,940	3,194	0.14558	3,624	527.6
Totals for period					74,669	2,143.0

* SOURCE: Data in columns I, II, and IV from *1946 S. of I.*, pp. 26–7. rows N, for net corporations; rows D, for no-net. Column V is III × IV.

and no-net categories, for each size class and for the "class" of non-balance-sheet corporations, by the method illustrated for allocations to the 1935–1939 period in table 44. A similar operation provides the estimate for each of the 20 age periods, columns I to III of table 44 being identical for all periods.

The totals of columns IV and V, the actual number of dated cor-

are to be carried out for only one type of classification, a choice must be made between size and line of industry. The choice of size is indicated because differences in age distribution among size classes are more emphatic and more systematic than those among lines of industry. Nevertheless, some testing of allowances in terms of line-of-industry classes was undertaken; but this did not point to an opposite conclusion, and the size basis was therefore chosen for the definitive allocation described in the text.

porations and the estimated number of Not-stated corporations, appear, for each period, in columns I and II of table 45. Column III of the table, which combines the items of columns I and II, gives the estimated distribution of all 1946-active corporations by age

TABLE 45

DISTRIBUTION OF ALL CORPORATIONS ACTIVE IN 1946 BY DATE-OF-INCORPORATION
PERIODS, COMPARED WITH CORRESPONDING DISTRIBUTION
OF DATED CORPORATIONS*

Period of incorporation	Number of corporations		Total	Fractions of aggregate	
	Dated	Not stated		All active	Dated
	(I)	(II)	(III)	(IV)	(V)
1946............	70,447	2,016	72,463	0.1475	0.1474
1945............	38,809	1,141	39,950	.0813	.0812
1944............	19,994	567	20,561	.0419	.0418
1943............	13,871	395	14,266	.0290	.0290
1942............	12,163	365	12,528	.0255	.0254
1941............	16,167	472	16,639	.0339	.0338
1940............	17,019	500	17,519	.0357	.0356
1935–1939......	74,669	2,143	76,812	.1564	.1562
1930–1934......	63,925	1,805	65,730	.1338	.1337
1925–1929......	48,023	1,295	49,318	.1004	.1005
1920–1924......	31,524	787	32,311	.0658	.0660
1915–1919......	19,451	480	19,931	.0406	.0407
1910–1914......	15,497	393	15,890	.0324	.0324
1905–1909......	14,607	363	14,970	.0305	.0306
1900–1904......	9,893	230	10,123	.0206	.0207
1890–1899......	6,827	153	6,980	.0142	.0143
1880–1899......	2,911	57	2,968	.0060	.0061
1870–1879......	778	15	793	.0016	.0016
1860–1869......	803	15	818	.0017	.0017
Before 1860.....	571	11	582	0.0012	0.0012

* IV is ratio of III to 491,152; V is ratio of I to 477,949.

periods. Column IV shows this distribution as fractions of the total, 491,152, of active corporations; and column V shows for comparison the corresponding fractions, taken from table 4 (to an additional decimal place), for the dated corporations alone. Table 46 shows corresponding figures, similarly derived, for 1945-active corporations.

If the allocation had been by the crude device first suggested above, the ratios in column IV would have been identical with those in column V. The more elaborate allocation, in terms of the net and no-net categories and of the size classes (and the nonbalance-sheet class), accounts for the very slight differences between the two columns—differences due to the different age structures for the two categories and for the various classes. In spite of the refinement,

TABLE 46

DISTRIBUTION OF ALL CORPORATIONS ACTIVE IN 1945 BY DATE-OF-INCORPORATION PERIODS, COMPARED WITH CORRESPONDING DISTRIBUTION OF DATED CORPORATIONS*

Period of incorporation	Number of corporations		Total	Fractions of aggregate	
	Dated	Not stated		All active	Dated
	(I)	(II)	(III)	(IV)	(V)
1945	22,543	965	23,508	0.0558	0.0556
1944	21,435	902	22,337	.0530	.0529
1943	14,962	604	15,566	.0370	.0369
1942	13,185	570	13,755	.0327	.0325
1941	17,062	726	17,788	.0422	.0421
1940	17,854	759	18,613	.0442	.0441
1935–1939	77,955	3,221	81,176	.1928	.1924
1930–1934	65,791	2,680	68,471	.1626	.1624
1925–1929	49,477	1,891	51,368	.1220	.1221
1920–1924	32,310	1,135	33,445	.0794	.0797
1915–1919	19,959	692	20,651	.0490	.0493
1910–1914	15,790	567	16,357	.0388	.0390
1905–1909	14,835	516	15,351	.0365	.0366
1900–1904	10,006	323	10,329	.0245	.0247
1890–1899	6,888	212	7,100	.0169	.0170
1880–1889	2,967	84	3,051	.0072	.0073
1870–1879	790	22	812	.0019	.0019
1860–1869	800	21	821	.0019	.0020
Before 1860	610	16	626	0.0015	0.0015

* IV is ratio of III to 421,125; V is ratio of I to 405,219.

in the allocation resulting from this more elaborate procedure, the figures of column II (and therefore of column III) remain estimates subject to possible error. They rest upon the assumption that, in each of the 22 classes allocated as in table 44, the age distribution is the same for Not-stated as for dated corporations. One may contend that the Not-stated corporations are more (or less) likely to be young than the dated corporations: that young corporations are more (or less) likely than old corporations to fail to state their dates of incorporation. No a priori reason appears for preferring the "more" or the "less" hypothesis, and I find no clear indication in the data pointing in one direction rather than the other.[97] In the absence of such reason or such statistical evidence, the assumption actually made appears to be the most probably valid. Moreover, some of whatever errors may be involved in the assumption are likely to affect the column V figures of table 44 for some of the 22 classes in one direction and some in the opposite direction, with the result that the net error in the total of the column may be small. This last point, however, loses some of its force when note is taken that the nonbalance-sheet classes have a very large effect upon that total, and that the allocation of these two classes inevitably fails to allow for size differences—and the relevant differences in age distribution—within the two classes. Whatever the errors in the assumption, they seem unlikely to damage seriously the validity of the findings in sections 28 and 29.

The age distribution for all active corporations is, for both 1946 and 1945 (columns IV and V of tables 45 and 46) somewhat younger than that for dated corporations: the concentration among younger corporations is somewhat greater for all active corporations than for the moderately less inclusive list of dated corporations. This implies corresponding small adjustments in the findings of chapter ii, if those findings are to be accepted for all active corporations; but it alters such findings in no fundamental respect.

28. *Death rates and age.*—We may now answer more precisely the question posed above, as to the number of corporations chartered in 1935–1939 which ceased to be active in 1946. The 1935–1939 figures from column III of tables 45 and 46 are 76,812 and 81,176. The difference, 4,364, is the number of corporations chartered in that period which became inactive in 1946; and a number of this sort is hereafter designated the number of "deaths" in 1946. Correspondingly, the ratio of the number of deaths in 1946 to the number active at the beginning of the year (the number active in 1945) is designated the current death rate in 1946. For corporations chartered in 1935–1939, the current death rate in 1946 is, accordingly, the ratio of 4,364 to 81,176, or 5.38 per cent.

---

[97] Of course, differences between column IV and column V of table 45 (and likewise table 46) imply that, for the entire list of corporations, the Not-stated group has a very slightly younger age distribution than the dated group. But this is a direct consequence of the facts that Not-stated corporations are more common in the no-net than in the net category, in small than in large-size classes, and among nonbalance-sheet returns than in most size classes; and the category and the classes in which Not-stated returns are most common are those having young age distributions. No such evidence exists for concluding that, *within* any one of the 22 classes, the Not-stated group has an exceptionally young age distribution.

The implications of this use of the term deaths must be borne in mind in connection with the remaining analysis in this chapter: the term means, subject to a single adjustment (in connection with consolidated returns) explained in section 29 and relevant also to section 30, the number of corporations which disappeared from the active list in a particular year (such as 1946) or other period.[98] In similar manner, as set forth in section 30, the number of corporate "births" in a year or other period means the number of corporations which became active in such period. Strictly, and in a legal sense, a corporation is born when its charter is granted; and it dies when it is dissolved, whether because of failure or for other reasons, and gives up its charter. For various reasons, a definition of birth and death in this sense would be preferable to the definition, in terms of becoming active or ceasing to be active, here adopted; but the definition here adopted is a practical necessity because of the form in which the data appear (and must necessarily appear, because they are based on tax returns) in *Statistics of Income*.

The number of deaths—in the sense of becoming inactive—in a particular year may differ markedly from the number of legal corporate deaths—the number of charters given up—in that year. The former number probably includes some corporations which also die legally in the same year, but includes also others which will not die legally until some later year—certain corporations may become inactive in 1946 but not give up their charter until after (in rare cases, long after) 1946. The latter number—the number of legal deaths in a particular year—may include, in addition to corporations which become inactive in the same year, some corporations which became inactive in some previous year (in rare cases, a much earlier year).

Similarly, the number of births—as here defined, in the sense of becoming active—in a particular year may include some corporations which were legally born in some earlier year (in rare cases, a much earlier year); and the number of legal births within a year may include some corporations which do not become active until a later year (in rare cases, a much later year). Hence, the number of births, as here defined, may differ greatly from the number of legal births during a particular year or other period.

A corporation which is legally born in a particular year may appear in our record as a "birth" for that year or for some later

---

[98] See section 2 for definition of the terms active and inactive, in reference to tax returns.

year, and a corporation which legally dies in a particular year may appear in our record as a "death" for that year or for some earlier year. The rare corporation which is legally born, is active for a brief time, and legally dies within a single year would appear in our record as a birth for that year and a death for the following year.

TABLE 47

CURRENT DEATH RATES IN 1946, by AGE PERIODS*

Period of incorporation	Number of deaths in 1946	Number active at beginning of 1946	Current death rate in 1946 (per cent)
	(I)	(II)	(III)
1945	−16,442	23,508	....
1944	1,776†	22,337	7.95†
1943	1,300†	15,566	8.35†
1942	1,227	13,755	8.92
1941	1,149	17,788	6.46
1940	1,094	18,613	5.88
1935–1939	4,364	81,176	5.38
1930–1934	2,741	68,471	4.00
1925–1929	2,050	51,368	3.99
1920–1924	1,134	33,445	3.39
1915–1919	720	20,651	3.49
1910–1914	467	16,357	2.86
1905–1909	381	15,351	2.48
1900–1904	206	10,329	1.99
1890–1899	120	7,100	1.69
1880–1889	83	3,051	2.72
1870–1879	19	812	2.34
1860–1869	3	821	0.37
Before 1860	44	626	7.03

* Column I is column III of Table 46 minus that of Table 45. Column II is column III of Table 46. Column III is I / II.
† Figures are not significant, as explained in the text.

The still rarer corporation which is legally born and legally dies within a single year without ever engaging actively in operations would never appear as either birth or death in our record. The differences here mentioned have an important bearing upon a comparison of our record of births with statistics of incorporations, as stated in section 30, and would have a similar bearing upon a comparison of our record of deaths with statistics of dissolutions, if such statistics were available on a comprehensive basis suitable for comparison.

Finally, notice may be taken of a technical peculiarity of the tax-return tabulations which results in the appearance in our record of certain fictitious births and deaths. Our data are based upon corporate tax *returns* as filed, and we have generally in the foregoing pages used the terms returns and corporations interchangeably. Here, however, the distinction becomes important, because the privilege of filing a consolidated return for a group of affiliated corporations means that only one return is counted whereas several corporations have a legal existence. Partly because of changes in the law respecting the consolidated-return privilege and partly because of the business and financial considerations determining whether a particular group of affiliated corporations will take advantage of the privilege, the number of consolidated returns—and therefore the number of legally existent corporate subsidiaries lost from our count through inclusion in such returns—varies from year to year. Whenever a particular corporation, which has heretofore filed a separate return, becomes covered under a consolidated return, that corporation disappears from the active list and would count as a death in our record. Likewise, when the consolidated-return privilege is given up or is taken away by the revenue act, the subsidiaries formerly covered under the consolidated return enter the active list on their own account, and would count as births in our record. This point has a slight bearing on the analysis of this section, as indicated below; but it is of greater relevance to section 29, where the appropriate adjustments of our record are set forth.

Column I of table 47 lists, for each period of incorporation, results corresponding to the 4,364 found above as the number of corporations chartered in 1935–1939 which died in 1946. These figures are obtained by subtraction of items in column III of table 45 from corresponding items of table 46 (the latter figures being repeated in column II of table 47). The corresponding current death rates, the percentage ratio of column I to column II, appear in column III.

We must at once note that the figures in columns I and III for periods 1945, 1944, and possibly 1943 are lacking in significance as deaths and death rates. The difficulty arises because the difference between a column III figure of table 46 and the corresponding figure of table 45 is a *net* figure—the net difference between the number of corporations, legally born (chartered) in a particular period such as 1945, which became inactive in 1946 and those which became active. Except for the most recent periods—1945 and 1944, and possibly 1943—the second of these items, corporations legally born in such period which first became active in 1946, may be taken as zero or negligibly small, since we have indicated above that only rarely does a corporation remain inactive long after it is legally born. For the very recent periods, and especially for 1945, this is not true. Many corporations actually chartered in 1945 were not active in that year and are not therefore counted in the 1945 item of column III of table 46 (column II of table 47).[90] Many, but probably not all, of these corporations did become active in 1946 and are therefore counted in the 1945 item of column III of table 45. The number of 1945-chartered corporations which became active in 1946 is not known; but it must have been larger, and perhaps much larger, than 16,442, because some deaths of 1945-chartered corporations must have occurred in 1946. The 1945 figure in column I of table 47 is, therefore, not the number of deaths of 1945-chartered corporations in 1946: the number of such deaths is offset, and more, to the extent of 16,442, by the number of corporations which became active in 1946. Although the 1944 and 1943 items in column I of table 47 are not negative, the former almost surely, and the latter possibly, understate the numbers of deaths in those years for the same reason: some 1944-chartered corporations almost surely became active in 1946, and some 1943-chartered corporations may have done so.

The result for 1945 certainly has no significance as an indicator of the number of deaths (and hence the current death rate), that for 1944 is probably a serious understatement of the number of deaths, and that for 1943 may be a considerable understatement. The results for those years in columns I and III of table 47 are therefore ignored. Whether the results for 1942 and possibly even for several still earlier periods are significantly understated cannot be known with certainty; but I assume that for all periods before 1943 the number of corporations becoming active in 1946 is negligible, and that the results in table 47 for such periods are valid.[100]

---

[19] See *1945 S. of I.*, p. 62, n. 46.

[100] These results may, however, be subject to certain other errors. Inaccuracies in reporting date of incorporation on the tax returns could damage the results, but such inaccuracies are not likely to be numerous. Errors in tabulation of the returns may exist; but, as *Statistics of Income* has an enviable reputation for accuracy in tabulation, these are surely negligible. Errors in the allocation, in section 27, of the Not-stated group may be more serious than either of the foregoing; but they are probably small and perhaps entirely negligible except possibly for certain age periods remote from 1946. For example, the remarkably high death rate for Before-1860 may be due to errors in allocation of the Not-stated group—only a small number of corporations in that group would need be shifted to this period (for 1946-active corporations) or away from this period (for 1945-active corporations) to change the rate sharply.

The deaths shown in table 47 include those which are fictitious, in the sense noted above: a corporation which becomes covered under a consolidated return in 1946 then ceases to file an active return on its own account. Undoubtedly, some such "deaths" occurred in 1946; but similarly fictitious births also occurred, because some corporations previously covered under consolidated returns filed separate active returns in 1946. As a matter of fact, more shifts of the latter sort than of the former occurred in 1946. The number of shifts of each sort cannot be determined from the published data, but the net difference between the two sorts is 1,056 in favor of shifts to the active list.[101] Hence, the estimated total number of deaths in 1946, regardless of date of incorporation, is understated by at least 1,056 because of changes in the filing of consolidated returns, and the understatement may be much greater than 1,056. No basis exists for allocating these 1,056 or more cases among the age periods; and the results in table 47 may therefore be distorted, but probably only in small degree for any age period.

The results in column III of table 47, for the age periods before 1943, show a fairly steady decline of the current death rate in 1946 as age increases, until periods far back in the record are reached. The chance of death generally declines with increasing age until age reaches more than fifty-five years (corporations chartered before 1890). Correspondingly, the chance of survival increases with age. With death defined as becoming inactive, this finding does not necessarily mean that the chance of dissolution of the typical corporation declines as age increases. As, however, becoming inactive is generally preliminary to an early, and often to an almost immediate, dissolution, the death rates here shown are probably not greatly different from similar rates based upon legal deaths (defined in terms of dissolution). To the extent that the finding may be thus extended, we may state that the risk of dissolution, whether because of failure or for other reasons, diminishes as age increases. Such a statement of the finding is in accord with the conclusion of chapter v that youth is the period of greatest danger for corporations.

The data of column III of table 47 are plotted in figure 8, for all periods before 1943, back to 1900–1904. The figure shows also a smooth curve, fitted by visual inspection to the points for periods 1942 to 1905–1909 and an "average" point (not shown in the figure,

[101] *1946 S. of I.*, p. 420, shows the number of subsidiaries (the number excludes the parent corporations) covered by consolidated returns at 6,093 for 1945 and 5,037 for 1946.

and centered in 1893) for periods before 1905. This curve is presented as a rough approximation to the "generally downward course" of the death rate with increasing age, and is the basis of a major step in the analysis of section 30.

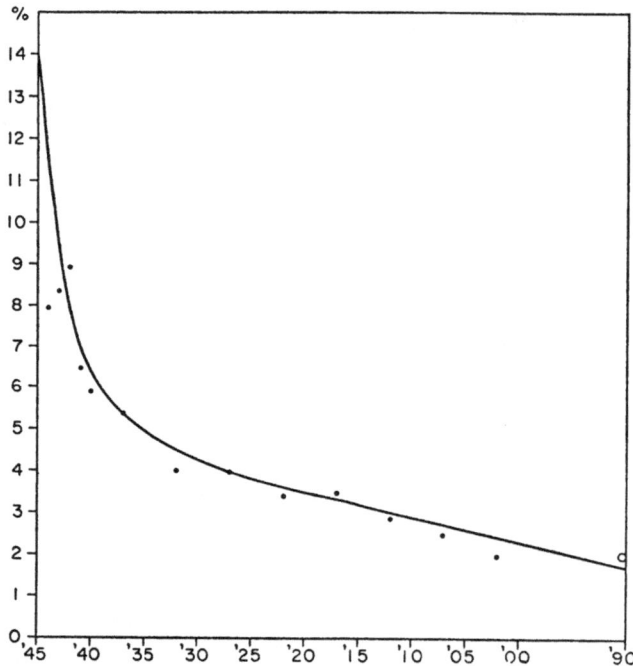

Fig. 8. Actual current death rates (dots) in 1946 of corporations active in 1945 which were chartered in indicated periods, and curve used for estimating such death rates for each year of incorporation since 1890.

SOURCE: Data for the dots from table 47. The circle at the right represents the average death rate in 1946 for corporations chartered in 1870–1899, and is centered in 1891.

One may seek explanations of some of the irregularities in figure 8. Why is the death rate for 1930–1934 below that for 1925–1929, why is that for 1920–1924 below that for 1915–1919, and why are the rates for certain very early periods substantially higher than the curve would suggest? No fully dependable explanations appear, but certain tentative explanations may be suggested. A death rate for a particular period may be higher (or lower) than would otherwise be expected because of an exceptional concentration in that period of incorporations in some lines of industry for which the chance of death in 1946 was higher (or lower) than for corporations in general, because of economic or other conditions affecting the situation or outlook in 1946 for such lines of industry. A similar suggestion can run in terms of an exceptional number of corporations, incorporated in a particular period, having some distinctive characteristic other than line of industry, such as size, capital structure, reliance upon research or technological developments, sponsorship by particularly powerful banking interests, and perhaps other factors which may have rendered death in 1946 exceptionally likely (or unlikely).

With respect to the abnormally low rates (abnormal in the sense of being below the curve of steady decline with advancing age), a special explanation may have some validity. Important periods of this sort are 1930–1934, 1920–1924, and 1890–1899 (not shown)— all periods in which severe depressions occurred, and which were followed by several years of sustained prosperity. Possibly corporations which were chartered in depressed periods were, because of the prevailing pessimism, confined to enterprises with exceptionally good prospects; and such corporations which survived into the ensuing period of prosperity may then have become so strong that they had exceptional resistance to death in some later year such as 1946. Conversely, some corporations chartered in a period of inflationary credit expansion and speculative boom such as 1925–1929 may have been less cautiously planned and, even if they managed to survive the ensuing depression, may have carried forward even to 1946 elements of weakness rendering them exceptionally liable to death. Consideration of this type of explanation should not be pushed too far until more detailed data than those here under study become available, especially as the date-of-incorporation periods are not timed to fit exactly periods of depression (or of boom). And general note should be taken of the fact that a corporation's capacity to resist death in a particular year such as 1946 is the composite result of many factors and experiences spread over the entire history of that corporation since birth.

We may remark finally that the results in table 47 pertain to deaths in a single year, 1946. Such deaths are, of course, partly the result of conditions in that year, or of prospects which were apparent in that year to corporate managers and others concerned with deciding whether activity should continue. Similar calculations for some other year, if the relevant data were available for making such calculations, might show a very different schedule of death rates.

A year of depression, for example, might show higher death rates for all or nearly all periods. But the general tendency of the death rate to decline with increasing age would almost surely appear for any year, however depressed or prosperous.

29. *The corporate population at various dates, and the chance of survival to 1946.*—We may now turn to a somewhat different ques-

TABLE 48

THE CORPORATE POPULATION FOR SPECIFIED YEARS, AS REPRESENTED BY RETURNS FILED, AND AS ADJUSTED TO THE 1946 BASIS OF CONSOLIDATION*

Year	Number of returns filed	Number of subsidiaries	Net increase in subsidiaries to 1946	Population adjustedfto 1946 basis
	(I)	(II)	(III)	(IV)
1946.	526,363	5,037	0	526,363
1945.	454,460	6,093	−1,056	455,516
1944.	446,796	5,780	−743	447,539
1943.	455,894	6,165	−1,128	457,022
1942.	479,677	5,584	−547	480,224
1941.	509,066	706	4,331	504,735
1940.	516,783	709	4,328	512,455
1939.	515,960	715	4,322	511,638
1934.	528,898	2,522	2,515	526,383
1929.	509,436	30,112	−25,075	534,511
1924.	417,421	24,720	−19,683	437,104
1919.	320,198	18,962	−13,925	334,123
1914†	331,000	0	5,037	326,000†
1909.	262,490	0	5,037	257,453

* SOURCES: Column I, *1946 S. of I.*, pp. 352–3; column II, since 1928, *1946 S. of I.*, p. 420; before 1929 estimated as explained in accompanying text.
Column III is 5,037 − II. Column IV is I − III.
† Rounded figure. See *1946 S. of I.*, p. 423, n. 8, for inclusion of 32,000 returns in 1914 not shown on p. 352 of *S. of I.*

tion: What is the chance of survival into 1946 for the population of corporations existing in any specified year? Answer to the question must be limited to the annual-period years since 1939 and to the terminal years of five-year periods from 1935–1939 back to 1905–1909, because certain of the relevant statistics are not available before 1909 when the corporate excise tax, which was the forerunner of the corporate income tax, went into effect.[102]

The total number of corporation returns, active and inactive,

---

[102] The years specified for the corporate population, and also 1946, are here taxable years. These may differ, for certain corporations, from the calendar year by as much as 6 months. See section 3.

See also *1946 S. of I.*, p. 423, n. 8, concerning the original source of data here used for 1909 and 1915—years before publication of *Statistics of Income* began.

covered by *Statistics of Income* tabulations appear in column I of table 48 for each of the above-specified years. Column IV restates these figures for the corporate population adjusted to a basis excluding the same number of subsidiaries, because of consolidated returns, as was excluded in 1946.

The details for these adjustments are provided in columns II and III. As shown in column II, 5,037 corporations were lost from the count shown in column I of table 48 for 1946, because they were covered by consolidated returns. Likewise, 30,112 corporations were lost from the count in 1929. The decrease in number of subsidiaries thus excluded from the count, from 1929 to 1946, was 25,075 (column III); and this figure is added to the 509,439 returns of 1929 to put the figure in column IV on a basis comparable with 1945.[103] Similar adjustments to the 1946 basis are made for other dates.[104] These adjusted figures in column IV of table 48 state the size of the corporate population in specified years, on a basis comparable with 1946.

[103] The adjustments thus made, for 1929 and other years, may not be wholly adequate, because the stated number of subsidiaries apparently excludes inactive subsidiaries, if any—see *1945 S. of I.*, p. 444, n. 82, for implication to this effect. Such subsidiaries are probably few in number, and ignoring them may not seriously damage the adjustments.

[104] The relevant figures on number of subsidiaries, column II of table 48, have to be estimated for years before 1929. Such estimates are secured for 1924 and 1919 by taking, as the number of subsidiaries, 5.922 per cent of the total number of returns (417,421 and 320,198, respectively) in those years. The 5.922 per cent rests upon data for 1929–1933:

Years	Number of subsidiaries	Number of returns	Ratio, I/II, in per cent
	(I)	(II)	(III)
1929	30,112	509,436	5.911
1930	32,209	518,736	6.209
1931	31,307	516,404	6.063
1932	29,232	508,636	5.747
1933	28,589	504,080	5.672
Total	151,449	2,557,292	5.922

The five annual percentages cluster very closely about that for the five-year totals. Even in a period marked by transition from high prosperity to deep depression—a period in which no drastic changes occurred in the law respecting the consolidated-return privilege—the relative numerical importance of the subsidiaries excluded from the count did not change noticeably. Although minor changes in these provisions of the law occurred between 1918 and 1929, assumption is made that the percentage for 1929–1933 is approximately valid for 1919 and 1924; and the percentage was applied to the number of returns for each of those years, to yield figures given in table 48. (*1946 S. of I.*, pp. 448–454, gives a summary of the changes in law concerning the consolidated-return privilege.)

Consolidated returns were not permitted for 1909 and 1914, and the number of subsidiaries is therefore zero for each of those years.

Unfortunately, the population so stated is not precisely relevant for our intended calculation of the rate of survival to 1946. Before explaining this difficulty, we may make a preliminary calculation of the survival rate on the basis of the population as stated in table 48. Suppose the question is asked: What fraction of the population in 1939 survived in 1946? The number of survivors to 1946 (number still active in 1946) is obtained by cumulating, from Before-1860 to 1935–1939, the figures in column III of table 45 and is 297,226. Division of this figure by 511,638, the 1939 population shown in column IV of table 48, yields 58.1 per cent as the fraction surviving. Or suppose the question is: What fraction of the population in 1945 survived in 1946? In a similar manner, division of 418,689 by 455,516 yields 91.9 per cent as the desired fraction.

But both of these percentages are understated, because both divisors (the population figures) are overstated; and the error is greater for the 1945 than for the 1939 case. The reason is that the population figure for any specified year is the number of corporations (after the pertinent adjustment for number of subsidiaries) which were in existence in a legal sense in that year—the number which had been chartered in or before that year and had not yet been dissolved.[105] *Some* of the corporations thus in existence were not exposed to risk of death—in our sense of becoming inactive—in the years following the specified year. The point at issue concerns the inactive returns in the specified year, of which 46,343 in 1939 and 33,335 in 1945 are included in the population figures, together with the active corporations. These inactive returns comprise—for example, in 1939—two categories: (1) those which had already become inactive (died, in our sense) mainly in 1939 or immediately preceding years, and had not yet been dissolved (died, in the legal sense); and, (2) those which had been chartered (born, in the legal sense) mainly in 1939 or the immediately preceding years, and had not yet become active (been born, in our sense). Members of the first category were no longer (after 1939) exposed to risk of death (in our sense). Hence, in determining the rate of survival to 1946, the number of survivors should be divided by the population figure reduced by the number in the first category. Many of the members of the second category, however, became active soon after 1939, and nearly all had probably become active well before 1946, and

---

[105] The assumption is here made that all corporations in existence in such year filed returns—whether active or inactive—as required by law. This assumption may be greatly in error, particularly in the case of inactive corporations; and the error may vary substantially from year to year.

were therefore exposed to risk of death in (or perhaps before) 1946.[106] Hence, with negligible error, the population figure for 1939 does not need to be reduced by the number in the second category, or any part thereof. The only adjustment needed for 1939 is for the number of inactive returns of the first category.[107]

The conclusion concerning the second category must be revised for a year, such as 1945, close to the terminal year 1946. The 33,335 inactive returns for 1945 also include the two categories described above; and the above conclusion for the first category applies: the population figure must be reduced by the number in the first category. As respects the second category, we can no longer assert that "nearly all had become active before 1946." In fact, as 1945 was the last year before 1946, *none* of them became active *before* 1946; and therefore none of the second category was exposed to risk of death (becoming inactive) in 1946. Hence, all the second category must also be subtracted from the population for 1945, before calculating the rate of survival. This means that the entire inactive list—both categories—must be subtracted from the 1945 population. The 1945 population exposed to risk of death in 1946 then becomes 422,181; and the rate of survival becomes 99.2 per cent.

If a year less close than 1945 to the terminal year 1946 is chosen—for example, 1944—some but probably not all members of the second category had become active before 1946 and were therefore exposed to risk of death in 1946. Accordingly, only a fraction of the second category needs to be excluded from the 1944 population. For 1943, the fraction to be excluded is still smaller, and possibly for 1942 and all earlier years the fraction is negligible.

The conclusions may now be summarized. The population shown in table 48 is overstated—for the purpose of calculating survival rates in 1946—for every specified year by the number of inactive returns of the first category. It is also overstated for recent specified years—beginning probably with 1943—by a fraction (increasing as the specified year comes closer to the terminal year, until it reaches 100 per cent for the specified year preceding the terminal year) of the number of inactive returns of the second category.

[106] A very small number of the second category may in fact not have become active until after 1945, and some few of them might never become active; but these cases are negligible for the above purpose.

[107] The population figures actually involved in the survival-rate calculations are those adjusted to the 1946 basis of consolidation, column IV of table 48. The process of adjustment may cause some shifts in the number of inactive returns—shifts from or to the 46,343 for the unadjusted population of 1939, for example—but these shifts are probably negligible.

If, for each specified year, we could determine the number of inactive returns in each category, and if, for each recent year, we could determine the number in the second category which did not become active before the terminal year, the appropriate numerical reductions could be made in the population figures of table 48. These facts cannot be determined from the *S. of I.* data.[108]

In the absence of a clear determination, the following assumptions are made. First, for every specified year, the first category

---

[108] We do know, from the 1945 line of table 47 and the relevant text, that, among the unknown number of corporations chartered in 1945, 23,508 became active in 1945 and *at least* 16,442 became active in 1946. Therefore, the second category in 1945 included at least 16,442 members; and, as the total inactive list in 1945 was 33,335, the first category included not more than 16,893 members. If we may assume, in line with the curve of figure 8, that 14 per cent of the 23,508 1945-active corporations chartered in 1945 became inactive in 1946, the above figure 16,442 must be raised to 19,733. Then the second category in 1945 included at least 19,733, and the first category not more than 13,602. If, as is probably the case, some corporations chartered in 1944 and even in 1943, which were not active in 1945, became active in 1946, the 19,733 needs to be increased, and the 13,602 correspondingly decreased. These results are, however, of no direct use in calculating the 1946 survival rate for the 1945 population, since we have already seen that the 1945 population must be reduced by the entire 33,335, regardless of the relative sizes of the two categories.

The results are, nevertheless, somewhat informing. They show that the number of charters in 1945 was *at least* the sum of 23,508 and 16,442, which is 39,950. This figure is an absolute minimum: the true number of incorporations in 1945 probably runs much above this because (1) the 16,442 is too small since it does not allow for the deaths in 1946 (estimated above at 3,291); and (2) it takes no account of those corporations chartered in 1945 which did not become active until after 1946. But even taking the minimum number of 1945 charters at 39,950 implies that less than 59 per cent of the corporations chartered in 1945 became active in that year, and the percentage is lower if a higher number of charters is assumed.

The results also show that, for such a year as 1945, the second category was at least 49 per cent of all inactive corporations; and, if allowance is also made for the estimated deaths in 1946, the percentage is at least 59. Allowance for corporations chartered in 1944 and possibly 1943 which became active in 1946 would raise the percentage even higher. This suggests that, in a year like 1945, the second category might easily have accounted for two-thirds of the inactive corporations, and the first category only one third. As economic conditions were fairly favorable in 1945, the number of incorporations may have been abnormally large (although it was far below that of 1946) and the number of failures and other discontinuances may have been abnormally low. In a year of depressed economic conditions, these two situations may have been reversed, and consequently the importance of the second category might have been smaller, and that of the first category greater, than in 1945. Fortunately, no specified year in the list in table 48 is marked by deep depression; though several years—1914, 1924, 1934, and certain wartime years—may have been less favorable than 1945. Hence, the allocation in the text of one third of the inactive group to the first category may not be seriously in error for any specified year.

Certain facts from other sources than *S. of I.* might supplement our information concerning the allocation between the first and second categories; but attempted use for this purpose of such facts as the record of new incorporations, published in *Survey of Current Business,* has involved such dubious assumptions and led to such perplexing contradictions that I do not report the results.

comprises 33 per cent of all inactive corporations. Second, for specified years close to the terminal year the following percentages of
the second category do not become active before the terminal year:
for the first preceding year, 100; for the second preceding year, 24;
for the third preceding year, 6. This second assumption is in accord
with the following more basic assumption: of the corporations
chartered in any year, 46 per cent became active in that year, 41
per cent in the next year, 10 per cent in the second following year,
and 2 per cent in the third following year. The combined exclusions
from the population, on account of both categories, therefore constitute the following percentages of total inactive corporations:

> First preceding year, 1945 100
> Second preceding year, 1944 49
> Third preceding year, 1943 37
> All earlier years 33

Table 49 adjusts column IV of table 48 in accordance with these
assumptions. Column I shows the number of inactive corporations
in each specified year, the figures before 1929 being estimated as
10 per cent of the total number of returns in those years as shown
in column I of table 48. This percentage is the approximate average
of the ratio of inactive to all returns in the 14 years 1927–1940.[109]

In column II, the estimated number of inactive returns which
were not exposed to death in or before 1946 is obtained by applying
the percentages listed above to the figures of column I. Column III
shows the finally adjusted figures for population, in each specified
year, exposed to risk of death (in the sense of becoming inactive)
in or before 1946: it is obtained by subtracting column II of table

---

[109] The percentage ranges from 8.5 to 11.4 in those 14 years, the highest being for
1933. After 1933, the percentage declines gradually, and without interruption to 6.7
in 1946. The high figure in 1933 may reflect the depression which had been in progress
for several years, and imply that the first category of inactive returns was much higher
at that time than the 33 per cent (of total inactive returns) assumed above for 1934
and other years. The low figures during the war years occurred at a time when,
though business was not depressed, discontinuances of enterprises—corporate and
other—were very numerous. The first category may therefore have been unusually
large in such years as 1942–1944, but the second category was probably greatly reduced
because new incorporations were at a low level. In 1946, however, new incorporations
were at an unprecedented level, and the relatively small number of inactive returns
cannot easily be explained. I am impelled to suspect that compliance with the requirement that even inactive corporations must file returns had declined in recent years
and may have been seriously deficient in 1946.

Some question exists as to whether the estimate of inactive returns for 1909, when
the modern income tax was not in effect, is dependable.

49 from column IV of table 48. These population figures are the divisors for the calculation, below, of survival rates in 1946.

Table 49 also shows in column IV the net increase in number of active corporations (adjusted to the 1946 basis of consolidation) from one specified year to the next. These figures are derived by subtracting column I of table 49 from column IV of table 48 and

TABLE 49

The Corporate Population Exposed to Death in or Before 1946, for Each Specified Year, and Excess of Births Over Deaths Between Beginning of Each Specified Year and That Succeeding*

| Year | Inactive corporations | | Population exposed to death in or before 1946 | Excess of births over deaths |
	Total	Not exposed to death in 1946		
	(I)	(II)	(III)	(IV)
1946	35,211	35,211	. . . . . .	68,971
1945	33,335	33,335	422,181	8,971
1944	34,329	16,821	430,718	−8,439
1943	35,373	13,088	443,934	−21,563
1942	37,012	12,214	468,010	−21,363
1941	40,160	13,253	491,482	−4,139
1940	43,741	14,435	498,020	3,419
1939	46,343	15,293	496,345	−1,994
1934	59,094	19,501	506,882	−13,807
1929	53,415	17,627	516,884	85,734
1924	41,742	13,775	423,329	93,259
1919	32,020	10,567	323,556	9,000†
1914	33,100	10,923	315,000†	62,000†
1909	26,249	8,662	248,791	. . . . . .

* Column I: since 1926, derived by subtraction from *1946 S. of I.*, pp. 352–353; before 1927, estimated at 10 per cent of column I of table 48. Column II estimated as explained in accompanying text. Column III is column IV of table 48 − II. Column IV is successive differences of (column IV of table 48 reduced by I of this table).
† Rounded figures.

then taking successive differences. As the net increase in active corporations between two years is the difference between the numbers of births and of deaths (both as here defined, in terms of entering or withdrawing from the active list), the figures of column IV show the excess of births over deaths for each period between two successive specified years.[110] The figures show an enormous growth

[110] The figures for 1914 and 1919 are in question because the basic figure for 1914 in column I of table 48 may be in question. See note † to table 48. The indicated excess, 62,000, of births over deaths between 1909 and 1914 may reflect in part the somewhat uncertain inclusion of 32,000 returns actually filed in 1915 as part of the 1914 total; but it may reflect also a greater coverage of the corporate system by the income tax than by the preceding corporate excise tax.

in the active corporate population from 1919 to 1929, a substantial contraction during the depression years 1929–1934, and a much greater contraction in the war years. Expansion was resumed in 1945 and became striking in 1946.

Table 50 presents the survival rates in 1946 of corporations in the population at various specified dates. Column I gives the number surviving as active in 1946, among all the corporations born in or before the relevant specified year.[111] This number is obtained by cumulating the figures in column III of table 45 from Before-1860 to and including the specified year. These figures of column I are divided by corresponding figures of column III in table 49 to yield the survival-rate percentages of column II. As is to be expected, the percentage declines steadily as the specified year becomes more remote from 1946: as time passes, the corporate population of any specified year contracts steadily because of losses through death. Even if the record were much longer than the thirty-seven years from 1909 to 1946, we may suspect that the percentage would not decline to zero for a much more remote specified year, since some corporations, as shown by the date-of-incorporation statistics, are known to have survived more than eighty-six years. But that the survival percentage among the population existing thirty-seven years before 1946 should be as low as 15 per cent is striking evidence that the great bulk of the corporate system at any given date passes out of existence within about one-third of a century.[112]

30. *Preliminary estimates of births during specified periods.*— The preceding sections of this chapter present analyses which rest in a limited degree upon certain assumptions which are debatable, but those analyses rest mainly upon the recorded data which are presumed to be tolerably free of error. In this section and section 31, however, certain new assumptions must be made; and these are not only more in doubt than those made previously, but they also determine in much greater degree the results of analysis. The following results therefore rest upon a much more tenuous basis than those of previous sections, and they must be regarded as highly tentative findings. Nevertheless, I venture to present them

---

[111] The term "born" is used here in the sense of having been legally born (chartered) by the specified year, for the number is based upon date-of-incorporation of survivors in 1946.

[112] An analysis along lines parallel to those followed above for 1946 survivals can be carried out similarly for survivals in 1945; but the resulting survival percentages, though differing in detail, would show the same general course—a steady and fairly rapid decline as the specified year recedes from 1945.

for two reasons: (1) they are not entirely without value as results, since they are approximations, and perhaps fairly good approximations, to the unknown facts; and (2) the method used in deriving them is of general applicability and may be applied to other data which may become available later, with a view to removing some and perhaps much of the doubt surrounding the fundamental assumptions.

The purpose of the first part of the analysis is to estimate the total number of corporations chartered in various years or other

TABLE 50

Percentage Surviving in 1946, of the Population in Specified Years*

Year	Number surviving in 1946	Per cent of population	Year	Number surviving in 1946	Per cent of population
	(I)	(II)		(I)	(II)
1945.........	418,689	99.2	1934.........	220,414	43.5
1944.........	378,739	87.9	1929.........	154,684	29.9
1943.........	358,178	80.7	1924.........	105,366	24.9
1942.........	343,912	73.5	1919.........	73,055	22.6
1941.........	331,384	67.4	1914.........	53,124	16.9
1940.........	314,745	63.2	1909.........	37,234	15.0
1939.........	297,226	59.9	....	....	....

* Column I is cumulation, from Before 1860 through specified year, of column III of table 45. Column II is ratio of I to column III of table 49.

periods of incorporation.[113] We already know (from estimates in column III of table 45) the number of corporations, among those chartered in any specified period, which survived as active in 1946. Therefore, if we can estimate the fraction, of all corporations chartered in that period, which survived in 1946, we can at once calculate the total number so chartered. This merely involves dividing the number of survivors by such fraction. We now proceed to a preliminary estimate of this decisive fraction.

For this purpose, an estimate is needed of the part, among all corporations chartered in any particular year and surviving at the beginning of each successive year (until 1946) after that initial year, which die in such successive year. A beginning can be made by examining column III of table 47. It shows that, of those corporations chartered in 1940 which survived to 1945, 5.88 per cent died in 1946—in the sixth year following the birth year. It like-

---

[113] This number is the number of births in the legal sense, not in the sense of becoming active. Strictly, it may deviate slightly from total legal births, because of consolidated returns; but this minor error is ignored.

wise shows that, of the corporations chartered in 1941 which survived to 1945, 6.46 per cent died in 1946—in the fifth year following
the birth year. And of the corporations chartered in 1942 which
survived to 1945, 8.92 per cent died in 1946—in the fourth year
following the birth year. Unfortunately, the figures in table 47
cannot supply the full schedule of such results needed for our purpose, for two reasons. As already stated, the figures in table 47 are
defective for periods since 1942 and cannot give the percentages
for the third, second, and first year after birth. Also, the table does
not give figures by years before 1940, but only by five-year or ten-
year periods. To supply this missing information, the smooth curve
of figure 8 may be used to estimate, for corporations chartered in
any year (covered by the curve) which survived in 1945, the percentage which died in 1946.[114]

The curve of figure 8 has been fitted by visual inspection, as
explained above; and it does not pass exactly through the various
points plotted from column III of table 47. Moreover, since no
such points can be plotted left of 1942, the extreme left part of the
curve is decisively determined by the opinion of the investigator.[115]
A first assumption is that the curve shows the current death rate
in 1946 for corporations chartered in 1943, 1944, and 1945—years
for which table 47 yields no clear results.

The fact that the plotted points for various years and other
periods lie off the curve—and this is especially true of some of the
very early periods for which the percentages in table 47 may be
somewhat undependable because they rest upon very few cases—
can be ignored on the ground that the curve is intended to be
generalized whereas table 47 is specific. That is: the curve is in-

---

[114] Use of these estimates from the curve also modifies somewhat the above figures
for 1940, 1941, and 1942, since those points do not lie exactly on the curve.

[115] I am aware that other opinions might differ widely from mine, in locating the
curve for years 1945, 1944, and even 1943; and I make no detailed attempt here to
"justify" the position selected. One may remark, however, that raising the curve so
that it would come closer to the plotted point for 1943 would imply very high percentages (unless one accepts a sharp bend to the left at 1943) for 1944 and 1945.
The curve indicates 14 per cent for 1945—14 per cent die in the first year after
the birth year. My own opinion is that this figure is as likely to be too high as too
low, but such opinion admittedly rests upon very meager facts. If the curve were
swung downward left of 1940 to make the 1945 figure 12 per cent, the survival ratios
(in table 51, below) for all ages more than six years would be increased by about 5
per cent (of the tabulated ratios) and for ages less than seven years by percentages
decreasing from about 5 to about 2 (for year 1). If the curve were swung upward to
make the 1945 figure 16 per cent, corresponding changes in the survival ratios would
occur in the opposite direction.

tended to show the percentages of deaths in the (for example) sixth
year after birth, among the survivors in the fifth year, for *any* year
of birth, whereas the 1940 figure (for example) of table 47 shows
specifically the sixth-year percentage only for corporations born
(chartered) in 1940.

TABLE 51

CALCULATION OF THE PERCENTAGE, AMONG CORPORATIONS CHARTERED
IN YEAR ZERO, WHICH SURVIVE IN YEAR a*

Year counted from birth year as 0	Per cent, among corporations surviving in year 1, which:		Per cent, among all chartered in year 0, which survive in year a
	Die in year a	Survive in year a	
(a)	(b)	(c)	(d)
1	6.44	93.56	93.56
2	9.88	90.12	84.32
3	9.12	90.88	76.63
4	8.00	92.00	70.50
5	7.02	92.98	65.55
6	6.35	93.65	61.39
7	5.90	94.10	57.76
8	5.60	94.40	54.53
9	5.34	94.66	51.62
10	5.12	94.88	48.97
11	4.94	95.06	46.55
12	4.78	95.22	44.33
13	4.63	95.37	42.28
14	4.50	95.50	40.37
15	4.38	95.62	38.61
16	4.27	95.73	36.96
17	4.17	95.83	35.42
18	4.07	95.93	33.98
19	3.98	96.02	32.62
20	3.89	96.11	31.35
21	3.80	96.20	30.16

* *b* is read from fig. 8, with adjustments, explained in text, for years 1, 2, and 3; *c* is 100-*b*; *d* is cumulative
product of *c*, from year 1.

In fact, a second and more fundamental assumption—which is
preliminary, and will be replaced in section 31—may now be stated
as follows: the indication of the curve, as to the percentage dying
in some specified year after birth, from among the corporations
chartered in a particular birth year which survive to the year next
preceding the specified year of death, is valid for *any* year of birth.
Thus, if the curve shows that, among the corporations chartered in

1936 which survived to 1945, 5.12 per cent died in 1946—in the tenth year after the birth year—that same 5.12 is valid for tenth-year deaths of corporations chartered in *any* particular year of the entire historical period. For example, among corporations chartered in 1929 which survived to 1938, 5.12 per cent are assumed to die in 1939. The curve is *based,* subject to matters of opinion listed above and to the smooth course of the curve by which it misses various plotted points, upon the record of deaths in 1946; but it is *used,* in the preliminary analysis of this section, to estimate deaths in any year. When the assumption is viewed in these terms, its validity is obviously debatable; and section 31 undertakes to modify the assumption in view of this defect. One may well urge that the conditions tending to induce corporate deaths may have been different in 1946 from those in some other year—some year, for example, not disturbed by certain abnormal factors present in 1946, or some year in which economic conditions were much less (or more) favorable than in 1946. Moreover, the relative impact of the prevailing conditions upon corporations of various ages may have differed between 1946 and some other year. That the curve of figure 8 truthfully indicates the current death rate in the first, second, third, etc., year after birth for *any* selected year of birth is therefore an assumption subject to error, and perhaps large error.[116] Nevertheless, the assumption is provisionally accepted in the remainder of the highly tentative analysis of this section.

The current death rates, as read from the curve of figure 8 for each year since 1924, are shown in column *b* of table 51. In accordance with the above assumption, the lines of the table are labeled, not with the year in which births occurred according to the figure, but with the serial number (counting the birth year as zero) of the year (1946) in which death occurred (in which corporations disappeared from the active list). Thus, the 5.12 read from figure 8 for 1936 (year of birth) is entered in column 10 of the table, indicating that the relevant deaths occurred in the tenth year after the birth year; and likewise the 3.80 read from the figure for 1925 is entered in line 21. Column *c* gives the corresponding percentage,

[116] Fortunately, some chance exists that minor specific errors tend to cancel out, in the use made of these figures in table 51. That use involves linking together, for any selected birth year, a succession of current survival rates (derived directly from the current death rates, and therefore subject to the same errors), one for each year after the birth year. As some of the death rates may be overstated by the curve, and some understated, the error in the combined result may be somewhat reduced. But any *general* understatement in the death rates, for a particular birth year will not be thus corrected, even in part, as shown in section 31.

among the survivors in the next preceding year, which survived in the year specified by column *a*. Column *d* gives the percentage resulting from the cumulative multiplication of figures in column *c*. For example, the column *d* figure for line 2 is the product of 0.9356 and 0.9012, stated in percentage form; and that for line 3 is the product of 0.9356, 0.9012, and 0.9088, stated in percentage form.

Hence, the figures of column *d* show, for any year of birth, the percentage, of corporations chartered in that year, which survived

TABLE 52

PRELIMINARY ESTIMATE OF NUMBER OF CORPORATIONS CHARTERED
IN SPECIFIED PERIODS*

Period of incorporation	Per cent surviving in 1946	Number surviving in 1946	Estimated number of charters in period
	(I)	(II)	(III)
1945...........................	93.56	39,950	42,700
1944...........................	84.32	20,561	24,400
1943...........................	76.63	14,266	18,600
1942...........................	70.50	12,528	17,800
1941...........................	65.55	16,639	25,400
1940...........................	61.39	17,519	28,500
1935–1939......................	51.89	76,812	148,000
1930–1934......................	40.51	65,730	162,300
1925–1929......................	32.71	49,318	150,800

* Column I from column *d* of table 51, stated as averages in the 3 five-year periods. Column II from column III of table 45. Column III is II / I.

(were active) in the first following year, the second following year, and so on to the twenty-first following year. Therefore, if we know that, among the corporations chartered in 1940, 17,519 (from column III of table 45) survived as active in 1946—the sixth following year—division of 17,519 by 61.39 per cent (from line 6 of table 51) provides our preliminary estimate of the births in 1940 as 28,537.

Operations of this sort are shown in table 52. Since the date-of-incorporation figures (as in table 45) before 1940 are stated in five-year intervals, an average of the five corresponding figures of column *d* of table 51 is entered for each such interval in column I of table 52.[117] The results in column III may be compared with an inde-

---

[117] The estimates in table 52 are carried back only to the period 1925–1929, though the five-year periods extend back to 1900–1904. Before 1900, each period is ten years long until 1860; and before 1860 the length is indefinite. The annual analysis of table 51 was carried back not only to 1925, but to 1862. Between 1861 and 1862, the

pendent series of estimates of incorporations, for periods since 1924. Unfortunately, such figures on incorporations relate to charters granted in only four states—Delaware, Illinois, Maine and New York.[118] Aggregate reported incorporations in these four states, for the specified years and other periods, are divided by 0.373 to yield the estimated totals of incorporations shown in column I of table 53. The estimates in table 52 are carried over, for comparison, to column II of table 53, where an estimate for 1946 is also included.[119]

---

curve of figure 8 reaches o: column *b* of table 51 becomes o. This implies that all corporations which survive their 85th year survive indefinitely thereafter. This conclusion is surely suspect; but, as the estimates of table 52 need not go back earlier than 1925 (because the relevant figures in column II of table 53, below, are not available before that date), the possible error in the extreme right-hand part of figure 8 may be ignored.

[118] *Survey of Current Business,* 1947 Supplement, p. 21 and p. 189, n. 2. Figures are available beginning with 1925. The *Survey* now publishes—see issue of May, 1950, p. 21, and current issues for more recent data—a monthly record of incorporations in 48 states, beginning with 1946 (47 states, for the last six months of 1945); but this more comprehensive series is unfortunately not available for comparisons over the years covered by table 52. Examination of the records for the three years, 1946–1948, for which both the 4-state and the 48-state series are available, shows, however, that the former is not an entirely consistent sample of the charters for the entire United States. Annual incorporations in the 4 states, expressed as a percentage of incorporations in the 48 states, were: 37.3 in 1946, 32.1 in 1947, and 32.2 in 1948. The corresponding percentages for the monthly figures show the following ranges from low to high: 32.9 to 42.4 in 1946, 28.7 to 35.2 in 1947, and 30.6 to 34.5 in 1948. For July to December, 1945, incorporations in the 4 states were 41.7 per cent of those in 47 states (with a range for the monthly figures from 39.1 to 43.3); and, as the missing state (Louisiana) seems unlikely to account for a substantial number of charters, the 4-state percentage of the 48-state total in this period must have been well above the 1946 figure of 37.3, though, of course, somewhat below 41.7. Some chance exists, therefore, that the estimate in table 53 of total incorporations for the years 1925–1945—based upon application of the 1946 ratio of 0.373 to the annual figures for the 4 states—may be in error, and that the error tends to be an overstatement. Such overstatement may be exceptionally large in the 1925–1929 period of financial boom, because incorporations in such states as Delaware and New York may have been a more significant fraction of the total in those years than in certain later years, especially 1945 and 1946.

We may remark also that even the comprehensive (48-state) figures on incorporations may not be strictly comparable with figures derived from *S. of I.* tabulations. Under the Internal Revenue Code, certain classes of corporations are not required to file returns, whereas the incorporation figures for some states may include some of these corporations. For example, Delaware incorporations apparently include nonprofit corporations. Discrepancies on this account are, however, not likely to be seriously large.

[119] This last estimate rests on an assumption, in line with the text above (p. 143), that the 72,463 corporations chartered in 1946 which were active in 1946 constituted 46 per cent of the total chartered in that year. Actually, 46 per cent is probably too low for 1946: actual incorporations were much heavier early than late in 1946 (the part, of the year's total, incorporated in the first six months was 57 per cent for the 4 states, 54 per cent for the 48 states), and the percentage which became active before the end of the year was probably greater than the 46 assumed for a "normal" year in

The figures in column III of table 53 indicate, for all periods before 1946, an important apparent deficiency in the estimates of table 52 (column II of table 53), and the deficiency increases steadily as the period becomes more remote from 1946. One might at once infer that the survival percentages in column I of table 52 must be too high, and that the degree of their overstatement increases as the period becomes more remote from 1946. In order, for example, for the column III estimate in table 52 for the period 1925–1929 to coincide with the table 53 estimate of 506,200 reported incorporations in that period, the survival ratio for 1925–1929 would need to be 9.74 instead of 32.71 per cent.[120] Such a change in the survival ratio, from 0.3271 to 0.0974, would imply that the figures for lines 17 to 21 of column *d* of table 51 are far too high. But these figures are the cumulative products, from line 1, of the current survival rates in column *c;* and therefore all or many of those rates must be far too high. This implies that all or many of the current death rates of column *b,* for lines 1 to 21, are far too low.

This last conclusion seems inescapable, unless we are to accept the highly improbable conclusion that the estimate of total incorporations in 1925–1929 at 506.2 thousand is very greatly overstated. A corresponding conclusion appears similarly inescapable for the more recent periods, such as 1930–1934, 1935–1939, and so on; although, as the period becomes less remote from 1946, the deficiency of column II below column I of table 53 becomes relatively smaller. Even as recently as 1945 that deficiency is so great that explaining it fully by assuming an overstatement in the estimate (column I of table 53) of incorporations is highly improbable. In other words, our provisional estimates in column II are almost

---

which incorporations were at a steady rate through the year. Such higher percentage would reduce the estimate for 1946 below the 157,500 shown in table 53, column II—perhaps to a figure close to the 133,000 of reported incorporations (this would require the percentage becoming active within the year to be 54).

[120] This assumes that the 49,318 survivals in 1946 of corporations chartered in 1925–1929, as shown in column II of table 52, is correct. Strong presumption exists that it cannot be seriously in error. The only element of estimate introduced by this analysis into that figure is through the allocation of 1,295 Not-stated cases to the 1925–1929 period (column II of table 45). Although that allocation may be somewhat in error, the maximum error cannot exceed a very small percentage of 49,318. The only other possible sources of error are: failure of various active corporations chartered in 1925–1929 to file returns in 1946, inaccuracies in the returns filed (specifically, in the stating of date of incorporation), and inaccuracies in the *S. of I.* tabulations from such returns. Errors due to the first and second causes are almost certainly not large, and the third type is either nonexistent or negligible. I conclude that the figure of 49,318 survivals must be very close to exact.

certainly too low, and their degree of understatement appears to increase as the period becomes more remote from 1946. This understatement presumably implies that the current death rates at various ages, assumed in table 51 for corporations born in *any* year, are seriously understated for corporations born in the earlier years. This means that the fundamental assumption made provisionally above (p. 148) is seriously in error: one cannot validly assume that

TABLE 53

PROVISIONAL ESTIMATES OF TOTAL NUMBER OF CORPORATE CHARTERS ISSUED IN SPECIFIED PERIODS, BASED UPON INCORPORATIONS IN FOUR STATES AND UPON ANALYSIS IN TABLE 52, IN THOUSANDS*

Period of incorporation	From incorporation data	By analysis of 1946 survivors	Per cent ratio II/I
	(I)	(II)	(III)
1946	133.0	157.5a	118
1945	65.4	42.7	65
1944	39.1	24.4	62
1943	32.3	18.6	58
1942	32.6	17.8	55
1941	51.1	25.4	50
1940	59.2	28.5	48
1935–1939	333.3	148.0	44
1930–1934	440.5	162.3	37
1925–1929	506.2	150.8	30

* Column I derived from *Survey of Current Business* data on incorporations, as explained in text.
Column II from column IV of table 52, except that item *a* is 1946 item of column III of table 45 divided by 0.46.

the current death rates at various ages, derived for deaths in 1946 from figure 8, can be applied to deaths in earlier years.

31. *Revised estimates of births during specified periods.*—A revision of the provisional fundamental assumption of section 30 will now be attempted, and the estimates in column III of table 52 will be revised accordingly. One may properly suggest that, for deaths in various years between 1924 and 1946, the curve of figure 8 should be shifted upward and perhaps inclined more sharply downward to the right, in order to reflect greater general risk of death in such years than in 1946. Although risk of death in 1946 may have been influenced by various abnormal factors peculiar to that year, 1946 was certainly not a year of depression; and the death rates in 1946 were accordingly not raised above normal by the acute adversities ordinarily affecting corporate survival in a period of severe depression. On the contrary, 1946 was, by most previous standards, a

year of high prosperity; and the 1946 death rates (at various ages) were therefore probably below normal. On the other hand, in various preceding years since 1924, severe depression was a major, and perhaps the all-dominant, factor affecting chances of corporate death; and we may take it for granted that, in such depressed years, the current death rate (for corporations of any particular age) was higher, and perhaps very much higher, than that shown by figure 8 for 1946.

No direct data on the comparative risks of death in a particular year—for example, a severely depressed year like 1932—and in 1946 are, to my knowledge, available. Any adjustment of the 1946 death rates of figure 8 to a basis appropriate for some other year of death must accordingly rely upon an assumption which, if it rests upon any evidence, must rest upon indirect evidence. I now make the following assumption: the risk of death varies from year to year in the same way and to the same degree as does the risk of loss.[121] We have already used, in chapter v, the concept of the risk of loss in a particular year, defined as the ratio of the number of corporations in the no-net category to the total number (net and no-net categories combined) of active corporations. The present assumption is that year-to-year variations in that ratio are identical, on a relative basis, with year-to-year variations in the current death rate.

Table 54 derives, in column III, the loss ratio for each year 1925–1946; and column IV shows these ratios relative to the 1946 ratio as unity. One might not be surprised to find the loss ratio of 1932 more than three times as great as that of 1946, but to find the 1946 ratio lower than that in any of the other 21 years is perhaps unexpected. Even in the boom years 1928 and 1929, risk of showing a loss was much greater than in 1946. The assumption is now being made that the figures in column IV are also valid as comparisons of the risk of death in the various years 1925–1945 with that in 1946, not only for deaths in general within the corporate system, but also for deaths of corporations of any particular age. For example, in considering deaths in 1932, the current death rates for 1946 read

---

[121] Until far more extensive data than any now published in *S. of I.*, or in any other source known to me, become available, this assumption cannot be tested by any analysis of statistical evidence bearing directly upon the implied correlation between risk of loss and risk of death. The assumption in fact implies that risk of loss and risk of death are perfectly correlated: a change (presumably percentage change) in the risk of loss between one year and another is accompanied by an equal change in the risk of death. But a remarkably revealing *indirect* test, more or less convincing, arises as a by-product of the revision of our estimates of table 52 in the light of the assumption, as will be seen in the text below.

TABLE 54

CALCULATION OF RISK OF LOSS IN EACH YEAR 1925–1946, AS A
RELATIVE TO THE 1946 RISK AS ONE*

Year	Number of active returns	Number showing loss	Loss ratio II/I	Loss ratio relative to 1946
	(I)	(II)	(III)	(IV)
1925	387,065	134,731	0.3481	1.297
1926	409,788	151,654	.3701	1.379
1927	425,675	165,826	.3896	1.452
1928	443,611	174,828	.3941	1.468
1929	456,021	186,591	.4092	1.525
1930	463,036	241,616	.5218	1.944
1931	459,704	283,806	.6174	2.300
1932	451,884	369,238	.8171	3.044
1933	446,842	337,056	.7543	2.810
1934	469,804	324,703	.6911	2.575
1935	477,113	312,882	.6558	2.443
1936	478,857	275,696	.5757	2.145
1937	477,838	285,810	.5981	2.228
1938	471,032	301,148	.6393	2.382
1939	469,617	270,138	.5752	2.143
1940	473,042	252,065	.5329	1.985
1941	468,906	204,278	.4356	1.623
1942	442,665	172,723	.3902	1.454
1943	420,521	136,786	.3253	1.212
1944	412,467	123,563	.2996	1.116
1945	421,125	118,106	.2805	1.045
1946	491,152	131,842	0.2684	1.000

* Figures in columns I and II from *1946 S. of I.*, pp. 352–353; except that 1925 and 1926 figures are obtained by assuming that 10 per cent of all returns in each year were inactive—43,007 in 1925, 45,532 in 1926. Column IV is III divided by 0.2684.

from figure 8 for corporations of each age are multiplied by 3.044 to yield the assumed schedule of current death rates for 1932. This amounts, of course, to shifting the curve of figure 8 upward—with the same relative, not absolute, shift at all points—in order to yield the rates for 1932.

The application of such adjustments, for corporations born in any particular year, requires multiplying the various current death rates of 1946 (column *b* of table 51) by a succession of factors from column IV of table 54. Thus, in 1926, 1925-chartered corporations were in their first year after the birth year, and the relevant 1946

TABLE 55

CALCULATIONS, FOR CORPORATIONS CHARTERED IN 1925, OF THE ADJUSTED CURRENT
DEATH RATE, AND THE PERCENTAGE SURVIVING FROM THE GROUP ORIGINALLY
CHARTERED IN EACH YEAR TO 1946*

Year	Basic death rate	Relative loss ratio	Adjusted death rate	Current survival rate	Per cent of original group surviving
	(I)	(II)	(III)	(IV)	(V)
1926	6.44	1.379	08.88	91.12	91.12
1927	9.88	1.452	14.35	85.65	78.04
1928	9.12	1.468	13.39	86.61	67.59
1929	8.00	1.525	12.20	87.80	59.35
1930	7.02	1.944	13.65	86.35	51.25
1931	6.35	2.300	14.61	85.39	43.76
1932	5.90	3.044	17.96	82.04	35.90
1933	5.60	2.810	15.74	84.26	30.25
1934	5.34	2.575	13.75	86.25	26.09
1935	5.12	2.443	12.51	87.49	22.83
1936	4.94	2.145	10.60	89.40	20.41
1937	4.78	2.228	10.65	89.35	18.23
1938	4.63	2.382	11.03	88.97	16.22
1939	4.50	2.143	09.64	90.36	14.66
1940	4.38	1.985	08.69	91.31	13.38
1941	4.27	1.623	6.93	93.07	12.46
1942	4.17	1.454	6.06	93.94	11.70
1943	4.07	1.212	4.93	95.07	11.13
1944	3.98	1.116	4.44	95.56	10.63
1945	3.89	1.045	4.07	95.93	10.20
1946	3.80	1.000	3.80	96.20	09.81

* See accompanying text for explanation of items.

rate from table 51 is 6.44 per cent; this is multiplied by 1.379, the 1926 relative loss ratio of table 54, to yield 8.88 as the current death rate for these 1925-chartered corporations in 1926. Similarly, in 1932 those 1925-chartered corporations were in their seventh year after the birth year, and the relevant 1946 rate is 5.90 per cent; this is multiplied by 3.044, to yield 17.96 as the current death rate in 1932. The full schedule of such adjustments, for corporations chartered in 1925, appears in the first three columns of table 55. Column I shows, as the basic 1946 current death rates derived from figure 8, the evidence given in column *b* of table 51. Column II repeats the ratios of column IV of table 54. Column III gives the adjusted death rates—adjusted by allowing for differences in risk of death as compared with 1946—and is obtained by multiplying column I by column II.

Noticeable differences appear between the basic rates and the adjusted rates—the difference is, of course, greatest for 1932; and, except for a small rise reflecting the business recession of 1937–1938, it declines steadily after 1932 and becomes zero for 1946. The basic rates were used in the analysis of section 30; and, as the adjusted rates are now to be used in working out an estimate of births, we may expect that the results in this section will differ greatly from those of section 30.[122]

Columns IV and V of table 55 correspond, on the basis of these adjusted current death rates, to columns *c* and *d* of table 51. The final figure in column V, 9.81, is to be compared with the final 30.16 in table 51. Of all corporations chartered in 1925, table 55 estimates that 9.81 per cent survived as active in 1946; whereas table 51, resting upon the erroneous provisional assumption of section 30, estimates the per cent surviving in 1946 as 30.16.

Results, corresponding to column V of table 55, for corporations chartered in 1930—the age group of corporations which felt the heaviest impact of the great depression—are as follows:

1931........85.19		1939........16.78	
1932........59.57		1940........15.08	
1933........44.30		1941........13.87	
1934........35.17		1942........12.90	
1935........29.14		1943........12.18	
1936........25.18		1944........11.57	
1937........21.86		1945........11.04	
1938........18.95		1946........10.57	

Of the corporations chartered in 1930, more than 55 per cent had disappeared from the active list in the third year (1933) following

---

[122] Had a table like table 55 been shown for corporations chartered in 1930, the adjusted current death rate in 1932 would appear as 30.07. This means that, of the 1930 corporations which survived as active in 1931 (the year preceding 1932), more than 30 per cent died (disappeared from the active list) in 1932. Corporations chartered in the first full year of the decline into depression were particularly vulnerable to death in the worst year of the depression. No other adjusted death rate, among those calculated for various years of death for corporations chartered in the various years 1925–1945, was as high as 30 per cent.

TABLE 56

ESTIMATED NUMBER OF CHARTERS ISSUED IN SPECIFIED YEARS, BASED UPON SURVIVALS
IN 1946, AND UPON INCORPORATIONS REPORTED FOR FOUR STATES*

	Per cent surviving in 1946, of corporations chartered in specified		Number surviving in 1946	Estimated number of charters in period (thousands)	Estimated charters from reports of four states (thousands)
	Years	Five-year periods			
	(I)	(II)	(III)	(IV)	(V)
1945......	93.56	.....	39,950	42.7	65.4
1944......	84.05	.....	20,561	24.5	39.1
1943......	75.64	.....	14,266	18.9	32.3
1942......	68.27	.....	12,528	18.4	32.6
1941......	61.07	.....	16,639	27.2	51.1
1940......	53.90	.....	17,519	32.5	59.2
1939......	46.44	.....	.....	.....	.....
1938......	32.63	.....	.....	.....	.....
1937......	32.82	32.30	76,812	237.8	333.3
1936......	27.80	.....	.....	.....	.....
1935......	24.27	.....	.....	.....	.....
1934......	21.04	.....	......	.....	.....
1933......	17.89	.....	......	.....	.....
1932......	14.94	14.96	65,730	439.4	440.5
1931......	12.22	.....	......	.....	.....
1930......	10.57	.....	......	.....	.....
1929......	9.94	.....	......	.....	.....
1928......	9.86	.....	......	.....	.....
1927......	9.94	9.89	49,318	498.7	506.2
1926......	9.91	.....	......	.....	.....
1925......	9.81	.....	......	.....	.....

* See accompanying text for explanation of items.

birth; whereas, of those chartered in 1925, less than 33 per cent had ceased to be active by the third year (1928) following birth. By the sixth year after birth, more than 74 per cent of the 1930 corporations had become inactive, and less than 57 per cent of the 1925 corporations. These and similar comparisons show in a striking way that the fraction surviving a specified number of years after birth is decisively influenced by the succession of experiences—including especially those reflecting cyclical variations in general economic conditions—through which such corporations live from birth forward until they die or succeed in surviving for the specified number of years.

Results corresponding to column V of table 55 have been calculated for corporations born in each year 1925–1945 and are shown (to the nearest whole per cent) in full in table B of the Appendix; but discussion of the comparisons, among the survival percentages for various years of incorporation, along lines indicated above for the comparison between 1930 and 1925, is not here undertaken. Our immediate concern is solely with the final figure (for survivals in 1946) of each such schedule of survival percentages—figures corresponding to 9.81 for 1925 corporations and 10.57 for 1930 corporations. Such results appear in column I of table 56; and, for the three five-year periods, the annual figures of column I have been replaced in column II by their weighted averages.[123] Column III is identical with column II of table 52, column IV is the ratio of III to I (or II), and column V is identical with column I of table 53.

The figures in column IV are the revised estimates of births in the various periods and replace the estimates, derived on the basis of the erroneous provisional assumption, in column III of table 52. Comparison of column IV with column V for 1925–1929 and 1930–1934 shows an astonishing approach to identity. For those two periods, estimate of births by applying survival percentages based on our new assumption to the reported survivals in 1946 yields results astonishingly close to the incorporation figures estimated from reports of actual incorporations in the four states—Delaware, Illinois, Maine, and New York. This close similarity might be taken as weighty evidence that the new assumption, concerning the variation of risk of death with cyclical variations in general economic conditions, is probably valid, at least to a high degree of approximation.

The evidence is, however, not so favorable for the more recent periods; for the percentage ratio of column IV to column V in the successive periods from 1935–1939 to 1945 runs: 71, 55, 53, 56, 58, 63, and 65. These percentages imply a very substantial deficiency in coverage for our present estimates in all periods since 1934, with

[123] The weights used are the annual averages of monthly figures of incorporations reported in four states, as published in *Survey of Current Business* (see n. 118). These annual incorporation figures are:

1925–1929	1930–1934	1935–1939
2,978	2,977	2,240
3,004	2,970	2,259
3,099	2,860	2,108
3,300	2,658	1,871
3,341	2,214	1,874

the greatest deficiency appearing for 1941.[124] Why are the estimates
of column IV understated in these periods since 1934? My belief
is that the understatement results primarily from failure of the
present assumption—that risk of death is exactly correlated with
risk of loss—to account for changes in death rates during the war
years. During those years, many withdrawals of enterprises from
active operation occurred for reasons other than those reflecting
merely the impact of economic conditions upon earning power and
hence upon risk of loss. Such reasons included: limited availability
of manpower, shortages of materials for inventory and for new construction or replacement, obstacles to financing, extraordinary burdens of complying with governmental regulations, restrictions upon
marketing, and other similar factors affecting business operations,
and in addition, a tax burden which may in some cases have damaged incentives so severely as to lead to outright abandonment of
enterprise activity.[125] My belief is, therefore, that the adjusted current death rates in the years 1942–1944 and perhaps 1945 should
be higher than those obtained by applying the relative loss ratios
of column IV of table 54 to the basic death rates of figure 8. If a
further adjustment of the current death rates in those years could
be applied, to allow for the peculiar "noncyclical" adverse factors
influencing corporate survival which are listed above, such rates
would be substantially higher than those for 1942–1944 and perhaps 1945 used in analyses such as that of table 55. This would, of
course, reduce the final survival percentage—9.81 for 1946—of the
1925-chartered corporations and reduce corresponding figures for
corporations chartered in succeeding years. But, for corporations
chartered before 1941 or perhaps 1940, the final survival percentage
would be less affected by this new change in assumed death rates
than it would be for corporations chartered in 1941 and the immediately following years. For example, corporations chartered in
1925–1929 would have a survival experience which was dominated
by the great depression and only moderately affected by the peculiar
adversities of the war years. For corporations chartered in 1941, on
the contrary, survival to 1946 would be under the dominant in-
fluence of those peculiar adversities.

---

[124] This statement assumes that the estimates of reported incorporations in column
V are correct. As those estimates rest upon the actual data for only four states, some
error may in fact appear in any of the figures of column V; but such errors are unlikely
to account for all or even a major part of the deficiencies noted above.

[125] The tax burdens on corporations may also have led certain corporations to give
up their charters and assume an unincorporated form. Such transfers of form would
appear as deaths in our record.

Such further adjustment of the current death rates, if it were possible in numerical terms, might accordingly reduce all of the survival percentages shown in column I of table 56, but such reduction would probably be greatest in relative (percentage of the present figure) terms for a period close to the beginning of the war, such as 1941. The corresponding effect on the estimates of column IV would be a reduction—perhaps a very large reduction—in the apparent understatement for the periods since 1934, whereas the figures for 1925–1929 and 1930–1934 would become moderately overstated.[128] Viewing the record as a whole since 1924, we should then find fairly close similarity between column IV and column V; and this outcome would be strong evidence that the basic assumption of this section, after appropriate allowance for the peculiar adversities of the war years, is valid to a fairly high degree of approximation.

If that assumption were tempered by allowing for the probability that the correlation between risk of death and risk of loss is not exact but is subject to various deviations, the estimates might be further improved. Account needs also to be taken of the undoubted fact that the persons responsible for deciding whether a corporation shall remain active consider—together with other factors bearing upon their decision—not only the current risk of loss, but also anticipations of losses in the more or less immediate future as well as the experience as to losses in the more or less recent years. The relevant loss ratio, in estimating the risk of death in a particular year, is therefore not the loss ratio in that year, as implied by the assumption herein, but some sort of average of the actual and anticipated loss ratios over several years centering in that year. Moreover, not only in the war years, but in various other years certain peculiar adversities, not related to mere cyclical fluctuations in the risk of loss, may have raised the risk of death; and, of course, in some years certain peculiarly favorable noncyclical factors may have lowered the risk of death. Available data afford, so far as I am aware, no basis for making numerical allowances on these several counts, or even for making such allowances for the peculiar adversities of the war years. Conceivably, new data may come to hand which would fill or partly fill some of these gaps; but such data are more likely to be supplied with reference to adjustments which can be applied

[128] The various schedules of survival percentages in table B of the Appendix would be altered. Figures there shown would remain unchanged for years of death 1926–1941, but would be reduced, in successively increasing degree, in the following years.

to death rates in years after 1946 than with reference to the historical period here under study. In particular, further tabulations by *Statistics of Income* of date-of-incorporation figures for years after 1946, particularly if such tabulations were elaborated somewhat beyond the form used for 1945 and 1946, might add greatly to our knowledge of corporate vital statistics and might in particular permit further testing of the assumptions and conclusions here set forth.

I leave the estimates as they stand in table 56. Those estimates are manifestly defective, especially for the years since 1934, but they are sufficiently close to the indicated actual incorporations to justify the conclusion that the assumptions on which they rest are approximately valid.[127] As indicated early in section 30, the analysis here presented is offered partly because it yields results which have great significance, but primarily because it outlines a method of analysis which may be useful in further investigations. The discussion and results of sections 30 and 31 seem to establish that such a method of analysis is correct in principle and that the assumptions on which it rests are valid to a fairly high degree.

---

[127] The process of estimating could, of course, be carried back to years before 1925; but such results are not here reported. With such results, one might then, by obvious operations, attempt to reproduce—by combining estimated survivals in any year from the corporations chartered in all the preceding years or other periods—the "population" figures of table 48.

APPENDIX

TABLE A

CLASSIFICATION, BY LINE OF INDUSTRY, OF ACTIVE CORPORATION RETURNS FOR 1946, WITH DATA ON NUMBER OF RETURNS, TOTAL COMPILED RECEIPTS, AND TOTAL ASSETS*

Class title†	Number of active returns	Total compiled receipts	Total assets	Rank in terms of: Receipts	Rank in terms of: Assets
1 (1) All divisions combined (A)	491,152	288,954	454,705	..	..
A. The 9 divisions					
2 (2) Mining and quarrying (B)........	7,675	4,300	5,949	7	5
20 (9) Manufacturing (F).............	98,131	139,422	96,300	1	2
158 (33) Public utilities (Z).............	21,823	22,926	63,812	3	3
182 (37) Trade (DD)....................	151,511	96,734	31,958	2	4
214 (56) Service (JJ)...................	39,648	7,374	5,869	5	6
233 (66) Finance, etc. (NN)..........	144,373	12,392	246,364	4	1
275 (81) Construction (WW)..........	15,849	4,321	2,497	6	7
279 (82) Agriculture, etc. (XX)..........	6,663	1,275	1,583	8	8
283 (86) Not allocable.................	5,479	213	373	9	9
B. Mining and quarrying groups					
3 (3) Metal mining (C).............	857	673	1,535	3	2
10 (4) Anthracite mining.............	177	459	390	5	5
11 (5) Bituminous coal, etc.............	1,640	1,628	1,368	1	3
12 (6) Crude petroleum, etc. (D)........	3,413	1,048	2,045	2	1
15 (7) Nonmetallic mining, etc. (E)......	1,364	478	574	4	4
19 (8) Not allocable.................	224	15	36	6	6
C. Metal mining subgroups					
4 Iron.........................	69	185	......	1	..
5 Copper.......................	47	175	......	2	..
6 Lead and zinc....................	147	144	......	3	..
7 Gold and silver.................	350	45	......	6	..
8 Other metal mining.............	89	54	......	5	..
9 Not allocable...................	155	70	......	4	..
D. Crude petroleum, etc., subgroups					
13 Crude petroleum, natural gas, and natural gasoline production.....	2,873	787	......	1	..
14 Field service operations.........	540	260	......	2	..
E. Nonmetallic mining, etc., subgroups					
16 Stone, sand, and gravel..........	1,082	317	......	1	..
17 Other nonmetallic mining and quarrying...................	275	161	......	2	..
18 Not allocable.................	7	0	......	3	..

* Data compiled from *1946 S. of I.*, pp. 94–103 for number of returns and total compiled receipts, pp. 146–178 for total assets. Money figures stated in millions of dollars.
† Titles of classes, and the first serial numbers preceding the titles, are those given in *1946 S. of I.*, pp. 94–102. The second serial numbers (in parentheses) are those for the somewhat coarser classification shown in *1946 S. of I.*, pp. 18–25. Only for classes so numbered are total-assets figures available, and only for such classes are date-of-incorporation statistics (examined in chap. iv) available. The capital letters (in parentheses) succeeding the titles of certain classes refer to the sections of this table in which such classes are broken down into narrower classes.

TABLE A—*Continued*

Class title†	Number of active returns	Total compiled receipts	Total assets	Rank in terms of: Receipts	Rank in terms of: Assets
F. Manufacturing groups					
21 (10) Food and kindred products (G)....	9,842	23,404	8,653	1	4
32 (11) Beverages (H)................	2,864	4,837	2,577	11	13
38 (12) Tobacco manufactures..........	216	2,625	1,963	21	16
39 (13) Cotton manufactures...........	947	3,820	1,956	14	17
40 (14) Textile mill products, except cotton (I).....................	4,595	6,440	3,735	8	8
49 (15) Apparel, etc. (J)...............	11,714	6,694	2,185	6	15
56 (16) Leather and products (K)........	2,825	2,834	1,200	19	23
61 (17) Rubber products (L)...........	561	3,133	1,723	15	19
64 (18) Lumber and timber basic products (M).........................	3,010	2,097	1,698	22	20
67 (19) Furniture, etc. (N).............	5,173	2,770	1,482	20	21
74 (20) Paper and allied products (O).....	2,361	4,381	3,264	12	10
78 (21) Printing, etc. (P)...............	10,996	4,847	3,577	10	9
85 (22) Chemicals and allied products (Q).	6,837	10,830	8,673	3	3
96 (23) Petroleum and coal products (R)..	485	10,820	12,787	4	1
100 (24) Stone, etc. (S).................	3,627	2,950	2,386	16	14
109 (25) Iron, steel, and products (T)......	7,696	13,725	11,326	2	2
122 (26) Nonferrous metals, etc. (U).......	3,480	4,313	3,182	13	11
128 (27) Electrical machinery, etc. (V)....	2,549	5,517	4,668	9	7
135 (28) Machinery, etc. (W)............	7,511	9,149	7,933	5	5
145 (29) Automobiles, etc. (X)...........	900	6,581	5,269	7	6
149 (30) Transportation equipment, etc. (Y)	1,025	2,899	2,881	17	12
156 (31) Other manufacturing...........	5,523	2,897	1,842	18	18
157 (32) Not allocable..................	3,394	1,858	1,342	23	22
G. Food, etc., subgroups					
22 Bakery products................	1,494	2,008	......	5	..
23 Confectionery..................	603	986	......	7	..
24 Canning fruits, vegetables, and sea foods.......................	1,577	2,504	......	4	..
25 Meat products..................	1,016	7,062	......	1	..
26 Grain-mill products, except cereal preparations...................	1,099	3,624	......	2	..
27 Cereal preparations.............	36	489	......	10	..
28 Dairy products.................	1,734	3,343	......	3	..
29 Sugar........................	131	912	......	8	..
30 Other food, including ice and flavoring sirups..............	1,785	1,689	......	6	..
31 Not allocable..................	367	788	......	9	..
H. Beverages subgroups					
33 Malt liquors and malt...........	453	1,961	......	2	..
34 Distilled, rectified, and blended liquors....................	228	2,102	......	1	..

Class title†	Number of active returns	Total compiled receipts	Total assets	Rank in terms of:	
				Receipts	Assets
35 Wine........................	159	220	......	4	..
36 Non-alcoholic beverages..........	1,989	502	......	3	..
37 Not allocable..................	35	52	......	5	..
I. Textile-mill products, etc., subgroups					
41 Woolen and worsted manufactures, including dyeing and finishing...	614	1,696	......	1	..
42 Rayon and silk manufactures.....	508	951	......	3	..
43 Knit goods....................	1,706	1,533	......	2	..
44 Hats, except cloth and millinery...	203	236	......	8	..
45 Carpets and other floor coverings..	143	353	......	7	..
46 Dyeing and finishing textiles, except woolen and worsted.......	602	628	......	4	..
47 Other textile-mill products........	479	519	......	6	..
48 Not allocable..................	340	524	......	5	..
J. Apparel, etc., subgroups					
50 Men's clothing.................	2,324	2,192	......	2	..
51 Women's clothing..............	5,430	2,804	......	1	..
52 Fur garments and accessories.....	754	196	......	5	..
53 Millinery.....................	408	97	......	6	..
54 Other apparel and products made from fabrics..................	2,217	1,073	......	3	..
55 Not allocable..................	581	332	......	4	..
K. Leather and products subgroups					
57 Leather, tanned, curried, and finished.....................	394	710	......	2	..
58 Footwear, except rubber.........	1,325	1,678	......	1	..
59 Other leather products...........	1,058	420	......	3	..
60 Not allocable..................	48	25	......	4	..
L. Rubber products subgroups					
62 Tires and inner tubes............	49	2,543	......	1	..
63 Other rubber products, including rubberized fabrics and clothing..	512	590	......	2	..
M. Lumber, etc., subgroups					
65 Logging camps and sawmills......	2,131	1,523	......	1	..
66 Planing mills..................	879	574	......	2	..
N. Furniture, etc., subgroups					
68 Furniture (wood and metal)......	2,486	1,484	......	1	..
69 Partitions and fixtures...........	535	139	......	4	..
70 Wooden containers..............	529	317	......	3	..

Class title†		Number of active returns	Total compiled receipts	Total assets	Rank in terms of:	
					Receipts	Assets
71	Matches......................	18	91	......	5	..
72	Other finished lumber products, including cork products..........	1,424	656	......	2	..
73	Not allocable.................	181	83	......	6	..
	O. Paper, etc., subgroups					
75	Pulp, paper, and paperboard	438	2,423	......	1	..
76	Pulp goods and converted paper products...................	1,908	1,955	......	2	..
77	Not allocable.................	15	3	......	3	..
	P. Printing, etc., subgroups					
79	Newspapers...................	2,502	1,596	......	1	..
80	Periodicals...................	1,184	790	......	3	..
81	Books and music...............	889	453	......	4	..
82	Commercial printing............	3,242	1,220	......	2	..
83	Other printing and publishing.....	1,573	382	......	6	..
84	Not allocable.................	1,606	406	......	5	..
	Q. Chemicals, etc., subgroups					
86	Paints, varnishes, and colors......	896	1,208	......	3	..
87	Soap and glycerin..............	234	998	......	5	..
88	Drugs, toilet preparations, etc.....	2,364	1,661	......	2	..
89	Rayon (raw material) and allied products...................	7	237	......	9	..
90	Fertilizers....................	253	351	......	8	..
91	Oils, animal and vegetable, except lubricants and cooking oils......	261	1,062	......	4	..
92	Plastic materials...............	222	169	......	10	..
93	Industrial chemicals............	683	3,501	......	1	..
94	Other chemical products..........	1,257	649	......	7	..
95	Not allocable.................	660	992	......	6	..
	R. Petroleum, etc., subgroups					
97	Petroleum refining.............	291	10,237	......	1	..
98	Other petroleum and coal products	183	581	......	2	..
99	Not allocable.................	11	2	......	3	..
	S. Stone, etc., subgroups					
101	Cut-stone products.............	372	65	......	7	..
102	Structural clay products..........	697	353	......	4	..
103	Pottery and porcelain products....	262	235	......	6	..
104	Glass and glass products..........	542	883	......	1	..
105	Cement.......................	109	300	......	5	..
106	Concrete and gypsum products, wallboard....................	1,119	417	......	3	..

Class title†	Number of active returns	Total compiled receipts	Total assets	Rank in terms of: Receipts	Rank in terms of: Assets
107 Abrasives and asbestos products...	443	653	......	2	..
108 Not allocable..................	83	44	......	8	..
T. Iron, steel, etc., subgroups					
110 Blast furnaces and rolling mills....	135	5,739	......	1	..
111 Structural steel, fabricated; ornamental metal work...........	978	629	......	5	..
112 Tin cans and other tinware.......	80	551	......	7	..
113 Hand tools, cutlery, and hardware.	814	780	......	4	..
114 Heating apparatus, except electrical, and plumbers' supplies...	1,257	1,677	......	3	..
115 Firearms, guns, howitzers, mortars, and related equipment.....	23	31	......	9	..
116 Ammunition..................	17	121	......	8	..
117 Tanks........................	6	1	......	12	..
118 Sighting and fire-control equipment (except optical)..........	7	13	......	11	..
119 Ordnance and accessories, not elsewhere classified...........	14	25	......	10	..
120 Other iron, steel, and products (not classified below).............	3,948	3,584	......	2	..
121 Not allocable..................	417	574	......	6	..
U. Nonferrous metals, etc., subgroups					
123 Nonferrous metal basic products..	282	1,885	......	1	..
124 Clocks and watches.............	93	211	......	4	..
125 Jewelry (except costume), silverware, plated ware............	999	601	......	3	..
126 Other manufactures of nonferrous metals and their alloys........	2,086	1,596	......	2	..
127 Not allocable..................	20	19	......	5	..
V. Electrical machinery, etc., subgroups					
129 Electrical equipment for public utility, manufacturing, mining, transporation (except automobiles), and construction use.....	868	2,098	......	1	..
130 Automotive electrical equipment..	100	210	......	6	..
131 Communication equipment and phonographs................	665	1,945	......	2	..
132 Electrical appliances............	276	312	......	5	..
133 Other electrical machinery and equipment..................	409	361	......	4	..
134 Not allocable..................	231	591	......	3	..

Class title†	Number of active returns	Total compiled receipts	Total assets	Rank in terms of: Receipts	Rank in terms of: Assets
W. Machinery, etc., subgroups					
136 Special industry machinery.......	1,157	1,085	......	4	..
137 General industry machinery......	2,294	2,019	......	1	..
138 Metal-working machinery, including machine tools..............	1,907	1,313	......	3	..
139 Engines and turbines...........	91	296	......	9	..
140 Construction and mining machinery.....................	394	918	......	5	..
141 Agricultural machinery.........	374	1,338	......	2	..
142 Office and store machines........	231	683	......	7	..
143 Household and service-industry machines....................	463	664	......	8	..
144 Not allocable..................	600	834	......	6	..
X. Automobiles, etc., subgroups					
146 Automobiles and trucks (including bodies and industrial trailers)...	394	5,317	......	1	..
147 Automobile accessories, parts (except electrical), and passenger trailers....................	492	1,251	......	2	..
148 Not allocable.................	14	13	......	3	..
Y. Transportation equipment, etc., subgroups					
150 Railroad and railway equipment...	93	648	......	3	..
151 Aircraft and parts..............	274	1,173	......	1	..
152 Ship and boat building..........	593	1,012	......	2	..
153 Motorcycles and bicycles........	39	56	......	4	..
154 Other transportation equipment, except automobiles............	25	10	......	5	..
155 Not allocable..................	1	0	......	6	..
Z. Public utilities groups					
159 (34) Transportation (AA)............	15,142	14,378	33,576	1	1
171 (35) Communication (BB)............	3,761	3,160	9,391	3	3
176 (36) Other public utilities (CC)........	2,920	5,389	20,845	2	2
AA. Transportation subgroups					
160 Railroads, switching, terminal, and passenger car service companies.	635	8,576	......	1	..
161 Railway express companies.......	4	434	......	8	..
162 Railways, street, suburban, and interurban, including bus lines operated in conjunction therewith......................	121	613	......	5	..
163 Taxicab companies..............	930	209	......	9	..

Class title†	Number of active returns	Total compiled receipts	Total assets	Rank in terms of: Receipts	Rank in terms of: Assets
164 Other highway passenger transportation.	1,906	780	......	4	..
165 Highway freight transportation, warehousing, and storage.	7,628	1,577	......	2	..
166 Air transportation and allied services.	854	527	......	6	..
167 Pipe line transportation.	145	196	......	10	..
168 Water transportation.	1,308	956	......	3	..
169 Services incidental to transportation.	1,448	465	......	7	..
170 Not allocable.	163	45	......	11	..
BB. Communication subgroups					
172 Telephone (wire and radio).	2,868	2,582	......	1	..
173 Telegraph (wire and radio) and cable.	19	226	......	3	..
174 Radio broadcasting and television.	860	351	......	2	..
175 Other communication.	14	1	......	4	..
CC. Other public utilities subgroups					
177 Electric light and power.	700	4,159	......	1	..
178 Gas, distribution and manufacture	577	1,087	......	2	..
179 Water.	1,408	104	......	3	..
180 Public utilities not elsewhere classified.	182	34	......	4	..
181 Not allocable.	53	4	......	5	..
DD. Trade groups					
183 (38) Wholesale (EE).	47,657	47,573	13,878	1	2
194 (41) Retail (GG).	84,758	41,072	15,050	2	1
213 (55) Not allocable.	19,096	8,088	3,029	3	3
EE. Wholesale subgroups					
184 (39) Commission merchants.	6,800	2,463	1,088	2	2
185 (40) Other wholesalers (FF).	40,857	45,111	12,791	1	1
FF. Other wholesalers sub-subgroups					
186 Food, including market milk dealers.	6,968	9,972	......	2	..
187 Alcoholic beverages.	1,604	3,800	......	4	..
188 Apparel and dry goods.	4,982	3,970	......	3	..
189 Chemicals, paints, and drugs.	1,912	2,300	......	7	..
190 Hardware, electrical goods, plumbing and heating equipment.	3,678	3,723	......	5	..
191 Lumber and millwork.	1,247	943	......	8	..

Class, title†	Number of active returns	Total compiled receipts	Total assets	Rank in terms of: Receipts	Rank in terms of: Assets

	Class, title†	Number of active returns	Total compiled receipts	Total assets	Receipts	Assets
192	Wholesalers not elsewhere classified....................	17,952	17,652	......	1	..
193	Not allocable..................	2,514	2,750	......	6	..
	GG. Retail subgroups					
195 (42)	General merchandise (HH).......	5,894	12,627	5,553	1	1
199 (43)	Food stores, including market milk dealers..................	6,459	8,131	1,742	2	3
200 (44)	Package liquor stores...........	2,037	299	83	13	13
201 (45)	Drug stores....................	4,248	1,220	400	10	10
202 (46)	Apparel and accessories.........	12,058	4,676	1,788	3	2
203 (47)	Furniture and house furnishings...	6,398	1,656	902	8	6
204 (48)	Eating and drinking places.......	11,334	1,762	528	7	9
205 (49)	Automotive dealers (II)..........	11,875	4,440	1,380	4	4
208 (50)	Filling stations..................	1,866	371	154	11	12
209 (51)	Hardware......................	2,452	344	158	12	11
210 (52)	Building materials, fuel, and ice...	7,678	2,059	933	6	5
211 (53)	Other retail trade...............	8,193	2,081	890	5	7
212 (54)	Not allocable..................	4,266	1,407	538	9	8
	HH. General merchandise sub-subgroups					
196	Department, dry goods, other general merchandise...........	5,264	10,526	......	1	..
197	Limited-price variety stores.......	357	1,797	......	2	..
198	Mail-order houses..............	273	304	......	3	..
	II. Automotive dealers sub-subgroups					
206	Automobiles and trucks..........	10,276	3,950	......	1	..
207	Accessories, parts, etc...........	1,599	490	......	2	..
	JJ. Service groups					
215 (57)	Hotels and other lodging places....	4,805	1,339	1,590	3	2
216 (58)	Personal service (KK)..........	8,868	1,164	589	4	4
221 (59)	Business service (LL)...........	7,476	1,448	805	2	3
225 (60)	Automotive repair services and garages.....................	3,109	266	171	7	7
226 (61)	Miscellaneous repair services, hand trades..................	1,697	131	61	8	8
227 (62)	Motion pictures (MM)..........	4,278	1,949	1,854	1	1
230 (63)	Amusement, except motion pictures.....................	4,578	600	448	5	5
231 (64)	Other service, including schools....	4,543	450	320	6	6
232 (65)	Not allocable..................	294	26	31	9	9

Class title†	Number of active returns	Total compiled receipts	Total assets	Rank in terms of: Receipts	Rank in terms of: Assets

KK. Personal service subgroups

217	Laundries, cleaners, and dyers.....	4,758	880	......	1	..
218	Photographic studios............	956	78	......	3	..
219	Other personal service...........	3,139	205	......	2	..
220	Not allocable..................	15	2	......	4	..

LL. Business service subgroups

222	Advertising....................	2,029	866	......	1	..
223	Other business service...........	5,432	578	......	2	..
224	Not allocable..................	15	4	......	3	..

MM. Motion pictures subgroups

228	Motion-picture production.......	718	978	......	1	..
229	Motion-picture theaters..........	3,560	972	......	2	..

NN. Finance, etc., groups

234 (67)	Finance (OO)..................	34,975	4,944	170,439	1	1
254 (76)	Insurance carriers, agents, etc. (SS)	7,970	4,397	57,007	2	2
260 (79)	Real estate, including lessors of buildings (UU)...............	95,291	2,776	14,202	3	3
268 (80)	Lessors of real property, except buildings (VV)...............	6,137	273	4,716	4	4

OO. Finance subgroups

235 (68)	Banks and trust companies.......	14,911	3,247	152,220	1	1
236 (69)	Long-term credit agencies, mortgage companies, except banks...	2,738	43	381	8	7
237 (70)	Short-term credit agencies, except banks (PP)..................	3,859	348	2,713	4	4
242 (71)	Investment trusts and investment companies (QQ)...............	3,700	379	4,531	3	3
248 (72)	Other investment companies, including holding companies (RR)	1,947	562	7,477	2	2
251 (73)	Security and commodity-exchange brokers and dealers............	1,332	210	1,833	5	5
252 (74)	Other finance companies.........	1,349	88	241	6	8
253 (75)	Not allocable..................	5,139	68	1,042	7	6

PP. Short-term credit agencies, etc., sub-subgroups

238	Sales finance and industrial credit.	1,575	176	......	1	..
239	Personal credit..................	1,701	151	......	2	..
240	Other short-term credit agencies...	160	3	......	4	..
241	Not allocable..................	423	18	......	3	..

Class title†	Number of active returns	Total compiled receipts	Total assets	Rank in terms of:	
				Receipts	Assets
QQ. Investment trusts, etc., sub-subgroups					
243 Management type...............	535	225	......	1	..
244 Fixed or semifixed type.........	94	14	......	4	..
245 Installment investment plans and guaranteed face-amount certificates......................	87	25	......	3	..
246 Mineral, oil, and gas royalty companies......................	184	6	......	5	..
247 Not allocable..................	2,800	110	......	2	..
RR. Other investment companies, etc., sub-subgroups					
249 Holding companies..............	865	269	......	2	..
250 Operating-holding companies.....	1,082	293	......	1	..
SS. Insurance carriers, etc., subgroups					
255 (77) Insurance carriers (TT)..........	2,126	4,072	56,485	1	1
259 (78) Insurance agents, brokers, etc.....	5,844	325	523	2	2
TT. Insurance carriers sub-subgroups					
256 Life insurance companies........	777	1,457	......	2	..
257 Mutual insurance, except life or marine or fire insurance companies issuing perpetual policies.	515	34	......	3	..
258 Other insurance carriers.........	834	2,581	......	1	..
UU. Real estate, etc., subgroups					
261 Owner operators and lessors of buildings....................	76,201	2,246	......	1	..
262 Lessee operators of buildings......	2,520	86	......	4	..
263 Owners for improvement........	5,981	133	......	3	..
264 Trading for own account........	2,679	39	......	7	..
265 Real estate agents, brokers, etc....	3,342	140	......	2	..
266 Title abstract companies	1,239	61	......	6	..
267 Not allocable..................	3,329	72	......	5	..
VV. Lessors of real property, etc., subgroups					
269 Agricultural, forest, etc., properties	1,019	16	......	4	..
270 Mining, oil, etc., properties.......	2,638	98	......	2	..
271 Railroad properties..............	356	119	......	1	..
272 Public-utility properties..........	164	25	......	3	..
273 Other real property, except buildings........................	1,687	9	......	5	..
274 Not allocable..................	273	6	......	6	..

TABLE A—*Concluded*

Class title†	Number of active returns	Total compiled receipts	Total assets	Rank in terms of:	
				Receipts	Assets
WW. Construction groups					
276 General contractors.............	7,303	2,751	......	I	..
277 Special trade contractors.........	8,168	1,532	.....	2	..
278 Not allocable..................	378	37	......	3	..
XX. Agriculture, etc., groups					
280 (83) Agriculture and services..........	6,041	1,207	1,445	I	I
281 (84) Forestry......................	321	31	107	3	2
282 (85) Fishery......................	301	36	31	2	3

TABLE B

Estimated Percentage, of the Corporations Born (in the Legal Sense: Chartered) in Each Year 1925–1945, Which Survived as Active in Each Year 1926–1946*

(Derived as Explained in Section 31)

	1925	1926	1927	1928	1929	1930	1931	1932	1933	1934	1935	1936	1937	1938	1939	1940	1941	1942	1943	1944	1945
1926	91	91																			
1927	78	78	91																		
1928	68	67	77	90																	
1929	59	56	63	73	87																
1930	51	47	52	58	68	85															
1931	44	38	41	44	49	60	80														
1932	36	32	33	35	38	44	58	82													
1933	30	27	28	29	31	35	44	61	83												
1934	26	24	24	25	26	29	36	47	63	84											
1935	23	21	22	22	23	25	30	39	51	66	86										
1936	20	19	19	19	20	22	26	33	42	53	67	86									
1937	18	17	17	17	17	19	22	28	35	43	53	65	85								
1938	16	15	15	15	16	17	20	25	30	36	44	53	67	86							
1939	15	14	14	14	14	15	18	22	27	32	38	44	55	69	87						
1940	13	13	13	13	13	14	16	20	24	29	34	39	48	59	73	90					
1941	12	12	12	12	12	13	15	18	22	26	31	36	43	48	64	77	91				
1942	12	12	11	11	11	12	14	17	20	25	29	33	39	40	57	68	80	92			
1943	11	11	11	11	11	12	13	16	19	23	27	31	37	37	53	62	72	82	93		
1944	11	11	10	10	10	11	13	16	18	22	26	29	35	37	49	58	66	74	83	93	
1945	10	10	10	10	10	11	13	16	19	22	24	28	33	35	46	54	61	66	76	84	
1946	10	10	10	10	10	11	12	15	18	21	24	28	33	33	46	54	61	68	76	84	94

* Year of birth heads each column, year of survival marks each line, of table.

INDEX

INDEX

Note.—Following the page references, f. refers to figure; n. to footnote; t. to table.

www.ingramcontent.com/pod-product-compliance
Lightning Source LLC
Chambersburg PA
CBHW021712210326
41599CB00013B/1619